Public Planet Books

A series edited by Dilip Gaonkar, Jane Kramer,
Benjamin Lee, and Michael Warner

Public Planet Books is a series designed by writers in and
outside the academy—writers working on what could be
called narratives of public culture—to explore questions that
urgently concern us all. It is an attempt to open the scholarly
discourses on contemporary public culture, both local and
international, and to illuminate that discourse with the kinds
of narrative that will challenge sophisticated readers, make
them think, and especially make them question. It is, most
importantly, an experiment in strategies of discourse, com-
bining reportage and critical reflection on unfolding issues
and events—one, we hope, that will provide a running narrative of our societies at this moment. Public Planet Books is
part of the Public Works publication project of the Center for
Transcultural Studies, which also includes the journal *Public
Culture* and the Public Worlds book series.

The Empire of Love ⎯⎯⎯⎯

public planet books

The Empire of Love

Toward a Theory of Intimacy, Genealogy, and Carnality

Elizabeth A. Povinelli

DUKE UNIVERSITY PRESS *Durham and London* 2006

© 2006 Duke University Press

All rights reserved

Printed in the United States of

America on acid-free paper ∞

Typeset in Bodoni by Tseng

Information Systems, Inc.

Library of Congress Cataloging-

in-Publication Data appear on

the last printed page of this

book.

For Stacey Marie D'Erasmo

Contents

Acknowledgments

Over the course of writing this book, numerous people in mangroves, workshops, lectures, and seminars; on beaches, telephones, and sides of the road; at subway stops; over cups of coffee; and across continents and languages have helped me understand what this book was about and to shape, focus, and revise its content.

Central to this work have been my friends and family at Belyuen and its hinterlands and in the United States. Many people at Belyuen have passed away, but many remain, including my mothers, Ruby Yarrowin, Marjorie, Binbin, and Jarim; my aunts and uncles, Alice, Teresa, Kabal; my husbands and wives, Kumu, Nicholas, Left Hand, Story, Ngapring, Patsy-Anne, Caroline; my siblings, Jojo, Daphne, Diane, Michelle, AA, Big Truck, Pelki, Elvis, Rossie, Chris, and Sharon; my sons and daughters, especially, Bronwyn, Anne-Marie, Ricky; and my nieces and nephews, especially Edwina. I'd like also to thank in particular Hush, Jai, Wicker, Daisy, Nuh-uh, and Jiggles, Paul and Pinto, Patti Sullivan and Jill Harris, Jonathan, and Layard for extensive conversation on spiritual and queer counterpublics.

The organizers and audiences in many workshops and seminars were also vital to sharpening and directing my thought, including those at: Department of Cultural Studies, Sabanci University; Department of Anthropology, Cornell University; Norwegian University of Science and Technology; London School of Economics and Birkbeck Law School; Department of Anthropology, Johns Hopkins University; Committee on Degrees in Studies of Women, Gender and Sexuality and Department of Anthropology, Harvard University; Department of Anthropology, Sydney University; Center for Advanced Studies, Charles Darwin University; Workshop on Gendered Bodies and Transnational Politics, American University at Cairo; Wiser Center, University of Witwatersrand; Center for the Study of Women, University of California, Los Angeles; Graduate Student Conference on the Boundaries of Feeling, Departments of Anthropology and History, University of Michigan; Center for the Study of Sexual Culture, University of California, Berkeley; Semiotics Workshop, University of Chicago; and the Institute for Research on Women and Gender, Columbia University.

Colleagues in the Center for Transnational Culture Studies, the Department of Anthropology, the Center for Study of Law and Culture, and the Institute for Research on Women and Gender, at Columbia University, have provided constant support for this project, including: Nadia Abu El Haj, Lila Abu Lughod, Craig Calhoun, Vincent Crapanzano, Katherine Franke, Susan Gal, Dilip Gaonkar, Ben Lee, Rosalind Morris,

Michael Silverstein, Charles Taylor, Kendall Thomas, Greg Urban, and Michael Warner.

Duke University Press and its books editor, Ken Wissoker, have provided me with continuous support for my work, for which I am thoroughly indebted.

Several people have read drafts of various parts of this book, in some cases more than once. To them I am particularly indebted: the two anonymous reviewers at Duke University Press, Anjali Arondekar, Veena Das, Susan Gal, Dilip Gaonkar, Andrew Graan, Laura-Zoe Humphreys, Janet Jakobsen, Dicle Kogacioglu, Emma Kowal, Yin Paradies, and, especially, Michael Warner, Susan Edmunds, and Stacey D'Erasmo.

Empires of Love: An Introduction

One

This short book arises from a certain hope and a certain frustration. The hope is that we can conceptualize a set of systematic relations between forms of love and forms of liberal governance in empire without reducing these relations to a singular kind or scale of power, to analogy, description, or rumor. The frustration is that this kind of project is doomed—and rightly so—before it can begin for several reasons, not the least of which are: that the concrete linkages between forms of love and forms of governance are too many and too dispersed to be of much use for a theoretical or practical political anthropology; that the way I am conceptualizing love, intimacy, and sociality removes this work from the very field it seeks to address; and that we can never agree about the referent of liberalism. Indeed, there are many ways that I could frame this study—as a study about sexuality, sovereignty, death and life worlds, and new social imaginaries. So what am I trying to do, and why?

Perhaps the first thing to note is that this book is a theoretical reflection, but it is also the product of my own experiences in what would appear to be two very different social worlds: on the one hand, the social worlds of indigenous men and women living at Belyuen, a small community in the Northern Territory of Australia, and its hinterlands; and, on the other, the social worlds of progressive queers in the United States who identify as or with radical faeries. In many ways these two worlds are incommensurate, the one based on thick kinship and face-to-face socialities, the other on stranger sociality. And in many ways the various members within these two worlds would seem to misuse each other. Some indigenous people with whom I am quite close reject homosexuality as a legitimate mode of social life; some progressive queers are uncritically culturally appropriative. For the past twenty years I have moved back and forth between these two worlds and across the racial and sexual discourses that locate me most self-evidently within one of them, no matter how my personal history might locate me within the other. The incommensurate nature of these social worlds and of the racial and sexual discourses that apprehend them make it difficult for me to do such normal things as express joy and grief in one world for the people I have found and lost in another and for me to make sense of my insertion in either.

No matter this incommensurability, I have come to see these two worlds as vitally related. This book attempts to explain why by critically exploring how the liberal, binary concepts of individual freedom and social constraint—concepts that were continually pressed on me as I moved back and forth across these worlds—contribute to the ways that intimacy in these two worlds is apprehended and what alternative practices of intimacy are found in each, especially as these modes of intimacy move us beyond the choice between freedom and constraint. Thus this book is not interested in the study of identities so much as it is interested in the social matrix out of which these identities and their divisions emerge, including: where and what sexuality is; where and when a person is a token of a type of social identity, for instance, an indigenous person or an "indigenous person"; which forms of intimate dependency count as freedom and which count as undue social constraint; which forms of intimacy involve moral judgment rather than mere choice; and which forms of intimate sociality distribute life and material goods and evoke moral certainty, if not moral sanctimoniousness. This approach to intimacy and governance does not collapse these two worlds; it does not make them two versions of the same thing. Instead it allows us to see how their differences emerge diagonally to the deafening drum of liberal figurations of freedom and its others and their racial and civilizational inflections.

3

The second thing to note is that this is an essay, a trial, an attempt to provide some preliminary flesh to an intuition about how a set of ethical and normative claims about the governance of love, sociality, and the body circulate in *liberal settler colonies* in such a way that life and death, rights and recognition, goods and resources are unevenly distributed there. I examine how discourses of individual freedom and social constraint—what I refer to as *autological* and *genealogical* imaginaries—animate and enflesh love, sociality, and bodies; how they operate as strategic maneuvers of power whose purpose—or result—is to distribute life, goods, and values across social space; and how they contribute to the hardiness of liberalism as a normative horizon. In previously published papers, as well as in talks and conferences, I have referred to these discourses in a variety of ways, mainly by the terms "intimacy" and "genealogy." In this little book, I use the terms "autological subject" and "genealogical society" and "intimate event" and "intimacy" to refer to specific aspects of liberal sociality. By the *autological subject*, I am referring to discourses, practices, and fantasies about self-making, self-sovereignty, and the value of individual freedom associated with the Enlightenment project of contractual constitutional democracy and capitalism. By *genealogical society*, I am referring to discourses, practices, and fantasies about social constraints placed on the autological subject by various kinds of inheritances. The *intimate event*, as opposed to *intimacy*, is simply the way in which the event of normative love is formed at the intersection—and crisis—of these two discourses.[1]

These definitions are meant to be no more than the minimal groundwork on which the following discussion can begin to be built. In his late notes, published in the volume *On Certainty*, Ludwig Wittgenstein calls on but never defines the concept of a language game. And how could he, when these meditations argue that even a rule is merely the effect of a chain of questions and answers that make sense and nonsense, an inherited background against which we distinguish between truth and falsity. Sounding a bit like Gilles Deleuze and Felix Guattari in *A Thousand Plateaus*, Wittgenstein writes, "I do not explicitly learn the propositions that stand fast for me. I can *discover* them subsequently like the axis around which a body rotates. This axis is not fixed in the sense that anything holds it fast, but the movement around it determines its mobility."[2] It is thus for the intimate event and the genealogical society. These are not rules that can be defined outside of their practice of usage, removed from the chain of questions and answers that invest them with sense and truth, nonsense and falsity, or held fixed by some property internal to them. Instead, the intimate event and genealogical society are the phantasmagorical axis cast by discourses about individual freedom and social constraint. It is to these discourses that we must turn to understand the real world effects of the phantoms rather than to a set of unworldly rules and definitions.

5

What I argue in this book, what I try to show through a *Thesis* series of ethnographic, juridical, and historical readings, is that these discourses and their material anchors are a key means by which people in liberal settler colonies articulate their most intimate relations to their most robust governmental and economic institutions, make sense of how others do the same, account for the internal incoherence of these discourses, and distribute life and death internationally. Autological and genealogical discourses are not in this view different in kind even though they are used to differentiate kinds of people, societies, and civilizational orders. They both presuppose a liberal humanist claim that what makes us most human is our capacity to base our most intimate relations, our most robust governmental institutions, and our economic relations on mutual and free recognition of the worth and value of another person, rather than basing these connections on, for example, social status or the bare facts of the body. These presuppositions circulate through the subjects and institutions of liberal settler colonies, informing how people talk about themselves and others, how they govern themselves and others, and who they think they are or who they think they should be. As people go about their ordinary lives—their practices of love, work, and civic life—they continually constitute these discourses as if the *discourses* were the agents of social life, as if there were such a thing as the sovereign subject and the genealogical society, as individual freedom and social constraint, and as if the choice between these Manichean positions were the only real choice available to us. They do this as if all other actual and potential positions and practices were impractical, politically perverse, or socially aberrant.

As an alternative to this way of practicing and analyzing intimacy, this book explores a number of immanent dependencies among indigenous and queer people I know, some of which emerge from actual human encounters within and between these groups, some of which emerge from the legal and medical regulations that members of these groups encounter, and some of which emerge from the material and affective dynamics that are artifacts of these encounters. Thinking of the social relations within and among the people I know as *immanent dependencies* allows me to dislodge certain commonsense views of the social matrix of indigenous and queer people in which the dependencies of indigenous persons are so saturated by determination that the immanent is only a sign of the breakdown of the indigenous order and in which the dependencies of queer persons are so annulled by portraits of stranger sociality that dependency itself is hard to imagine.

Because the following ethnographic, legal, and historical readings are oriented to discourses *and* their material anchors, I am especially interested in an aspect of social life that I am calling *carnality*: the socially built space between flesh and environment. I distinguish *corporeality* from *carnality* in terms of the difference between flesh as a juridical and political maneuver and flesh as a physical mattering forth of these maneuvers. What I am claiming, and try to show throughout this book, is that the uneven constitution of the flesh is not merely an effect of a liberal biopolitics, or merely the disciplinary means by which the discourses of autology and genealogy are secured, maintained, and reproduced, but also an independent, unruly vector at play within these biopolitics. In other words, the flesh may be an effect of these discourses but it is not reducible to them. To make sense is to shape, etch, and engenre discourse as much as it is to direct and frame physicalities, fabricate habitudes, habituate vision, and leave behind new material habitats that will be called on to replicate, justify, defy, and interfere with given sense-making and with the distribution of life and death, wealth and poverty, that this sense-making makes possible. In this way I am merely following a line of thought stretching from Althusser's attempt to locate ideology in practice to Deleuze's attempt to produce a radical pragmatics of the body. Contemporary critical theory has attempted to model the material of all social mediation without reducing this material mediation to the same mode, the same qualities of durability, transposibility, and detachability or the same level of force, intentionality, and efficacy. Thus, this book is less interested in the meaning and semantics of love, sociality, and the body, and more interested in their forms, fits, materialities, moorings, anchors, and landings.

Talking about bodies and materialities as actual fleshy things can produce strong ambivalence among feminists, queer theorists, and progressive scholars in part because it is assumed that to mention bodies and their materialities is to forget that these are always stretching, reacting, and forming their physiology in the domain of discourse. Further, it would seem to forget that even if there were flesh on one side and discourse on the other, neither of these sides is singular, homogeneous, or reducible to a singular axis. What flesh, where and when? And which discourse, where and when?

The multiplicity of discourses wound into any one object meets the multiplicity of the object as it changes over time, is stretched by any given discourse, and winds others as it twists away from them. The aim of my emphasis on the physical matter of the body—the ways discourses leave bodies behind them in a certain condition—is neither to reach the fact of the flesh as opposed to discourse, nor to establish a discursive separation of flesh and self. Instead, I want to show how the uneven distribution of the flesh—the creation of life-worlds, death-worlds, and rotting worlds—is a key way in which autology, genealogy, and their intimacies are felt, known, and expressed. The dynamic between carnality and the discourses of the autological subject and the genealogical society is in this sense more like a skein than a skin—like a length of yarn or thread wound loosely and coiled together, a flock of birds flying across the sky in a line, or a tangled or complex mass of material.

In a short book on the psychosomatics of Freudian psycho-analysis, Elizabeth Wilson elaborates nicely on what is at stake here when she reflects on what Freud might have meant by the term "obligation." Freud wrote, in relation to his theory of neurasthenic melancholia, that the "associated neurones are obliged to give up their excitation, *which produces pain*."[3] Wilson asks, "What is the character of the psychosomatic structure such that soma and psyche are bound by obligation rather than unilateral control" and such that a binding re-lation, a mutuality of cause, influence and orientation, is at-tributed to non-human agents?[4] What Wilson suggests, and what is conceptually useful here, is that Freud is attempting to sketch a system of governance in which the mutual consti-tution of soma and psyche, flesh and discourse, are no longer captured by the usual mechanics of "cause and effect, origin and derivation."[5] They are instead the literal material of each other, different from each other but mutually obliged rather than caused or affected, *vulnerable to* rather than *subject of*.[6] For Wilson, the point of reading Freud in this way is to break through a certain resistance in feminist theory to consider the physiological aspects of psychological process, not to reduce psyche to soma or soma to psyche, but to map the strange elasticity of each as it finds itself obligated by the other—a leg obligated to a psychic paralysis, psyche to the pain of a hysterical facial tic.

In seeking to resist the choice between individual freedom and social determination as the only foundation for governing love, sociality, and the body—a choice presented as natural, vital, and irreplaceable in liberal settler colonies—the aspira-tion of this little book is not so different from the biopolitical project that Michel Foucault outlined over a quarter of a century ago.[7] As we know, the point of his histories of sexuality (as well as of his histories of the clinic, the prison, and madness) was not to study discourses of sexuality, for example, for the sake of knowing sexuality but for the sake of investigating power and the discursive matrixes that underpinned it. Similarly, the aspiration was not merely to know how power disciplined sexuality, sexual expression, or sexual identity, but to understand how all of these were the means by which power in a robust sense — power over life and death, power to cripple and rot certain worlds while over-investing others with wealth and hope — is produced, reproduced, and distributed when we seem to be doing nothing more than kissing our lovers goodbye as we leave for the day.

It is at the intersection of questions of power and exploitation that my approach to love, sociality, and the body and my approach to liberalism converge. In this book, love, intimacy, and sexuality are not about desire, pleasure, or sex per se, but about things like geography, history, culpability, and obligation; the extraction of wealth and the distribution of life and death; hope and despair; and the seemingly self-evident fact and value of freedom. So, when I speak of love and its socialities, I am referring to the processes by which the dialectic of individual freedom and social bondage is distributed geographically, how social phenomena that contest this distribution are made commensurate with it, and how discourses that arise from this distribution circulate, are localized, and are contested.

Approaching the international division of life and death in liberal settler colonies in this way would, I think, change how we go about studying sexuality and the social imaginary. My original motivation for writing this book was to address what I saw as a certain literalism of the referent hovering over Euro-American studies of sexuality as they opened themselves to their transnational conditions. We were witnessing, I thought, an example of what Judith Butler described as the disciplinary function of the "proper object."[8] The study of "woman," "Third-World women," "men," "the third sex," "new masculinities," "gay worlds," "lesbian worlds," and "straight worlds," and the globalization of the hetero-homo binary were considered to be the proper object of scholars, academic programs, and activists who study sexuality and gender as transnational phenomena. Progressive politics and scholarship addressing, for example, indigenous worlds, the international division of labor, emergent Islamic theocracies and reformations, fundamentalist Christian social politics, postcolonial racializations, and other aspects of social life not explicitly self-characterizing as sexuality or gender per se tend to enter sexuality studies either through a grammar of concatenation or through a transformational grammar of pleasure, desire, and sexual identity. What do I mean by grammars of "concatenation" and "transformation"? Something quite simple. Either gender and sexuality are added to nominalized social phenomena (so we get race *and* sexuality or indigeneity *and* gender) or an aspect of social life is treated as transformed by sex and gender — as being sexualized, feminized, or engendered.

Some conservative critics, and others just outright hostile to sexuality studies, have seized on the distance between social phenomena that have an obvious relationship to sexuality

11

and gender and those that have a more attenuated relationship to the same in order to accuse queer theorists and feminists of making linkages and intersections between phenomena based on nothing more than their own theoretically over-heated and slightly salacious minds. For example, although scholarly books on sexuality have had a certain commercial success in university presses, scholars of sexual studies find it increasingly hard to support their research.[9] This is just fine from the point of view of conservative critics. For them, if sexuality studies and gender studies have a place at the table of scholarship, it is on condition that they discipline their object and not overstep their proper domain. To be sure, the call for carefully differentiating various kinds of social struggles — racial struggles from queer struggles and both from indigenous struggles — has not come only from conservative critics within and outside the academy. As recent debates over same-sex marriage in the United States and over gender parity in France (*le Mouvement pour la parité*) suggest, progressive academics and critics may see the social foundations and dynamics of queer, feminist, and racial demands for cultural civil rights to be utterly distinct. These conservative and progressive critics are right, in one sense. Contemporary sexuality studies and gender studies have engaged in what we might call a *politics of trespass*. They have refused to sequester, to ghettoize, women's issues, gender issues, and queer issues to a subset of social life. The best of these trespass studies have demonstrated decisively how discourses and practices of gender and sexuality are critical to the maintenance of liberal and illiberal forms of power and domination and are at the gov-

Counter

12

ernmental heart of capitalism, secularism, civil society, and new and old religiosities.[10]

For all the good these studies have done, and I think that they have done tremendous good, this book investigates what happens when we move away from a language of trespass where it is based on grammars of concatenation and transformation, without capitulating to the conservative demand that feminist and sexuality theorists either simply go away or define more narrowly their domain of study.[11] Rather than narrowing the field of study, I am advocating a far more robust model of "sexuality" which would examine the distributive linkages among the social struggles of indigenous Australians, queer Americans, and others by more than mere metaphor, by more than the conjunctive "and," or a quasiuniversal economy of pleasure and desire. In short, I want to suggest a different way of approaching love, intimacy, and sexuality in the wake of settler colonialism that includes how various subjects of liberal diasporic sexuality have resisted the pervasive politics of cultural recognition.

Two

One serious impediment to the project I am proposing is the phantom-like nature of liberalism itself. Liberalism is not a thing. It is a moving target developed in the European empire and used to secure power in the contemporary world. It is located nowhere but in its continual citation as the motivating logic and aspiration of dispersed and competing social and cultural experiments. The same can be said of the liberal discourses this book is tracking. Individual freedom, social constraint, autology, genealogy, the intimate event: These are not things but moving targets. When, for instance, does the event of intimate love actually happen? What are the criteria we use to decide whether this event has happened? One thing I want to show is that, as a result of the strategic shape-shifting partnership of autology and genealogy, discourses of the autological subject, the genealogical society, and their putative modes of intimacy are at best incommensurate discourses, multiple rather than singular; they are undecidable and, at times, incoherent events. Although they are used to distinguish social and civilizational orders on which they themselves are dependent, they are, at the same time, destabilized and invaginated by the very sites they seek to discipline. They describe neither the actual worlds of liberalism nor the actual worlds of others. Rather than studying liberalism, I want to understand how these discourses and their material anchors act as a means of moving among an array of disparate and multidimensional, multifunctional phenomena; a means of organizing these disparate phenomena into a definite relation of values and a thing called Liberalism; and a means of making other kinds of social phenomena commensurate or incommensurate, comparable or incomparable with this phantom Liberalism.

The mysterious "now you see it, now you don't" quality of discourses of autology and genealogy derives in part from two kinds of performativity. On the one hand, the fantasy of Liberalism is tightly associated with the fantasy of the performative subject, a point I elaborate on more fully in the last essay. On the other hand, the fantasy of Liberalism is tightly dependent on the ability of these discourses and their material institutions to transform the world into an image of its own normative horizon. In other words, these discourses must, and do, continually change the facts on the ground. Though these discourses may not have had any substantial hold in many places to which they initially referred, over time the actual material and discursive conditions of places change to meet and mirror the presumptions of these discourses. What at first was a misrepresentation becomes an accurate description. Instead of asking, where are the discourses? we might ask, what is being done to produce the world in their image? The dynamic transformation of the facts on the ground is not merely a transformation of social values, economy, and political institutions, but the transformation of life-forces, of ecology and environment, of disease trajectories. However, as much as these discourses change the material-subjective grounds of social life, because they are written into different kinds of materials — human bodies, ecological landscapes, and analogical and digital texts to name just three — the ground itself is extraordinarily dynamic, with multiple rhythms and complex coordinations. These material dynamics continually cast autological and genealogical discourses into a spectral realm, halfway between being and becoming.

And so this book runs headfirst into the serious question of how to write an account of a historical formation without fetishizing that formation, without abstracting it from its immanent social contexts, and without collapsing the social reality of that formation into ideological accounts of that formation.

Where do we look to find discourses of autology, genealogy, and their intimacies if we are truly committed to studying their inter-digitation and immanence in processes of circulation and processes of localization rather than merely engaging in a comparative study? Where to look if we are to study them as interdependent discourses rather than as comparative ones? Where to look if we see the objects of comparison as emergent in these circulations rather than as concrete, bounded units that are circulating? Are these discourses operating at a particular scale of sociality? Are they only in certain sorts of institutions, only in certain regimes of disciplinarity? Or are they more ubiquitous, secreted in practices that seem to have nothing to do with love? To answer these kinds of questions we need to ask, first, what constitutes the borders, interiors, and dynamics of autology, genealogy, and intimacy, and their relation with other objects. What are the conditions of circulation placed on these discourses, what are their habitats and habitudes, what are the densities of their interconnectivities such that a culture of circulation comes to be the general equivalent, resisted only with great risk? What are the barricades and incentives to their circulation and its effects? How are populations constituted and stabilized by such circulations? Who takes and is assigned responsibility for the effects of these circulations?

Three

The strong argument of this book is that the social imaginaries of the autological subject, the genealogical society, their modes of intimacy, and their material anchors emerged from European Empire as a mode and maneuver of domination and exploitation and continue to operate as such. This book claims that the intimate couple is a key transfer point between, on the one hand, liberal imaginaries of contractual economics, politics, and sociality and, on the other, liberal forms of power in the contemporary world. Love, as an intimate event, secures the self-evident good of social institutions, social distributions of life and death, and social responsibilities for these institutions and distributions. If you want to locate the hegemonic home of liberal logics and aspirations, look to love in settler colonies.

If the intimate couple is a key transfer point within liberalism, this couple is already conditioned by liberalism's emergence and dispersion in empire. At the same time that people spread the good news of the singular world-historic value of these freedom-producing subjects and institutions, they claim this singular heritage for the North Atlantic and Western Europe. Such claims may seem particularly loud in British settler colonies such as Canada, Australia, and the United States. But, as with the concept of the colonial subject, so with the referent of the liberal settler colony—the reach of settler colonialism stretches way beyond the self-evident site of colonial settlement itself. As W. E. B. Du Bois long ago insisted, the location of the United States and Europe and their economic and discursive wealth, capital, and political power was not self-evident and was certainly not anchored in their own borders.[12] Nor are the effects of Western accumulation of economic and discursive capital felt solely within the offshoots of Western Europe and the North Atlantic, a point that Dipesh Chakrabarty has more recently elaborated on in *Provincializing Europe*. For this reason, the referent of *liberal settler colonies* is much wider than nation-states literally founded on the basis of colonial settlement, encompassing what I sometimes describe as the *liberal diaspora*— an origin-less or origin-obscuring process of transformation in circulation that retroactively constitutes its beginning and center.[13]

Europe's economic, discursive, and political power was begged, borrowed, and stolen from subjects of empire, then twisted and turned to a Western advantage. Empire created and circulated poverty, trauma, and death globally while claiming to create and foster wealth, happiness, and life, and it claimed a universal origin and end even as it was partial about its values and goals. Part of the way particular colonial regimes secured their universal claims was to absorb local languages and life-worlds. This absorption was not, however, seamless. The history of absorption filled liberalism's institutions and discourses with jagged edges and very fine cracks, cleavages, and fissures that marked the nontranslation of discursive orders, ideal norms, and actual practices, that is, the various ways bodies were left behind. As a result, the more life-worlds and languages that liberal institutions and discourses absorbed, the more the tensions and contradictions between its ideal image and its actual practice increased, while suspicion grew that liberalism was an incoherent, ideology-driven system of exploitation.

No matter the multiplicity, incoherence, and indeterminacy of these discourses, they are extraordinarily productive and mobile. The exact articulation among elements within the dynamic of individual freedom and social constraint can radically shift shapes even as the self-evident nature of this opposition is itself conserved. One of the difficult tasks facing this book, then, is trying to capture and explore both sides of the governance of love, sociality, and the body in liberal settler colonies—its disciplinary effects and its disciplinary failures in the face of a set of social refusals. After all, if the discourses and imaginaries of individual freedom and social constraint remain surprisingly resilient and absorptive in settler colonies, they do so in spite of multiple heterogeneous challenges to their legitimacy in local worlds. One of the most pressing questions we face is how the challenges of these actual-world heterogeneous ways of living are subdued and redirected, or not; why they have such a hard time becoming expansive alternatives—or why they may not wish to be so. In the first and second chapters, therefore, I return these discourses of the intimate event and the genealogical society to the thick actual worlds from which they were pulled.

Though I am reflecting on the capture of sociality in liberal settler colonies through queer and indigenous communities, this is not intended as a comparative study.[14] I do not attempt to illuminate comparative aspects of queer and indigenous forms of sociality per se, but rather to show the co-constitution of worlds where before we saw separate populations, dynamics, and problematics. I hope that this approach allows us to see new forms of life that contest, elaborate, or ignore these discourses, and how these new forms of life do, or do not, disrupt deep channels of exploitation and domination. In short, I hope to open up a social politics that goes beyond saying yes or no to the intimate event and the genealogical society by cutting across these fields of regularity. This said, the ethnographic ground of this book comes from two very different social worlds and two very different kinds of experience on my part. My discussion of the indigenous northwest coast is based on twenty years during which I have lived and traveled at least a month or two a year there (along with much longer, year-length trips, at several points). Generally, indigenous communities absorb strangers into local languages of kinship and moiety relations. This certainly was the case when I first arrived at Belyuen in 1984. There, kinship relations—with specific norms for how various kinds of kin are treated—are the presumed backdrop of every relationship of any longstanding nature. I will, therefore, often refer to various people from Belyuen and beyond as my mother, sister, husband, brother, et cetera. This is not merely an issue of reference, however. Part of what I am exploring in this book is where, why, and how these relations are made real and fictive forms of kinship. I have spent much less time living and traveling with men, and some women, who identify as radical faeries. Moreover, the ways strangers are absorbed into radical faerie communities and publics are quite different from the ways strangers are absorbed into indigenous communities. Thus, alongside my examination of how, why, and where indigenous-nonindigenous relations of kinship are figured as real or fictive, is another: what are the legal, economic, and social dynamics between these two forms of social absorption?

And yet for all this complexity, in the end, I think what makes the approach I am advocating in this set of essays difficult is not the density of the thought or the partiality of the object, but the absence of any clean moral or political stance toward any piece of the lives I discuss. My goal is not to say yes or no to individual freedom and social constraint, the intimate event or the genealogical society. All I can hope is that by understanding how these discourses work to shape social life, we can begin to formulate a positive political program—something I have begun to describe as a politics of "thick life"—in which the density of social representation is increased to meet the density of actual social worlds. The goal is not to produce a hermeneutics of the Self and Other, but to shatter the foundations on which this supposedly simple relay of apprehension has historically established a differential of power as a differential of knowledge.

Four

I have organized this book to replicate and tackle the ways in which liberal discourses of freedom and constraint and intimacy and governance discipline the immanent nature of social dependencies in settler colonies. The book consists of three essays, each of which maps a different network of liberal love, intimacy, and sociality and liberal governance and each of which presents somewhat different narrative styles and strategies. Though different in tone and archive, the chapters of the book are best understood as a loop that begins with ethnographically thick accounts of the governance of

21

bodies across settler colonies—Australia, the United States, and Canada along with the indigenous and queer worlds found there—and ends with a general account of the discourses of the intimate event and the genealogical society as an epiphenomenon to the dialectic of individual freedom and social constraint, its dynamic relationship to carnality, its ideological borders, its internal incoherence, and its techniques of commensuration.

The first chapter pivots on a tropical ulcer that I contracted in the far north of Australia and how it was medically treated in the United States, Canada, and Australia. This physical condition would seem to have little to do with love, intimacy, or sexuality. But the sore provides me with a way of making visible a set of interpenetrating legal, cultural, and medical disciplines of the body that presuppose and entail the forms of the autological subject and the genealogical society, their disciplinary modes of intimacy and sociality, and their carnal anchorings. The suggestion is that the operation of these discourses is weakest where it is most apparent, most tenacious where we would never dream it could be organizing bodies, their authorized voicing, and circulations. In other words, the sore gives me some traction in making sense of how the discourses of autology and genealogy, and the different intimacies they presuppose and demand, are reproduced not merely in domains explicitly identified as love or sexual, but in domains having seemingly little or nothing to do with love, intimacy, or sexuality per se and everything to do with who can be free without harm. The chapter focuses on how, through a politics of cultural recognition and sensitivity, discourses of genealogy make and unmake the voices and bodies of my indigenous friends and family even though these discourses do not describe the contours of their actual social worlds and relations *even where these relations can be described as relations of kinship*. The purpose of this chapter is to make visible how the disciplinary operation of these discourses is lodged in the deep tissue—the background conditions—of social interpretation and practice.

The weight of the second chapter falls on the other side of the discipline of individual freedom and social constraint. I track the disciplinary effects of discourses of autology and genealogy in the experimental social worlds of friends of mine who identify as radical faeries and their allies. To do so, I first outline some of the thickly contested aspirational and practical horizons that constitute the "radical faeries" as a social genre. The point is to demonstrate that there is not "a" radical faerie movement, but rather a set of allegiances to a moving and contested set of qualities and stances toward normative masculinity and sociality. The motivating question of the chapter is, then, Why and how do legal, public, cultural, and many progressive indigenous activists intern this eclectic counter-public within a particular negative model of intimacy and sexuality? To this end, I then place these practices of social making in the contested interior terrain of the faerie movement, the critical indigenous public, and the jurisprudence of religious certification and cultural copyright. I examine how discourses of the autological subject and the genealogical society interpret these social worlds as mere ideological cover for illicit sex acts, as mere appropriation of other people's culture, or as seriously intended but legally dubious modes of religiosity. The essay ends by trying to understand how the disciplining of radical faeries through a discourse of freedom paradoxically reanimates the self-evident good of liberal democratic forms of freedom and how, in this context, a politics of espionage emerges as the foil of the cunning of recognition. As in the first chapter, my discussion of this social genre is not merely discursive, if by discursive we mean the play of signs outside their material inhabitations. Even as radical faeries are creatively coordinating a social identity made sensible in and by an entire field of possible social positions and practices, they are also physically and affectively made and haunted by these makings.

The last chapter is an extended theoretical meditation on the discursive terrain of the intimate event and the genealogical society. It seeks to provide a thicker description of these as a set of interpenetrating discourses about the geographical origins and destinations of individual freedom and social bondage and of these discourses as a vital aspect of liberal legitimacy and power. I suggest how this approach to reading the emergence of the intimate event in Empire would allow us to rethink a set of philosophical and historical questions that have been central to the story of liberalism's exceptionalism. To do so I animate these theoretical and historical discussions by placing them in dialectic tension with contemporary problems and tactics of building intimacy outside the North/West. I draw on the previous chapters as well as other postcolonial and settler colonial criticism to suggest the ways in which these figurations of the self and other have been and are still being refigured, divested, and diverted. To a certain extent I am agnostic about the local historical details of the emergence of the intimate event in Empire, choosing instead to move from a theoretical argument to a historical rethinking—how my argument about the intimate event and the genealogical society would recast the typical ways we have written the history of the enlightenment and its core social institutions and dynamics.

One last thing. As much as this book describes various tactics of intimacy and sociality emerging diagonally to liberal discourses of individual freedom and social constraint, this book does not present a redemptive narrative. I do not think these practices are redemptive, for at least two reasons. First, the options presented to those persons who choose, or must, live at the end of liberalism's tolerance and capitalism's trickle, are often not great options. To pretend they are is to ignore the actual harms that liberal forms of social tolerance and capital forms of life- and wealth-extraction produce. Second, to wish for a redemptive narrative, to seek it, is to wish that social experiments fulfill rather than upset given conditions, that they emerge in a form that given conditions recognize as good, and that they comply to a hegemony of love rather than truly challenge its hold over social life. It is to wish for a redemptive narrative authored by those who suffer most viciously from the hegemony of this form of intimacy. Instead of redemption's break from social life, I track the immanent dependencies that emerge in actual life.

1 Rotten Worlds

One

Montreal, 6 August 2000. I am quite sick; definitely sicker than I was in the Sydney airport last week, more nauseous in the day, and then there are these night sweats. I am sitting in a conference on globalization and multiple modernities, but I cannot concentrate on the conversation. I am too busy monitoring my body, waiting to see if these new antibiotics kick in and hoping the diarrhea set off by the previous antibiotics abates. As I sit here, I wonder if this entire medical fiasco is the result of my following too assiduously medical instructions or religiously ignoring them over the last sixteen years, placing too much trust in the local knowledge of my indigenous friends and family in Australia. Yesterday I went to a Montreal clinic on instructions from the physician I saw in the University of Chicago Hospital emergency room, where I had gone right after landing in the United States. "Have a doctor in Montreal change the dressing I've put on your shoulder," he said. And so I did. But along with changing the dressing, the Montreal physician switched my medication from Septrim (co-trimoxazole: Septrim, Bactrim) to Novopen, a semi-synthetic penicillin with a host of other popular brand names: Pen-vee K, Beepen-K, V-Cillin K, Nadopen-V. As a result, I can no longer tell if the infection or the antibiotic cocktail is causing my nausea and night sweats. As my body erupts, I wonder whether I have placed too much trust in people whom I have known longer and more intimately than almost anyone else in my life. In wondering, an affective separation emerges, if only as a slight fissure, between them and me.

When the Montreal physician pressed me for more details about the origin of the sore, I told him the somewhat incoherent medical narrative about "sores" that I had standardized during the sixteen years I had been working, on and off, year after year, in northern Australia. I gave a similar narrative to the Chicago doctor when he asked me where and how I had acquired this sore. It went something like this: I am an anthropologist. The sores are endemic in the indigenous communities I visit. They seem to appear and disappear with the seasons, more when it is hot, humid, and wet, less in the cool dry season. They are not obviously related to any previously existing cut or abrasion. This sore on my shoulder, for instance, did not seem to have been caused by any previous cut. Sores just "bubble up" like volcanoes from under the skin, or, using the language of my Emiyenggal-speaking friends in northwest Australia, like *pumanim*, fresh water springs that bubble up from the ground. Sometimes they stay hidden inside you, growing and growing. We call those blind boilers, or just "boilers" in creole and *tenmi* in Emiyenggal. Adults get both kinds. Kids get them, too. Babies can be covered with them, as if the sore were a bad case of chicken pox. Some boilers grow so large and hang on so tenaciously that they require a hospital stay, invasive surgery, and skin grafts. My indigenous friends are pretty cavalier about them. But so are most of the non-indigenous nurses and doctors whom I have met in various indigenous communities. Over the years, they have told me that the sores are "just" streptococcus or "just" staphylococcus. One doctor, many years ago, told me he thought the sores were a strain of leishmaniasis, caused by sand fly bites, but not to worry about it.[1] Worry has its own social distribution—it might be needed elsewhere.

> *New York Times*: Hundreds of American troops in Iraq have been infected with a parasite spread by biting sand flies, and the long-term consequences are still unknown, Army doctors said Friday. The resulting disease, leishmaniasis, has been diagnosed in about 150 military personnel so far, but that is sure to climb in the coming months, the doctors said. All have only the skin form of the disease, which creates ugly "volcano crater" lesions that may last for months, but usually clear up by themselves. None have developed the visceral form that attacks the liver and spleen and is fatal if untreated.[2]

The Montreal physician was quite curious about the sore on my left shoulder. And he became as cautious after seeing it, asking me a series of questions. "Where did you get this sore?" "Who cut into your shoulder like this?" "Why are you on Septrim?" "Is it helping?" Answering the last question was easy enough, and I was brief in my reply. "No. The sore is unchanged and I am desperately ill." The questions of why I was on Septrim, how my shoulder came to look like this, and the origins of the sore would take more time. I described the carnival scene in the Chicago emergency clinic when the bandage I had placed over the sore in Australia was removed. I described how the physician recoiled from me, literally, and shouted to the nurses to bring protective goggles, gowns, and a pair of forceps—as if I were about to give birth to the Andromeda strain.

Or perhaps the up-to-date reference for this young physician would be Ebola, as if I were about to dissolve in my own bloody juices from a virus picked up in a remote part of the world. I told the Montreal doctor, "I couldn't tell if he was freaked out because the flesh was necrotic or because I seemed so blasé about that fact." "He didn't seem to believe me that these sores are commonplace where I work, though I labored hard to convince him that they were no big deal and could be cured with a few shots of penicillin." To be honest, I had told the Chicago emergency room physician, "*I think* I just need a few shots of penicillin, *I think* it's penicillin, or in the tablet form, *maybe* something called amoxa-something. I know it rhymes with Bob Dylan." The imprecision of my pharmacological language was one index of the deep recess of everyday life in which these sores fester for many indigenous and non-indigenous residents in northern Australia. Familiarity breeds this nervous system. "You think," the Chicago doctor repeated, nonplussed. Not surprisingly, he did not give me penicillin or amoxicillin. Instead, he cut into my shoulder for what felt like an hour, took a culture from the core, and packed the hole with a "wick" to allow the fluids to drain out. (As he put it, he "packed it like a gunshot wound." As the assisting nurses put it outside his earshot, he packed it "like a ghetto wrap.") He then gave me a prescription for Septrim. He had wanted me to stay in Chicago until the culture came back, but I insisted I had a plane to catch.

Do you always take antibiotics that rhyme with Dylan, the Montreal physician asked. "Yes, why is that?" He didn't answer me, asking instead whether I had ever been given Septrim before—in Australia. "No. Why?" He answered me this time. "Because Septrim doesn't kill subcutaneous anthrax."

It was his hunch that anthrax was dispersed throughout pastoral northern Australia and that anthrax spores were the cause of the sore on my shoulder. If the Chicago doctor had no immediate referent for this sore, the Montreal doctor did. Opening one of his textbooks, he explained to me that he had heard about these kinds of sores on people working in the cattle and sheep industry.

I have to admit that in the beginning I thought it was cool to have anthrax, to have had anthrax all along without knowing it. I told everyone, including, later that same week on a phone in a Montreal airport terminal, my older sister, who is a microbiologist. She wisely cautioned me not to shout this information too loudly before passing through customs. This was a year before my girlfriend and I had watched the Twin Towers collapse from my studio in Williamsburg, Brooklyn; before anthrax was mailed to media offices along the East Coast and to members of Congress; and, in the shadow cast by these attacks, before international terrorism became an articulation point between the medical and legal subject of anthrax. Anthrax Man was just a comic figure, Judge Dredd, spun from the heavy metal band, Anthrax. In August 2000, my Chicago doctor would have been hard-pressed legally to constrain my movements, not knowing what it was that I had. The Montreal doctor, believing I had anthrax, did not have "international terrorism" as an immediate or self-evident referent. I appeared before them, and was treated by them, as a woman making perhaps a foolish but nevertheless a sovereign choice about how to treat her own body and its health. It was my body, my health, as long as it was not a public menace.

Even after these events, I made jokes about anthrax being passé, or got furious that, when the professional classes in the United States acquired anthrax, vast arrays of governmental and discursive resources were immediately mobilized, but the treatment of the same in poor indigenous communities is apparently left to a dedicated few health activists. Of course, this is not fair. Middle-class postal workers were most often at risk. Besides, what I noticed had been noticed long before. The differences between ordinary and extraordinary illnesses are dependent on a biosocial spacing — often organized as a *geophysical* distribution of ordinary and exceptional bodies and of ordinary and exceptional life, death, and rotting worlds.[3] The geographical component of this biosocial spacing of environmental harm presupposes and constitutes the connection between race, class, and health, but these presuppositions in turn lean on legal, medical, and social distinctions between *intentional harms* and *unintentional* or *unconsidered harms*. Intentionality — whether personal or corporate—is one of the key legal pivots in tort law that distinguishes ecological *pollution* such as that found in poor Australian Aboriginal communities and in poor African American neighborhoods from ecological *terrorism* as it was practiced or threatened after September 11, 2001.[4]

As for my sore, the Novopen that the Montreal doctor prescribed did not rid me of the infection, whatever its biological cause. Just as the largest sore began to heal, satellite sores emerged around the central infection. By this time, I was heading back to Darwin, and so I decided to put my faith in local doctors. Perhaps their casual, deeply familiar approach to these sores was just the remedy I needed. As I predicted, the doctor in Darwin laughed, at times uproariously, as he listened to my stories, especially the anthrax punch line. "It's not anthrax. Just tell them it's a bad case of streptococcus or staphylococcus." "But what is it, really?" I asked the doctor. "I've never taken a culture, but I'm sure it's just staph," he said. He explained that he, too, had been shocked when first witnessing one of these sores soon after his arrival in Darwin from Sydney. All his medical colleagues had reassured him that they were just staphylococcus or streptococcus and easily treated with penicillin. He found, over time, this diagnosis to be true; and so, while not cavalier about the sores, he was no longer shocked by them. "O.K.," I said, "but how do I get them? Doesn't there have to be a pre-existing abrasion to get staph?" He replied, "You can't see every little pinprick you get on your body. Who knows, maybe a mosquito bit you on your shoulder and you scratched. The real reason you get sores, though, is because you're living in an Aboriginal community and they're filthy places. You can't break the cycle of infection in those places. If you give Aborigines antibiotics, they start them and then they leave them on the shelf to rot."

By the time I arrived in Darwin, I had already come to think that the sores were just a bad case of staphylococcus or streptococcus, or some nasty combination of both. Right after my conversation with the Montreal physician, my Chicago doctor left a message on my home phone machine saying that my sore had cultured for staphylococcus. And while I was still in the United States, a friend who had co-written an early textbook on HIV/AIDS prevention looked up anthrax on the Centers for Disease Control and Prevention's Web site. It noted that once anthrax seeps into an environment it is hard to get it out—and expensive to do so. Schooled by HIV/AIDS activism, she observed that the incentive for a government or a business to diagnose a contaminated environment was small, because they would then have to clean it up for a poor black population or justify not cleaning it up. She also pointed out that the CDC said a doctor had to culture specifically for anthrax and that culturing anthrax was not especially easy, and certainly not routine. Even so, the anthrax theory, if interesting for a moment, seemed a bit far-fetched. The Chicago tests had come back with staphylococcus. The CDC described anthrax as having a telltale black scab. My sore, and all the sores I had ever had or seen, were volcanoes of rotted flesh, filled with greenish-yellowish squish, and without a scab. Moreover, the signs that dotted fences on the pastoral properties I routinely passed in northern Australia listed tuberculosis and drucellosis as the diseases of record, not anthrax. Tuberculosis I knew about. I had watched a Belyuen brother of mine die of it in 1987. And I am regularly tested for it because of its circulation in Aboriginal communities.

In any case, by the time I left Darwin, I had more than enough stories for my friends at Belyuen. I tucked them away in the backpack of my brain and headed across the harbor. They enjoyed my stories, as I had expected, and we shared them with other family and friends up and down the coast. I soon stopped caring what the biological agent of these sores was as long as they went away with the right treatment. Besides, in September 2000, the CDC were reporting that there were no long-term effects from having subcutaneous anthrax, so if it was anthrax, who cared? And if it was staphylococcus, or a bit of streptococcus, so what?[5]

This is an essay about that "so what." In it, I show how discourses of the autological subject and the genealogical society create attitudes of interest and disinterest, anxiety and dread, fault and innocence about certain lives, bodies, and voices and, in the process, form and deform lives, bodies, and voices. Recent innovations in research, theory, and method in medical anthropology and science studies are, of course, the necessary conditions for what I am doing here.[6] But this essay is not a medical anthropology of tropical ulcers or a science studies account of the social life of rotten things. My object is neither the medical sciences nor the medical subject, but a broader dynamic of discourses and practices that is continually shaping and directing bodies and voices in settler colonies such that some appear as coherent and others incoherent and such that the source of this coherence and incoherence seems to reside inside these various subjects and their social formations.

The sore is, on the one hand, simply a means by which I can make visible the various levels, modes, and forms by which these discourses of autology and genealogy saturate social life, allowing some voices to be heard, others dismissed, and allowing some bodies to be treated or left untreated. On the other hand, the sore is a challenge to this and any study seeking to grasp discourse in its materiality. Where, after all, is this sore? Whose is it? What is its biosocial nature? Are discourses of autology and genealogy obligated to this sore, constitutive of it, or merely in an accidental proximity to it? This is the question: In a post-essentialist theory how do we make the body matter? To answer this even partially, I track how modes of address and their material anchors presuppose and constitute the autological subject and genealogical society as if they were different in kind even though these subjects and social worlds are in fact thickly emotionally, socially, and discursively conjoined. And I track how these practices of address meet, order, and deform a multitude of material anchors —i.e., how they *enflesh* worlds; how they depend on previous *enfleshments* of the world; and how they apprehend this enfleshment both in the sense of the ability of these discourses to grasp the importance, significance, or meaning of this flesh and in the sense of the ability of these discourses to create a feeling of anxiety or excitement that something dangerous or unpleasant might happen in the vicinity of this flesh.

The narrative strategy of the essay is to remain as close as possible to the multitude of citational practices—law, medicine, medical ethics, research procedures, speculative pleasure, personal affection—and to the multitude of material anchors in which these citational practices emerge and are reinforced, challenged, or deemed irrelevant. My hope is that this tracking will better capture the immanent, performative struggle over how embodied social life is shaped and how these immanent dependencies steer material goods and resources.

However, the narrative strategy I have chosen for this essay runs into the very discursive trouble that I am trying to analyze. Two problems seem especially pressing. First, how and why these discourses show up in the following narrative have everything and nothing to do with my biography. If someone else were writing this piece who had the "same" sore and the same theoretical and methodological aspirations, the specific manifestations of these discourses might nevertheless show up differently—for instance, if this other writer were a white man, or straight, or African American, or indigenous Australian. My wager, however, is that discourses of autology and genealogy would still be the citational field in which this person played. Second, if I am interested in the ways that some voices and lives within settler colonies are made coherent and others incoherent in quotidian practices, then the coordination of narrative voice and narrative event in this very essay is a good example of exactly this. After all, I am the author of this essay; the authorial voice is my voice and this voice emerges from the intersection of the narrative event and the narrated event fairly coherently and unscathed, especially the more I try to demonstrate exactly where I am becoming unhinged.

No matter what I said to the Montreal and Chicago doctors, my Aboriginal friends are not cavalier about all kinds of sores, nor are they uninterested in the vectors of their transmission. They know that some kinds of sores can kill you whether or not you treat them with Western medicine and other kinds of sores can cripple or kill you if you do not treat them with local or Western pharmacies.[7] Indeed, they live in a landscape of sores built in part out of what is known in the anthropological literature and the English-speaking world as the Dreaming — what I will be referring to as the *geontology* — and in part out of the structural conditions of poverty and racism that constitute everyday life along the northwest coastal region.[8] It is important to note at the beginning that these two kinds of landscapes are tightly intertwined. Though ancestrally oriented, local *geontologies* are not mimetic to the genealogical imaginary of customary law. Instead, people I know treat the ancestral past as the geological material of the present, the flesh as it is now arranged. How people live within a structure of poverty has a direct effect on geontological sites. Who gets staphylococcal-infected sores, whose faucet works, and whose water is used to flush whose toilets? These mundane socioeconomic variables often determine who knows and is able to care for various sacred areas in the region. Irene Watson has made this point powerfully: The Law is not in the past as a pristine template, but is thoroughly within the worlds made and inhabited in the present.[9]

One outcropping of the geontological landscape is Maliya,

a small mudflat off the west coast of Anson Bay exposed during the huge king tides that help define the coastal ecology of the region. On 14 July 2000, just two weeks before traveling to the Montreal conference on multiple modernities, I was boating with some of my male brothers and husbands around Anson Bay, helping them map their respective countries and sacred sites in the region. We were boating during a nip tide—a tide that is neither up nor down—and as a result I do not know for sure whether we passed by the side of Maliya or accidentally passed directly over it. Perhaps I should mention that Maliya is an extremely dangerous sore Dreaming. I had first heard of the site in 1985, when men and women living in several Aboriginal communities stretching down the coast from Darwin were worried that one of their male relatives living at Balgal would release—some worried he had already released—the huge blowflies (*kalangak*) that live inside the site. Four years later, a Belyuen sister of mine, Daphne Yarrowin, asked her aunt if her *kuga* (uncle) had chucked the poison that the blowflies carried, but was reassured that he had not because he felt sorry for all the children who would never survive the plague. If released, the *kalangak*, which are as large as sea eagles, swarm from the site, enveloping people, biting them viciously on their lower backbone (*deditunggu*), and leaving them covered with horrible, fatal sores. I would subsequently learn that the first written reference to Maliya was by researchers working on a land claim in 1978.[10] They listed the site as *durlk moliyer* ("Dreaming Sore") and as belonging to the Emiyenggal people, specifically two men, Wanggi and Roy Young Miringa.

Not just anyone can properly release these *kalangak*. You have to know what to do and what language to use when doing it. Treated improperly, say if you have accidentally bumped Maliya while boating, the "poison" in the site can "come le [at] you." But even when releasing the *kalangak* properly, "in every country you name, no matter what place," innocent people fall, "die for good" — this according to Ruby Yarrowin, the daughter of Wanggi. Ten years after I first heard about Maliya, Ruby Yarrowin described to me the harrowing scene she had witnessed when she was young and living near Maliya.

> You try coverimim up, blanket. But they still biteimbet, *deditunggu* (backbone). People been lying down, dead, everywhere. Wula sore eatimupbet; bone, imliedown everywhere. I think hard now. I am going to finishup: *Ngayilewudanutheni, ngaladumari.*

Maggie Timber, who likewise traveled up and down the coast during the 1920s and 30s, told a similar story about Maliya before she died in the mid-1990s. She had a set of distinctive elements in her story, such as the existence of houses and window louvers, but her story shared elements of Ruby Yarrowin's version of the regional geontology—the same blanket, the same *kalangak*, the same *deditunggu*, the same reflexivity of imminent personal demise. "They try coverimup blanket, they try shutim louvers, that Banagula area, but wuliya getin, getin, wagaiyentha gaiya. You think hard now, 'I gana die.' "[11] Many factual elements of Maggie Timber's story could be disputed, from her assertion about the agency of the geontology to the factual problem that there were no houses in the Anson Bay coast during the 1920s, let alone louvers in their phantom windows. I remember thinking this when Maggie Timber first told me this story in 1989, pointing to the louvers in the community housing in which we were staying at the time, and saying to her, "Wulgaman, no louvers that Anson Bay." To which she replied, "that true," with the disturbing inflection that this fact intensified the power of the *kalangak*, rather than diminish it. When doing research for my first book, I learned that influenza epidemics had raged throughout the region during the same period in which Maggie Timber and Ruby Yarrowin saw the dead and the dying.

If I had told the Montreal doctor about Maliya, I would have told him of only one of the many active ancestral-based sources of illness in the north. Take, for example, a set of conversations that occurred in August 2003 at Belyuen, Daly River, and Wadeye. These conversations described how a group of people from Oenpelli, an Aboriginal community in coastal Arnhem Land, *tjukpiya mungarra* at a funeral at Barangga; that is, they intentionally spread a bad cold from an Oenpelli sacred site at the funeral, reportedly because no one from Barangga had come to the funeral of a senior ceremonial man held earlier that same year at Oenpelli. From Barangga the bad cold spread from Aboriginal community to Aboriginal community as people traveled back to their respective homes after the funeral, eventually reaching the city of Darwin. When the local Darwin newspaper reported on the severity of the flu and pinpointed its origin to Beswick (another name used to refer to Barangga), women and men commented, "Don't say Barangga *munggarra*, that Oenpelli *munggarra*, that *durlg* (ancestral site)."

The sheer fact of the geontology is not, however, the beginning or end of many conversations among indigenous women and men I know. The speculative pleasure of the Dreaming as cosmology may rivet the social sciences and publicly provide just the kind of material necessary to animate theories of radical translation, undecidability, and indeterminacy at the intersections of cultural difference. But locally, the existential fact of Maliya, the Oenpelli *munggarra*, and other sites like them is usually placed in a kind of discursive bracket, giving way to other social concerns. Who knows how to release the dangerous powers of these sites? What are the personal motivations for doing so? What are the networks of social obligation, expectation, and exasperation that cause these geophysical catastrophes? Almost everyone agreed that, in the case of the Oenpelli *munggarra* as well as the Anson Bay Maliya, this form of punishment is, in the common parlance, "the hard side of the Aboriginal law." What rivets people I know — what intensifies their conversation beyond the sheer fact of the event-catastrophe — is the reason someone or some group, or the *durlg* itself, would resort to such a fatal and crippling mode of social retribution.

Answers to these questions focus on a set of social sentiments that men and women refer to as "jealousy" and "sorry business." [12] In their use of these words, to be jealous and to be sorry covers an intersecting emotional terrain that in part overlaps with the average English uses of the word "jealousy" and the word "grief." Thus, when people along the northwest coast use the term "jealousy" they are usually referring to emotions that occur when a desired object is possessed or taken by another. The desired object remains within the world of the person who desires it. The question is who possesses and has access to the thing, place, or person. In contrast, persons in a state of "sorry business" are claiming, or experiencing the fact, that a person or object has moved between ontological realms or that the vital connections between ontological orders have been ruptured. The desired subject or object is removed from the world in which living persons have regular and ordinary access. The "thing" might be a material object, a lover, or a landscape. And people can continue to be encountered in places thickly saturated with their sweat or ancestral presence.[13] But this does not change the fact that sorrow is experienced as the emotional response to the irrevocable passing of a thing from one ontological realm to another.

Men and women speculate that geontological catastrophes occur where jealousy and sorrow intersect. This intersection ruptures social ties and produces the experience of radical aloneness, isolation, and abandonment. The state of being alone (*gamaparrking*, "He is alone, isolated"), the severe isolation of the subject, is seen as the root cause and consequence of states of sorrow and jealousy and their subsequent geophysical catastrophes. There are various levels of catastrophe and various consequences of being jealous or sorry. Large catastrophes include the kind of geontological manipulations and shifts that can result when people or places feel abandoned, the kinds of catastrophe exemplified in people's worries that a grieving relative would activate Maliya. Smaller catastrophes resulting from sorrow and jealousy include the burning of clothes and domestic wares as a dramatic statement that persons have been ignored a bit too much by their families and left alone (*ngamaparrking*, "I am alone, isolated").[14]

People are not the only agents of such geophysical catastrophes, however. Ancestral sites often register their sorrow by literally moving—going underground, shattering, or shifting location—when a significant ritual leader, a family head, or the last member of a social group has died. From the point of view of the ancestral site, the death of the elder person severs the connection between the ontological orders of human space-time and ancestral space-time by removing the living human membrane.

Perhaps not surprisingly, conversations circle around how this emotional intersection can be avoided or contained, as conversations did in the wake of the Barangga *munggarra* attack. The answers to how the more devastating effects of this emotional terrain can be avoided are surprisingly simple—visit, sit, and live with each other. In this manner, men and women diagnose the cause, consequence, and cure of these catastrophes as running along the same axis. The severe isolation of the subject is the route into the problem and the resocialization of the subject is the route out. This tactic works as well with ancestral sites as it does with people. Men and women observe how a geontological site might be "building back up" or "falling away" depending on whether it is visited or neglected, just as they talk about the bodies of their relatives as building up or falling away according to the tides of social visitation.

Maximally embodied social relations—what I sometimes think of as *thick life*—make physically and psychologically healthy persons. From this perspective, we can see that these discussions about the causes and ameliorations of radical sorrow are not simply or primarily a hermeneutical exercise. They are not for the production of texts that then lend themselves to interpretation and the generation of meaning. Instead, these discussions and others like them, whether supporting or contesting the reason for sorrow and its remediation, constitute both local socialities and their enfleshments. These discussions are one means by which the social relations that constitute this mode of sorrow, the activities that surround it, and the fleshes that animate it continue to be relevant to local life. Referring to grief and sorrow, speculating on what pushes someone into acting catastrophically, and urging a mode of socially proximate emotional relief continually reconstitute the actual concrete world in which people live as a world where these things matter in terms of social and material supports.

Because these discussions occur within the present-time of the settler colony, they also are always already about the difference between the emphases that settler and indigenous people place on social relations and the self. At Belyuen this emphasis is sometimes put in terms of "clean skin" (skin without sores, lice, scabies, or scars). To be within a socially thick world is to expose the skin to its play and its care. "Who gave you those *mimbi* (lice), Beth? Patsy-Anne (*menggen*) or John Moreen (*nera*)?" In these scenes, intimacy is an intensified form of a social relation. It is to become more kin-like, more ritually oriented, more for and from an ancestrally or residentially saturated place. People with too many lice, too many sores, too much scabies have too few if any family, but so do people with no lice, sores, or scabies. For them, the sore on my body is not *my* sore, though whose sore it is may be unclear, may take social work to unpack, may lead me into the mud of Maliya or more simply to the kinship of husbands and wives. In any case, here at Belyuen, my flesh is always already stretched across multiple possible material anchors. In perhaps their most damning social analysis of settler society, indigenous men and women from the northwest coast observe how comfortable white people are living alone, how they seem satisfied by the thinnest embrace of the conjugal couple, how they would rather be alone (*gamaparrking*) than have one little louse.

Three

But even *here* at Belyuen some of these material anchors demand very different presuppositions about the body, its location, and its care. Belyuen friends and family might focus on the social and geontological conditions of enfleshment, and by doing so, iterate them, but they meet medical, legal, and economic institutions that address these social and geontological conditions in more or less diagonal and tangential terms. For instance, no one from Belyuen or from surrounding coastal communities has ever traveled with me to the United States, let alone to the clinics I visited in Chicago and Montreal. They do, however, regularly travel through local community clinics, hospitals in Darwin, and sometimes hospitals in southern cities. Over the course of their lives, they have encountered significant changes in how these clinics and hospitals approach their health care and indigenous health care generally. In recent years, particular attention has been paid to the dynamic relationship between culture and indigenous health. Aboriginal health activists have fought hard to place respect for cultural beliefs at the forefront of indigenous health care research and practice. And they have, in concrete institutional ways, installed a culturally sensitive, indigenously controlled approach to health into procedural and substantive aspects of research and policy. For example, in 1986, the Aboriginal Health Research Ethics Committee (AHREC) was implemented for all research in South Australia. The AHREC stipulated that

> the ethical guidelines set out by the National Health and Medical Research Council be adhered to in relation to securing individual and community consent to participate in the research. *Acceptability of Methodology*. That the culture and geography of the Aboriginal community be taken into consideration in developing research methodology that is acceptable. *Benefit to Community*. That research assists Health Workers in better management of health problems in the community and that intervention studies are preferred in that the community would benefit directly from the research being carried out as opposed to investigatory research. *Feedback to Community*. That the right of individuals to gain

access to information resulting from their participation in the research be acknowledged and provided by researcher and for the Aboriginal Health Research Ethics Committee to be furnished with data resulting from specific studies.[15]

In 2003, the National Health and Medical Research Council discussed some of the sociopolitical conditions for separating ethical guidelines pertaining to "all Australians, including Aboriginal and Torres Strait Islander People" from a "complementary set of guidelines covering research in Aboriginal and Torres Strait Islander Health."[16] The report notes a number of social changes that propelled this separation, including increasing collaborative partnerships among research institutes and communities, more Aboriginal and Torres Strait Islander people involved in research as researchers, and a general increase in the level of interest in indigenous health research. The immediate end of the new guidelines was to standardize the ethics of research in these new contexts. But the guidelines were also meant to establish a sense of trust in "the enterprise of research itself"[17] among indigenous people in the long run.

These new ethical protocols do not meet a virgin world, however. They circulate into indigenous worlds already conditioned by previous interactions with health research and care. The same Ruby Yarrowin who watched Maliya kill family members in the Banagula region experienced the irrelevance of her beliefs about death and dying when she was a young mother. In the 1940s, she was detained in a small Darwin jail cell without a translator because she had buried her baby boy in the bush after he died of a bronchial infection. Speaking no English, she had no idea why or to what end she was being held. In the early 1980s, Ruby Yarrowin, Maggie Timber, and other middle-aged and elderly women and men were sought out by academic and popular students of Aboriginal Bush Medicine to provide detailed accounts of their local pharmacopoeia. Ruby Yarrowin refused to participate, though others did.

In the late 1990s, Ruby Yarrowin also refused to have physicians remove a large lump from her arm and refused to say consistently why she refused—the reasons were her "secret." To be sure, in local vocabularies "secret" often signals an extra-physical, often geontological, reasoning. But her reasons could have been based on any number of things, including her sense, brewed in the mid-1940s, that white doctors lie or are cruel. The physicians called on her daughters to convince her that the lump was "just a physical condition" in case she was worried that it was associated with some other "cultural meaning." And, as in many such instances, indigenous health care workers and local family members were asked to mediate between the non-indigenous doctors and Ruby Yarrowin. The lump was eventually removed. In the process, sensitivity was shown to local social practices and cultural beliefs. Yet, here we see the precise point Emma Kowal and Yin Paradies have recently made, that researchers and practitioners trained in cultural sensitivity attempt "to escape neocolonialism" only to find that they are left in a "bind common to many postcolonial situations. They must relieve the ill-health of indigenous people without acting upon them; change them without declaring that change is required."[18]

This bind is not merely the result of an internal tension within the field of culturally sensitive medical research and delivery, but an effect of the impossibility of quarantining the medical subject from other types of subjects within the nation-state. For instance, if Ruby Yarrowin were to base the medical care of one of her children or grandchildren on her belief about Maliya or other sites like it, a medical condition might quickly change into a legal condition—social welfare policies or statutes pertaining to child abuse might suddenly be cited as the relevant framework for understanding such "care." And yet even though Maliya cannot maintain its status of truth in certain instances of medical treatment—its geontology cannot trump biomedical epistemologies—in other legal settings it is not merely the basis of casual pleasures and coffee table books on bush medicine, but the demand of law.

Take, for instance, Ruby Yarrowin's rendition of Maliya's powers during the Lower Daly River Land Claim hearing.

> Mr. Keely: He is dangerous one, you have said?
> Ruby Yarrowin: Yes, dangerous that one. If you chuck him, you will die. If you touch that people.
> Mr. Keely: If you chuck them?
> Ruby Yarrowin: Yeah.
> Mr. Keely: People?
> Ruby Yarrowin: Yeah, they're dreaming.
> Mr. Keely: If you chuck them, people might die?

Ruby Yarrowin: Everyone. People.

Mr. Keely: Right, what are you talking of—chucking? Chucking what?

Ruby Yarrowin: Chucking the water . . . or bamboo.

Mr. Keely: Chucking water or poking him with a bamboo, you are talking.

Ruby Yarrowin: Yeah.

Mr. Keely: In that dreamtime story, where does the blowfly bite you? He bite somebody?

Ruby Yarrowin: Yeah.

Mr. Keely: He bite people?

Ruby Yarrowin: Yeah, they are to kill him, killing you, and you fall down.

Mr. Keely: He kills you—

Ruby Yarrowin: Yeah, back one.

Mr. Keely:—by biting you in the back.

Ruby Yarrowin: Yeah. Everyone died. Didn't even look.

Mr. Keely: At Maliya.

Ruby Yarrowin: Yeah.

Mr. Keely:—there are some bones there? Before, did you look at some bones there, that place?

Ruby Yarrowin: Yeah, bones everywhere really, bone really—everywhere, taking my people everywhere. They fall down and die everywhere. Have a look bone.[19]

For her narrative to be effective in this legal setting, Ruby Yarrowin's voice needs to index—refer to and entail—discourses of the genealogical society that situate her within the counter-world of the autonomy of reason. The confirmation of this counter-world's conjuring pivots on an actual event that is transformed into a mythological event—Ruby Yarrowin's personal account of witnessing the horrific effects of sorrow is transformed into a "dreamtime story." In this narrative conjuring, "bone really" and "bones everywhere" become moments of speculative reason and speculative pleasure, the "what if" of a fairy tale. The pleasure of these "stories" arises in part from the figuration of the customary as rationality's receding horizon.[20] They become part mythological and part archaeological, even as they cease being about actual being and start being about the cultural encrustations of facts. Of course, legal assessments of the "traditional Aboriginal" do not draw only from these modal transformations. They draw equally on racial and sexual discourses—education level, skin pigmentation, marriage practices. The closer these and other indices come to creating a visual and sonic field compatible to current thematizations of the "traditional Aboriginal," the tighter the projection of Ruby Yarrowin into this field.

The kinds of transfigurations occurring in this land claim do not merely occur in land claims. In a doctor's office, Maliya and *munggarra* are interesting stories, a cultural *poesis*, but they are unable to maintain their status of truth or even practical knowledge when push comes to shove. In legal contexts other than land claims, the indigenous subject is stretched across an autological and genealogical divide rather than beached on one side of this divide. In criminal procedures in Australia, cultural beliefs and attitudes are not a basis for criminal charges but can be taken into consideration during sentencing. If a crime was committed because of a customary obligation then the sentence can be lightened — the crime is mitigated but not excused. Many younger indigenous men and women living along the northwest coast are well aware of this sentencing flexibility — one of my husbands steering the boat during our trip to Maliya has relied on this distinction between charge and sentencing to mitigate several assault charges.[21]

What is important here is not whether Ruby Yarrowin is or is not traditional or whether she did or did not see the devastating effects of *kalangak*. Ruby Yarrowin could remain silent about her beliefs and still be as "traditional" as she is when she is talking. Or she could not believe a hoot of what she was saying. But no matter what she does, the doing is already embedded in a network of discursive matrixes that apprehends her actions under the sign of the autological subject or genealogical society. *And she must do something.* She must care for herself at the multidimensional and multifunctional intersection of law, public culture, and practical knowledge. She must navigate clinics, dreaming sites, legal protocols, and camping grounds as well as navigate their games of truth about the indigenous self, even as she makes decisions in the context of very local debates about what knowledge should circulate through the community and beyond. She and others must continually ask and answer the question of exactly when a law, economy, or health care plan pertains to "all Australians, including Aboriginal and Torres Strait Islander People" and when it pertains only to Aboriginal and Torres Strait Islander people. In clinics, Ruby Yarrowin must act as if her knowledge and belief in Maliya and the Barangga *mungarra* did not *really* matter, in legal hearings as if it did. She must do so even though she cannot be sure what would happen if she actually acted on this knowledge and belief.

In other words, one aspect of the cunning of recognition is the transformation of a discourse of demand into a discourse of recognition—the demand that Ruby Yarrowin have a specific kind of knowledge about Maliya and a specific propositional attitude toward it if she is to be recognized as a "traditional Aboriginal subject." Another aspect of the cunning of recognition is the bracketing of the incoherence of these multiple external demands on the indigenous subject as she traverses the incommensurately coordinated social institutions. This second bracketing is especially significant since the ways that indigenous subjects move strategically across the various demanding environments of law, health, economy, and social welfare are recycled into the disciplinary apparatus of the state. The lack of traditional attitude toward health care and ritual practice can be, and has been, used to undermine land claims.

Equally important is the fact that this second bracket allows critics and practitioners some distance from the grotesque misalignment of the rhetorics of cultural preservation within the practices of life preservation. These critics and practitioners can claim that these other contexts are not relevant to the case in hand. But we must break this bracket if we are to see how legal imaginaries of the flesh and the actual temporality of indigenous flesh are out of joint. The speculative pleasure of the law of cultural recognition as well as its legislative force pivots on a delicate intersection of knowledge and age—old people with old knowledge. But because of the health collapse within Aboriginal society, age is the one thing people usually don't have. On the small boat mapping Maliya and other sites along the Anson Bay coast was a man, Trevor Bianamu, a brother of mine who was about thirty-five at the time. As we sailed along the coast, the men shared what they had learned from their relatives about its historical and spiritual contours. And they discussed the pressure that would fall on them if a legal contest over the land took place. My brother quipped that he was not worried because he would just make the "old people" do the talking. We were at that point passing by his country, Banagaiya. His brothers and I looked at him and said, "*Mana* (brother), you are the old person got your family, man side." And he had been, since he was 26, the oldest male member of his patrilineally defined family.

When Trevor Bianamu said he would make the old people talk, he was just repeating what he had heard and seen in other land claims and consultations over the years. He had witnessed several land claims by this time and knew that lawyers preferred to have the eldest members of a descent group speak for their family group—usually meaning people in their middle fifties or sixties, and, where possible, seventies and eighties: "*Pulupiya* people," or grey-headed people. He and his age mates had been endlessly passed over as "too young" or too drunk when lawyers and consultants arrived in the community looking for the proper people with whom to discuss traditional land issues. And whose fault is that? Most indigenous bureaucracies are grossly under-funded, chronically under-staffed, and constantly under political assault.

They do not have the time to find, move, feed, and nurture more than the most necessary people for any land-related issue. These tasks are said to reside properly within the indigenous family, clan, or community even as these families, clans, and communities are themselves struggling to find the means to pay for rent, food, and schooling.

Even as these incoherencies are written into the everyday fabric of indigenous life, other bodies and voices are being made articulate as they move across institutional spaces. They are not articulate; they are made articulate. Take me, for instance. I have discussed all of the above ways of thinking about bodies and their social and material conditions with the doctors and lawyers I have worked with over the last twenty-odd years. In these conversations I am addressed as an expert on cultural belief and its rational groundings. I am invited to speculate with them on the possibility, for instance, that flu epidemics and streptococcal infections may have been the vector of the deaths and illness that these women described, and perhaps also the cultural initialization of Maliya, *munggarra*, and other active ancestral sites. In these conversations, I can insist that these places and events have no need of radical translation and that they must simply be addressed on their own terms. I do not, however, become indigenous at this moment. I become "over-identified" with my indigenous friends and family or I become "belligerent" and "unreasonable." Or, more interestingly, I risk losing my status as an expert and someone interesting to talk with. Whatever I become, this becoming usually does not affect the diagnosis and government of my diseased body. I can say anything and receive care in a form that seems to fit my life because the institutions of care had "me" in mind.

All of which is to say little more than that the treatment of my sore is not dependent on the ontological presence or absence of Maliya, my existential encounter with Maliya, or my belief in Maliya. In fact, I live in the same complex, multiply structured world that my indigenous friends do. I, too, must decide whether sharing a life with my indigenous friends is more important than being exposed to low levels of infection. I, too, must decide whether I will inhabit a life-world in which sharing a sore is a necessary precondition of being together, side-by-side, one cup, food that travels from mouth to mouth. But I share this necessity differently even as I share it. I can produce myself as a stranger to it, as a self-governing subject of it, passively or actively—just being quiet in the doctor's office and letting him assume what he is likely to assume so that I can get my medicine quickly—without disrupting other distribution networks that make up the broad nervous system in which my body is produced. I will be made autological everywhere I go, qualified by the obvious difference of my sex and sexuality, but autological all the same. This is not so for my friends and colleagues in Australia. And it is exactly the *irrelevance* of Maliya to my clinic experience that suggests how autology and genealogy, and their carnal anchors, function most tenaciously, steering the course of action and the shape of discourse by functioning most invisibly in situations in which nothing more remarkable is going on than deciding which part of one's life is relevant to a doctor changing one's bandage.

Of course, none of this is true. None of these institutions of care has been formed with me in mind, but only with "me" in mind, insofar as "I" am closer or further from the regulatory norm and the normal body. To reach toward this norm, I, too, must contort my voice and body to fit its shifting horizon.

Four

The rendition of care, curiosity, and calamity that I provided the Chicago and Montreal doctors was anything but complete, even leaving aside the beliefs and practices of friends living along the northwest coast of Australia. As the physicians probed me about the source of my sore and about how it was usually treated, I left out another set of social worlds I regularly inhabit. I did not tell the Montreal doctor that, the night before coming to the public clinic, my friend and colleague Michael Warner, also at the conference, had agreed to change the bandage on my shoulder so that we could attend the last day of Divers/Cité, Montreal's lesbian, gay, bisexual, and transgendered PRIDE celebrations. Michael wanted to see the featured performer that evening, Mado Lamotte. It was a difficult job, changing my bandage. Michael struggled to distinguish which part of my shoulder was the wick, which was rotted flesh, and which was alive. He eventually gave up and carefully re-bandaged the entire mess. I don't remember if I told him the medication I was on. But we both would have known that Septrim was widely prescribed for the prevention of PCP (Pneumocystis pneumonia) in people with HIV/AIDS.

After the conference I was off to a date with an old friend

of Michael's. And so, as he and I worked on re-bandaging my shoulder for our night out, we discussed the ethics of dating with a sore as hideous looking and as fundamentally undiagnosed as mine, stumbling around for a genre into which we could insert and make sense of my sore and sexuality. We were, as Cindy Patton has put it, "thinking without a proper name."[22] Not surprisingly, given the sexual discourses and worlds we shared, we fairly rapidly made recourse to a language of sex-positive safe sex—the ethical and medical imperative to disclose one's health status to actual and potential sexual partners. We discussed this ethic in the casual way that so many people of a certain age do in the United States. Our conversation was not groundbreaking or world-shattering by any means, just two people engaged in a mundane review of the importance of taking individual responsibility for the transmission of disease in a society structured by stranger sociality. (Which, parenthetically, may well be what irks many on the religious right—the casualness of this way of thinking ethically in the domain of sex.) Casual or profound, our conversation cross-hatched elements from the various social worlds that we were a part of, and in the process sutured together, if only for a moment, a new bodily matrix. Sores acquired from one social world entered into another, and as they did so, they were refigured by local discourses.

Although Michael and I spoke of my sore in the everyday language of safe sex, the sociomedical history of the sore rattled the intelligibility of this discursive move—no less in its presuppositions about individual disclosure and stranger publics than in its biomedical nature. What, after all, was I supposed to disclose to the woman I was dating? I wasn't even sure what the source or agent of these sores was, what risk I was exposing her to. I *could* tell her I was likely to continue to have these sores periodically because my life seemed inseparable from the lives of my indigenous friends and family in northern Australia and because their lives were likely to remain mired in the poverty and racism that helped cause these sores. But this explanatory frame—that poverty and racism are the cause if not the agent of these sores (not so different an explanation from that given to me by the Darwin physician) and that my health was now linked to their health via deeply felt kinship obligations—strains the flesh of the body that Michael and I inhabited. It stretches its skin and internal organs away from the biomedical and bioethical discourse of safe sex and the world of stranger sociality it presupposes, and re-grafts it onto geophysics of a different sort, a geophysics of thick ties of kinship, friendship, and ritual as well as the thick transfers of wealth, health, and power that these thick social worlds make possible and inhibit. In other words, a different supra-organic body is built when the inequalities of white and black, North and South, settler and indigenous are the primary axis of the body that exists between me and my indigenous family and friends. My sore stops being only a biological agent that needs to be treated and begins being also a social relation that needs to be addressed. It is this transnational body that Thabo Mbeki has controversially evoked in his HIV/AIDS policy, that Aboriginal artists have evoked in several well-known HIV/AIDS awareness posters, and that the Canadian Aboriginal AIDS Network has evoked in its harms-reduction approach to the epidemic.[23] It is also the body that indigenous friends evoke when they describe the difference between indigenous and white people as resting on the relative value of the skin and sociality—that whites care more about the smoothness of their skin ("clean skin") than the condition of their social relations. They would rather sleep far away from each other than risk getting lice, sores, and scabies.

Still, why wouldn't I tell the Montreal physician about the previous night's tampering of my bandage? What discursive forces were with me in that public clinic that helped shape and direct my language? One set of social vectors pressing onto this scene was a portrait with HIV/AIDS emerging at the intersection of two different portraits of social pathology. On the one hand, HIV/AIDS has been portrayed as the pathological product of genealogical sociability. Early medical bulletins, circulated across world health organizations, warned about the spread of HIV in indigenous communities through sexual laxity, ritual culture, and addiction; in other words, through either the continuity of customary kinship obligations or their breakdown. On the other hand, HIV/AIDS has long been portrayed as the pathological product of the autological subject at the extreme end of stranger sociality. Because I sit at the intersection of these two possibilities, the Montreal physician was less likely to dissect the intercommunal body that Michael and I had built than to tether it together more tightly with the two ends of the same pathological rope—too much genealogy, too much autology, too many kin, too many strangers. And so, if he wasn't thinking about the perverse sexual body, I wasn't going to help him waste our time by going down what I considered to be a misguided diagnostic path. True, I wanted this sore to go away and, given my upcoming date, I wanted a medically authorized judgment that these kinds of sores were not communicable. But I didn't want to get into a discussion about gay and indigenous sexual cultures. All of these motivations were part of the forces that shut my mouth and kept me silent. And all of these silences are part of the delicate apparatus by which the discourses of autology and genealogy are maintained in liberal worlds. In the effort to get the sore cleaned up and re-bandaged quickly so that I could get back to the conference, I, too, treated my sexuality, Maliya, and my Australian friends and family as irrelevant to the diagnosis and governance of my body. I managed, without anyone asking me to do so, a set of possible alignments between perverse "pathological" cultures—the ritual pathology of Aboriginality and the sexual pathology of undomesticated gay stranger sociality. Friends in indigenous Australia manage other alignments—creating, or not, genealogical spaces and times that do not disturb autological ideologies.

Adelaide, Australia (AP)—Because of ceremonial sharing of blood, as well as a general absence of safe sex practices, Australian aborigines are at high risk of devastation by AIDS, according to the findings of a state inquiry. HIV is spreading rapidly, and some aborigines have already died from the disease, said the report by South Australian Parliament's Social Development Committee. Alcohol abuse and the lack of "cultural sanctions against multiple sex partners" contribute to unsafe sex and transmission of the virus, stated the report. Also, in many rituals, aborigines cut themselves with a stick or rock and risk spreading the disease by sharing the cutting object, the report concluded.[24]

I am not cavalier about the danger that HIV/AIDS poses to indigenous people and communities. HIV/AIDS prevention in Australia has been far more aggressive than in the United States. The 1980s and 1990s saw a massive safe-sex campaign addressed to the general public and to gay and indigenous communities that helped to reduce the spread of HIV/AIDS in Australia. Face-to-face encounters were one of the textual means by which information about HIV/AIDS circulated through indigenous worlds. Aboriginal and non-Aboriginal video directors and screenwriters such as Ruth Carr, Catherine Adams, Mimi Pulka, and Tracey Moffat also produced works about and directed to indigenous communities. Infection rates are, as a consequence, relatively low, and seem to have peaked in the 1980s. In 1999, about one hundred people died of AIDS and about fourteen thousand were living with HIV/AIDS, around 0.15 percent of the adult population.[25] However, from 1994 to 2000, according to the CDC, the rate of new cases among urban indigenous Australians was four times higher than the average in the general population.[26]

These calculations of risk and the comparative epidemiology on which they rest presuppose a certain level of homogeneity within population groups even as, according to Stacy Leigh Pigg, they "promulgate a particular set of ideas about the sexual and reproductive body."[27] And yet, these populations and their discursive and material grounds are quite diverse. In some indigenous social networks, the difference between being and not being Aboriginal is a defining feature of daily interactional space. Because this kind of social distinction lies in the foreground, the struggle to define "Aboriginal" —its explicable and numerable cultural, social, and environmental dimensions—defines local cultural politics. Who is and is not indigenous is the struggle of identity. In other social networks, Aboriginality is the daily backdrop of interactional space—nearly everyone is Aboriginal—and so other regional, ecological, ritual, clan, community, and language identities are more important for defining and navigating everyday life. In many indigenous communities along the northwest coast, for instance, the question is usually not what defines an Aboriginal person but rather what it is to be a coastal rather than an inland person, with all the kinship and ritual ramifications of this ecological distinction. As a result, the dispersion of discourses of safe sex, sexual identity, and sexuality through indigenous worlds varies significantly from urban to suburban to rural spaces, from the heavily populated south to the more sparsely populated north. And when discourses of safe sex, sexual identity, and sexuality circulate in places like the northwest coast, they circulate among, and articulate, already existing life-worlds. The thematics of safe sex, sexual identity, and sexuality meet life-worlds with specific notions about how social goods and harms are distributed across age, gender, and kinship, about where the body is and how it can or cannot extend across physical and mental space.

Take, for instance, a conversation that occurred in 1989.

A group of indigenous women and I were sitting on the north coast of the Cox Peninsula, whiling away the late morning discussing the syntax of Emiyenggal, when a Toyota Land Cruiser filled with strangers drove up. Several women, some white, some indigenous, popped out of the truck, and after a brief introduction began to discuss with us the importance and mechanics of safe sex in the prevention of sexually transmitted diseases and HIV/AIDS. To demonstrate the use of condoms, they pulled a dildo from one of their bags and attached it to a piece of plywood. It was quite an uncanny sight—the white flesh-colored dildo swaying back and forth on the piece of plywood, my linguistic notes flapping in the breeze, the remains of half-eaten fish and bread from our morning breakfast attracting the interest of flies and dogs. Very quickly, as was their way, the women began entertaining each other with a particular coastal ribaldry in a mixture of Emiyenggal and Aboriginal English not parsable to the strangers. The women joked about whether the visitors were suggesting that we not only put the condom on the dildo, but that we then test out the entire contraption on each other.

When the older women joked about strapping on the dildo, they relied on, and entailed, the continuing relevance of the social distinction between what anthropologists term cross-cousins and parallel cousins, and what the women term in Emiyenggal *panen/menggen* and *mane/edje* or in creole husband/wife and brother/sister. Because of the dense kinship networks that compose their lives, every woman on that beach had several *menggen* sitting next to her. Speakers chose specific women as the address of their discursive play (*erere*), not a *menggen* in general, but a specific *menggen*. These modes of play intensify kinship relations, turning a dead category into a more intimate affair, not an intimacy that punctures kinship, but an intimacy that constitutes retroactively the truth of kinship as a persistent and relevant category of social life. In this way, these modes of address are creative and productive as much as they are normative and disciplinary. They pull immanent desires and alliances into actual social worlds, creating actual affective and discursive dependencies where before there were only potential dependencies. They mobilize

kinship, age grades, and gender to sweeten certain same-sex and cross-sex relations through a rough, sexually explicit discursive play (*erere, yedametj*). Is this sexuality? Only in the most reduced and decontextualized sense. These women are not choosing between homosexuality and heterosexuality, or between discourses of alliance and discourses of sexuality. They are instead constituting social dependencies beyond the conjugal couple; reducing harm through the formation of broader social networks; and enjoying each other's wit.

These women cannot hermetically seal off their practices of sociality from discourses of hetero- and homosexuality and stranger sociality, however, even if they wanted to. After all, discourses of sexuality were already within the languages and practices of safe sex circulating across countless beaches and community clinics as well as in newspapers and on television, radio, and Internet sites by the time we were discussing the syntax of Emiyenggal. An incident with two girls, each about ten in 1989, suggests some of the ways these discourses are coordinated, contested, and absorbed locally. One day, as we were fishing along a creek, one of the girls, Anna, declared to the other, and to everyone gathered around, that when she grew up she was going to marry her cross-cousin (*I gana marry you menggen when I get bigger*). A mother of Anna—who was about twenty at the time—corrected her daughter, saying that girls marry boys, not other girls, to which Anna replied, turning to her grandmother, "Neh, I can marry her. I call her wife. I can marry her. Eh Nana?" Anna's grandmother, who was sitting nearby, agreed, saying, "That her wife, that her proper *menggen*, finished, you can't make im different." The older women's statement did not end the argument, for Anna's mother retorted, "wulgamen you no more sebi, that different, that not *menggen* that lesbian." For Anna's grandmother, these were absolutely different social skins, but not the way her daughter had suggested: "No, no, don't say that, you wrong yourself, you say *menggen*, you say wife, that girl can play with that other girl, that not lesbian that *menggen*."

It would be easy to claim that Anna's grandmother constituted the separation between *menggen* and lesbian on the basis of the difference between kinship and stranger socialities and that, as she did so, Anna's grandmother was constituting the continual relevance of local modes of desire and association in the face of the globalization of the hetero-homo binary.[28] But the separation that Anna's grandmother made was supported by much more than the mere distinction between kin and strangers. It rested on an entire set of presuppositions about the body and its possible extensions—on a more general way of thinking about the body as a material extension into and out of the physical and social world *as that world is now organized*.

For some the tensile nature of kinship mediates social life. Kinship wires the deep recesses of the body. A complex coordination of muscles, organs, and joints signal the wellbeing of various kin, sacred ancestral sites, and ritual events. For others, the body extends more generally across quotidian materiality. For instance, in 1989, one of my brothers, Anthony Bilbil, who was about fifteen at the time, got furious with his older brother. Anthony claimed his brother cut his foot. The proximate cause of his injury was a piece of glass he accidentally stepped on. But what really caused his injury, according to Anthony, was that his older brother had touched his sleeping blanket, violating the bodily separation of siblings. These kinds of extensions of the body affect women and men. But once into their maturity, men and women tend to face these extensions in different ways. Men are usually the victims of social predators such as *munggul* — men who use young pretty women from other areas as bait to capture local men, removing their kidney fat and filling the void with dry grass. The victims have hollow backs, like large mudcrabs, light and without any beef inside, liable to death from the slightest wound. Women are more likely to be the victims of *tjukpiya* — the use of ritually imbued spit to cause traumatic deafness. Women warn men against traveling to certain places after reports of *munggul*, or socializing and sexualizing with women with "different faces." Men tell women not to take certain roads to hunt or to visit relatives lest they interrupt male ceremonies and become a victim of *tjukpiya* or worse.

Of course, these kinds of accounts of the body and its difference are just the kinds of things that medical and legal regimes of recognition wish to support, perhaps through copyright.[29] When culture/custom is considered to have positive social or moral values, then *demanding* this *determination* is seen as merely recognizing facts on the ground. Take, for example, two exchanges in a land claim between Betty Bilawag, Ester Barradjap, and their respective lawyers on the subject of kinship and marriage.

> Mr. Keely: Which mob do you belong to, Betty?
> Betty Bilawag: Marriamu, my tribe.
> Mr. Keely: When you got married to that old man Mosec, was that a promised marriage or not?
> Betty Bilawag: Yes, that my promised husband.
> Mr. Keely: He was promised by whom?
> Betty Bilawag: By my father promised to Mosec.[30]

> Mr. Young: Okay, good. Was that marriage between Agnes Lippo and Tom Lippo, was that a promised marriage?
> Ester Barradjap: Yes.
> Mr. Young: And what about your marriage to Tom?
> Ester Barradjap: It promised, same.
> Mr. Young: Promised marriage, same. Now, is there— who arranged your marriage to Tom?
> Ester Barradjap: My father.[31]

Note the various levels of genealogical discourse indexed in this exchange—the law of paternity, the law of custom, and the law of obligation. Other women, who did not marry promised husbands, or for whom no promised husband was arranged for various reasons (not least because of the social chaos of the colonial period and its aftermaths in the post-colony), are not equally "good subjects" of the law of recognition. In an exploratory discussion for this claim another woman was asked if her husband was promised. She replied that he wasn't but qualified this reply with the statement that he was nevertheless her proper cousin, i.e., lawful according to the custom of kinship and marriage. This form of address is found not only in this particular land claim, or in land claims in particular. It is a field of address in which a regime of recognition demands a regime of genealogical determination as the condition for authenticity.

It is precisely here that we need to remember that all of these bodily extensions into the physical and social world occur within the actual worlds where people live, not in some other world — not some counter-factual world of an enchanted Dreamtime. And we need to remember that all of these languages and practices of kinship, the body, and desire are also interpreted with regard to how indigenous men and women imagine settler subjects apprehending them and with regard to the power they have in shaping these imaginaries. Indigenous women and men have sharply critical positions on how they are inserted into discourses of the genealogical society and the proper indigenous subject. A few years ago, I was engaged in a conversation about "proper marriage forms" with a middle-aged mother of mine, Marjorie Bilbil, who had refused her own arranged marriage. We were discussing among which language groups it had been "proper" (also "right way") for younger women to marry their mother's father's brother and why it was proper for women to marry certain men in their grandparents' generation but not for men to do the same ("women go up, men go down"). At the very moment that I created a knot between traditional marriage and modern sexism, Marjorie Bilbil—whom I had known closely for eighteen years at that point—observed, without much of a transition, "White people marry anyone, like dog really, eh Bet." I qualified this statement by saying that, properly, they married anyone except members of their immediate family; they were qualified dogs. She responded that this was true, that white people were "back to front" in almost every conceivable way. Given the local emphasis on indirect forms of social critique, "white people" included anyone asking these kinds of questions—including me.

In short, when the group of women argued about the meaning of marriage, kinship, and sexuality, they did so on the edge of a creek that spilled into all of these local and translocal discourses—the sexual proclivity of various ancestral sites, the ongoing drama of *Will and Grace* broadcast on the local television channels, the coverage of white pedophiles in the local Murdoch-owned newspaper, the drinking parties that crisscross Aboriginal communities in which reggae, hip hop, and *wangga* are combined. The ubiquitous nature of the mass media and the longstanding social relations across indigenous and settler personal and institutional spaces have long ago invaginated kinship with other organizations of social life, desire, the body, and stranger intimacy. In these ways, local bodies are not merely open to kin, ancestral sites, and ritual events. They are also open to the drama of Western sexuality with its antagonisms and phobias, opportunities and exasperations. The binary opposition between heterosexuality and homosexuality, and the presumptions of stranger sociality that subtend them both, enter through very local discourses and practices, thickening one set of social relays, thinning others, displacing and unhinging the binary of hetero- and homosexuality itself. The multiplicity of discourses of sexuality provides the occasion for discursive contradictions, contractions, conflicts, and creative invaginations as well as new forms of the social skin, new social phobias, and new social aspirations.

It is within these thick possibilities that homophobia reappears as a powerful affective and discursive disciplinary tool and is as present in urban and rural indigenous spaces as sexualities per se. Along with the emergence of the identity of heterosexuality and homosexuality as a thing one can be and can be independent of kinship has come homophobia as a thing one can also be, creating a separation between people. Along with this sexual difference has come a thing that must remain hidden or demand visibility: discourse about loss, gain, and ethics, about the gay international and the politics of human rights, and about the difference between strangers and kin. In the face of the weak citizenship foundation of homosexuality and the strongly negative affective foundation, many urban-based self-identified gay indigenes, both men and women, struggle to reconcile their sexual identity with the notion of traditional Aboriginality.[32]

All of this is to make a simple point: indigenous men and

women are not the passive subjects of these discourses. They constantly disturb settler discourses of the body and its conditions of desire, integrity, and viability as these discourses circulate through their lives. And they disturb the people who are carrying these discourses, such as me. They disturb me not merely because they are homophobic but because I find retrospectively that being bound to my friends and family along the coast means that I can neither be with them nor with myself easily. I can tell my date that I am likely to continue to get these sores because I am likely to continue to return year after year to people whom I have known longer and more intimately than many in my biological family. But I also return there on the condition that I leave some aspects of my sexuality behind.

As a result, this deeply personal relation has made me personally implausible, my political allegiances awkward. If I locate myself within a world of stranger sociality and the sexuality it entails, then I have separated myself from them. But I also separate myself from myself because at this point who I am is unimaginable outside these twenty-one years of being in this family. All of which is to say little more than what Judith Butler said before—that all identities are risible, are disturbed by the play of citationality.[33] But in so saying we have only just begun. We have merely chalked the starting line of our social analysis. While it is certainly true that "I" am as disturbed by the discourses and expectations of autology and genealogy as my Belyuen friends and family, I am disturbed differently, and the effects of this disturbance are different. We are all vulnerable, but not equally so.

Part of what produces these different vulnerabilities is the intersection of discourses of genealogy and autology and the actual materialities of social life. I mentioned one intersection earlier—the legal prejudice for old people, old knowledge, and old practice in the context of a low life expectancy. But there are much less formal ways in which these discourses touch material life. My sore is not mine in any sense that really matters, after all. It belongs to a cascading set of social harms and attitudes toward these harms that have emerged in the wake of settler colonialism. Noel Pearson, an Aboriginal activist, has famously and forcefully argued that state welfare, when applied to indigenous peoples, is a technique of numbing indigenous and non-indigenous people to the radical "state of dysfunction" in Aboriginal communities.

74

> Imagine if the average life expectancy of the town of Gatton was only 50 years and sliding. Imagine if the population of Cairns was in prison to the same proportion as the people of Hopevale or Arrakun or Lockhart River. Imagine if over 38 per cent of the 15-to-40-year-olds in the town of Atherton had a sexually transmitted disease. Imagine if kidney or liver failures or heart disease were proportionally the same for Gympie as it is for Cape York. Would we be as numb and complacent about the statistics as we are when faced with the reality of the social disaster of aboriginal society on Cape York Peninsula? No. There would be nothing less than a state of emergency, with government initiatives that had pre-

vailed and failed being fundamentally questioned and radically revisited.[34]

Pearson's proposals for solving this numbing are controversial in large part because he claims that the malevolence of social welfare will stop only when social welfare itself ends. As a result, Pearson has joined forces with the conservative Liberal-National Party to declare self-determination a failed social experiment and to advance "shared responsibility agreements" between state bureaucracies and indigenous communities.[35] These packages condition the receipt of such essential governmental services as remote education and housing on the maintenance of personal hygiene and school attendance. Clearly, these packages smack of an earlier, paternalistic attitude toward indigenous self-governance. And it is unclear how these packages can be "mutual" in any sense given the extreme social, political, and economic inequalities that exist between indigenous and non-indigenous people. When it comes to non-indigenous health and mortality, indigenous Australians inhabit turn-of-the-century Australia, when the life expectancy of a European newborn boy was 55.2 years, and a newborn girl 58.8 years. These remained the high end of the life expectancies of indigenous men and women in 2004, even as that of their non-indigenous co-citizens climbed to 75.9 and 81.5, respectively.[36] These statistics of life and death, though neatly fitting the epistemology of the body count, barely capture life at the margins of markets, the bad faith of liberal capitalism's trickle-down economy, and the failure of cultural recognition to evolve an ethics of mutual life.

Pearson notwithstanding, the social welfare net has not been shredded in Australia, at least not yet. In rural indigenous communities, social welfare is managed through a variety of programs, including those for aged pensioners, women with children, the unemployed, and community development projects. The Community Development Employment Project (CDEP) is a work plan established in 1977. As Jon Altman and M.C. Gray note, CDEP has been described as "a labor market program, an alternative income support scheme, and a community development scheme," but whatever it is, CDEP has raised the personal income of rural indigenous men and women.[37] Even so, the standard measurements of social wellbeing—employment, income, housing, health, education—indicate that indigenous men and women inhabit by far the lowest rung of Australian society.[38] The CDEP was run by the Aboriginal and Torres Strait Islander Commission (ATSIC) until 2005, when the Liberal-National government under John Howard dissolved ATSIC. Since its founding, ATSIC had been roiled by a number of funding scandals, though whether these scandals evidence more or less corruption than non-indigenous government is an open question. ATSIC was hailed as the primary place where indigenous issues would be resolved through self-management and was disparaged as riddled with mismanagement and corruption. It is not clear whether the problem ATSIC faced was one of overfunding or underfunding, one of too much or too little self-management. On the one hand, under the Labor government of Paul Keating, responsibilities that initially rested in ATSIC were transferred to other departments, notably control over health care.

On the other hand, a large majority of funding within ATSIC was non-discretionary spending on programs that the Commonwealth government had determined and shaped, such as CDEP.[39]

In the shadow of these statistics Pearson's rage is understandable. All of the physicians with whom I spoke as I traveled from Belyuen to Chicago to Montreal to Darwin and then back to Belyuen assured me I shouldn't worry about getting sores because they would go away when I returned to the colder North American climate and a sanitary environment, or, if necessary, after a round of antibiotics. If it were staphylococcus, or a bit of streptococcus, so what?

To say that in 2003 I discovered that Group A streptococcus can lead to serious, sometimes fatal, health conditions is a sad commentary on my research skills. But sadder still is the fact that I fell for one of the oldest tricks of the capitalist organization of global medicine—*ghoul health*. Ghoul health refers to the global organization of the biomedical establishment, and its imaginary, around the idea that the big scary bug, the new plague, is the real threat that haunts the contemporary global division, distribution, and circulation of health, that it will decisively render the distribution of *jus vitae ac necris*, and that this big scary bug will track empire back to its source in an end-game of geophysical bad faith. Ghoul health plays on the real fear that the material distribution of life and death arising from the structural impoverishment of postcolonial and settler colonial worlds may have accidentally or purposefully brewed an unstoppable bio-virulence from the bad faith of liberal capital and its multiple geophysical tactics and partners. Even if the Chicago doctor who took the time to treat my shoulder, and whom I have repaid unfairly by pillorying him internationally, was not thinking about the Andromeda strain or Ebola so much as the more mundane possibility that my shoulder harbored a new strain of flesh-eating streptococcus, someone like me remains the worry of ghoul health—the innocent bystander, the casual traveler, back from the inter-space of empire, the tourist as biological means of transit, stopping here and there on the way to and from, with no certain origin and no certain end. The density of human circulation has created a new biosocial space and time, and it seems that opportunistic infections can strike anyone, anywhere, anytime.

The temporality of ghoul health stands in stark contrast to the state of health crises at the seams of global capitalism. There, sores and diarrhea mark the timing of life and death—an exceedingly slow, hard to quantify, cumulatively acting health collapse. Sore after sore, bronchial flu after bronchial flu, broken toilet after broken toilet wear down the body's immune system and help account for the quantifiable difference in life expectancy between Aboriginal and non-Aboriginal Australians and the less easily quantified difference in quality of life. Diseases of poverty are not usually medical rarities; they demand neither high technology nor new movies to apprehend them. Rather they demand choices about wealth and resource distribution and political sensitivity to a different kind of corporeality.

In short, ghoul health is ideological in the sense that Althusser used this term: the imaginary relationship of people to their real conditions of existence. The material back-drops of these imaginary relations are multiple, the patterns of structural impoverishment many. The withdrawal of capital from regions after the severe extraction of resources and the resulting pollution of the environment—such as seen in Papuan mining regions, the Brazilian rainforest, and Nigerian oil fields—has left over-crowding, incipient starvation, environmental harm, and appalling sanitation.[40] The encouragement of a region to enter capitalist development quickly, bypassing the economic "drag" of social services such as health care that would threaten or stifle the sufficient bottom line (as if profit operated according to the limit of sufficiency in capital accumulation), has also led to a steep curve in health failures, such as we have seen in China and the post-Soviet world.[41] In still other regions, such as the interior lining of First World settler colonies, the continuing state of carnal collapse has led to calls for new strategies and experiments in life.

In other words, Pearson's rage, as an echo of the carnal collapse in indigenous worlds, is not alone and does not register the only intersection of callous prejudice and ghoul health. We heard a similar outrage in Greg Bordowitz's film, *Fast Trip Long Drop*, which explores his response to ACT-UP's inability to stem the tide of death before so many of his friends and lovers had died. The film is a cry of a failed dream and a waking nightmare in which he cannot depend on having the normal stages of a normal life: birth, childhood, adolescence, middle age, and old age. He no longer has the privilege of a certain kind of youthful amnesia around the transitory nature of life. He lives within a deathscape, and no one cares. And yet, the sheer volume of Bordowitz's outrage is also a subtle sign of just how thoroughly life is distributed in the liberal diaspora—not life in a simple numerical, demographic sense; but life as an experiential state. His justified shock signals a certain privilege—that many people consider life as something that can be counted on, at least for a certain length of time, for long enough to be able to forget about its limited nature. This amnesia does not infect many others. If you are an indigenous person in Australia, you know you are likely to die fifteen to twenty years earlier than your white counterpart; that your household income probably will never rise above the poverty level; that you probably will be sent to prison (though they account for only 2.2 percent of the population, indigenous people make up 20 percent of the prison population); that you and your children probably will have life-imperiling addictions; and that you probably will have sky-rocketing levels of diabetes, renal failure, and Group A streptococcus that will cause you or your children to suffer from rheumatic fever and heart failure.

In short, the cause of ghoul health and its solutions telescope a certain tension between international poverty and profit, statesmanship, robber capitalism, liberal capitalism, gangster capitalism, and socialism, and they increase the pressure on subjects of these value regimes to conform or risk being left behind in a vastly reduced, nearly uninhabitable landscape. In the language of a post-recognition politics of shared responsibility: Wash your face or funding for your school will vanish. As progressive health programs challenge the normalizing routines of ghoul health, the ways in which ghoul health fixes certain populations into a normative *geophysics* consolidates the distinctions between ordinary and exceptional bodies, providing different expectations about which forms of remedial care are likely to work for whom, and why. This routinization of public expectations, mediated by government, NGOs, and public reports about the persistence of a set of negative biostatistics, creates a normative expectation about where it would be normal to see a sore such as the one on my shoulder, and where not—what Allan Feldman has described as a discourse of "in place and out of place bodies."[42] After all, part of the disturbing nature of the sore on my shoulder was where it was seen and on what kind of body—in Chicago/Montreal and on a highly educated white woman. One aspect of the disturbing nature of Aboriginal health is also its location—a biosocial fold of the Third World within the imaginary healthy body of the First World. Unless, of course, what I had was a symptom of HIV/AIDS, in which case I would cease being an effect of a biosocial fold and start being a cause.

Ghoul health does not characterize the world-views or practices of all world health activists—nor of most indigenous health workers and activists in Australia. A host of competing national and international state agencies and NGOs have built a set of interlocking, more or less functional institutions and protocols for rapidly apprehending actual and possible infectious types and trajectories, both to forestall pending epidemics and to address the cultural and material inequalities that help foster them. But they build these programs within a context of limited and unevenly distributed resources dedicated to national and international health. As indigenous families and friends of mine in the northwest coastal regime negotiate their lives in landscapes of sores, the extralocal institutions meant to remedy their situation are skimming surplus value off their ill health. In a study of the Aboriginal health care system in the Northern Territory under the conservative Country Liberal Party, Tess Lea has noted that even as it denounces the immense sum of resources consumed by Aboriginal health, "the Northern Territory Government receives a disproportionate share of national revenue in order to maintain most of its services, predominantly on the basis of the cost burden of supporting Aboriginal people. That is, the parlous state of Aboriginal people and the role of the nation in bearing responsibility for that sorry state form a key part of arguments for extra funding beyond what would ordinarily be distributed under strict per capita allocations."[43] The Northern Territory Government is, to use the social imaginary of my friends, a *munggul*, a person who feeds on other people's kidney fat. The state's extraction of wealth from indigenous ill-health is not the only game in town. Vaccines for Group A streptococcus, tested out in the laboratory of indigenous communities, may ultimately generate profits for large corporations, just as the results of bio-prospecting in Mexico generate profits for pharmaceutical companies far away from home.[44] The HIV/AIDS pandemic has already become a "lifestyle" illness for many in the First World, providing a permanent flow of cash to the pharmaceutical companies treating it. Power itself speaks this truth—potential, if deferred, profit is seen as the necessary incentive for companies to invest in biomedical research on so-called marginal diseases in the first place.

Progressive health care workers and advocates face not only the economy of health. They encounter the uneven national terrain in which this health is distributed. Within First World settler colonies such as Australia, the United States, and Canada, the state's organization of health care and the national imaginary of the indigenous subject vary significantly. The United States is alone among these three countries in lacking a universal health care system. I was able to have relatively quick access to the University of Chicago Hospital because of the kind of private health care policy I had. The aggressive diagnosis of the physician I met there may well have been influenced by my ability to pay, his relative unfamiliarity with anything indigenous, and the research quality of the hospital itself. The clinics I visited in Australia and Montreal were both public, and the indigenous subject there occupies a much larger segment of the national and health care imaginary. As a result their doctors displayed more, if varying, degrees of familiarity with the kind of sore that I was carrying, though they differed significantly in their diagnoses of the biological agent of the sore. But the doctor in Darwin, who was the most familiar with these kinds of sores, was also the least aggressive in terms of the treatment. Rather than resolving the triangle of diagnosis, treatment, and eradication, familiarity seems to have bred, if not contempt, then neglect. Indeed, what many medical anthropologists and health workers have long known is that the first order of business in these "zones of dysfunction" is to interrupt the nervous system of blame and bemusement among doctors ("they leave them on the shelf to rot") and the blasé attitudes among indigenous men and women. These pathologies of the body must be made pathological; they must be made unfamiliar to the subjects most familiar with them. I must begin to lose faith in my indigenous friends. My indigenous friends must lose faith in each other.

In *Notes on a Native Son,* James Baldwin reflected on a problem that he thought all African American parents faced: "How to prepare the child for the day when the child would be despised and how to *create* in the child—by what means?—a stronger antidote to the poison than one had found for oneself."[45] The ability of indigenous men and women to navigate the various autological and genealogical demands on them depends not merely on mastering a set of discourses. They must also navigate these discourses within the actual worlds in which they live. The speed with which people die, the violence attached to these deaths, or the slowness of a body's decay all present different temporal frameworks—cataclysmic and glacial—for the working out and working through of these different discourses of autology and genealogy. When a funeral occurs once a week or every fortnight in Aboriginal communities stretching across the Top End region of the Northern Territory, the social, monetary and physical stamina required to attend them all, let alone participate in ceremonial aspects of one or several of them, can quickly overwhelm people for whom the average yearly income is $10,000 —and that's if one is able to keep up with the paperwork of welfare. Yet, being absent, no matter what the financial reason, provides the emotional friction of the sort that led to the alleged *mungarra* attack—the intensification of feelings of severe isolation of the person (*gamaparrking*) that leads to biosocial catastrophes. It is within these actual worlds that new experiments in sociality emerge.

In other words, if extreme poverty and extreme sexuality signal the collapse of intimacy and genealogy, they also signal the availability of these states for experimentations in new forms of life. The normal has de-camped, and with it the presuppositions of an ethics of the norm. Another prefabricated ethics of crisis is excreted into the scene: the ethics of the extreme social reduction, and the ethics of living in unlivable conditions. Within these scenes, arguments are made for alternative regularities, in the beginning at least only for "here," where the old regularities make no sense, where they have become incoherent and inconvenient. In the end, who knows where and how these new regularities will migrate?

It should not surprise anyone that many of these experiments emerge in forms and terms that make them hard to digest. These experiments are awkward. They produce discomfort to many not living within these zones. They do not have an obvious redemptive moment. It is not clear—at all—whether they will produce anything that anyone could or would want to live within. So these kinds of experiments don't seem fair, because there is no way to know whether they will produce a good life for anyone. And yet, it is just these kinds of awkward, uncomfortable, off-kilter experiments in life that the carnality of liberalism produces.

We get a glimpse of the heterogeneity of these social experiments and the network of law and economy in which they are embedded by looking briefly at how, in 2003, a sister of mine used the $119,000 that she received in compensation for the accidental traffic death of her husband. He did not die from a sore. At least a sore was not the immediate cause of his death (although, it should be noted that many deaths are attributed to secret sores, inner sores that people who have given up on life are said to hide). Because a car hit him before life could, state resources could be mobilized for compensation. Within a few weeks, some said days, the money had been converted into cash and assets such as trucks, washing machines, and stereos, and then distributed across five different Aboriginal communities. Very quickly, the widow was in virtually the same state of poverty she had been in before she received the compensation.

What may well be interpreted as "waste" in one culture of circulation, however, was viewed as a proper form of sharing in another.[46] Jealousies and criticisms certainly abounded regarding who was given what and what sorts of things should have gone to what sorts of people. Many people whistled at the sheer speed of the distribution and were not surprised when, within just a few more weeks, the widow reclaimed several of the large assets (trucks and washing machines) and redistributed them along another line of kinship. And people commented on how quickly the widow transitioned from being the author of social ties to being dependent on these same social ties. She herself shrugged at times about this rapid transition, saying, rich or poor, she had kin. No one questioned, however, whether the widow should have disbursed these goods. Instead they questioned the calculus of the closeness of kin-

ship, residence, marriage, previous economic help, and ceremonial connections on which the giving was based. And they
adjusted how they thought about the degree and kind of relationship the widow had to various people based on her choices
of distribution. The widow, for instance, relied heavily on a
network of trained indigenous women, in a variety of indigenous communities, not merely to collect, fill out, and usher
the forms necessary for her compensation through the state
bureaucracy, but to tell her that such forms of compensation
existed in the first place. And these women used the fact that
they had activated this epistemological asset for the widow
because of their kinship, residential, marriage, or ceremonial
closeness as the basis for a claim on the resources that resulted.

This potlatch is matched by countless smaller instances
of financial redistribution that create and nurture networks
of interdependency and that calibrate and recalibrate types
and degrees of social closeness among people. In short, these
economic possibilities are part of the extendable, flexible,
and absorptive play of kinship relations in a region where an
actual relationship is never as settled as modernist accounts
of kinship studies suggest. Indeed, in this extreme example
we see something profoundly ordinary—the willingness to
act on a very different ideology of self in society, an ideology of "enough" and of the "will come." Kinship is not a
view from the nowhere of the genealogical chart. Rather, it is
made meaningful each and every time someone uses it to ma-
nipulate, chase, sweeten, pressure, or ignore specific people.
In disbursing the money she had received for her husband's

death, the widow creatively entailed, out of the deformations that composed her life, what might be called a network of trust — trust that provisions will come, that the severe nature of poverty in a capitalist society will not exile the self from the social.

In these biosocial environments, the comforting difference between worlds of fantasy and reality begin to bleed as subjects experiment with the limits of the body in a field of liberal deformation. For indigenous people I know, the relevant question is not what kind of harm is too much for what kind of person, but how does one produce a viable subject within these carnal worlds and mitigate the social numbing they inspire in others. Achille Mbembe pointed to this in his provocative reading of Amos Tutuola's *The Palm Wine Drinkard*.[47] The ghostly exchange of body parts that Tutuola describes has a real counterpart — the organ trade, the sex trade, and the less publicized profit in accidental maiming and death.[48]

Take, for instance, a front-page story that ran in the Darwin newspaper about a female maintenance worker who received $100,000 in compensation for the deformation of her hands after twenty-five years of using a floor polisher.[49] The article presented a picture of the woman's hand and invited its readers to decide whether the amount of the compensation award was justified. The article reflects the logic of tort law. Tort law asks not merely whether this harm is too much to ask of any citizen, but too much to ask of *this particular kind* of citizen doing this particular kind of job. These ordinary assessments rework a point made by the political philosopher Carl Schmitt that, although the liberal state has the right to demand that its citizens risk death, even die, in a war fought against its enemies, no one, neither state, court, nor business, could demand that anyone sacrifice his life for economic expediency.[50] The "no one" of Schmitt's abstract citizen is always someone particular in individual compensation claims. As a result the worth of a hand—whether it is really mangled or not that bad—depends on how you look at it. The visual field of judgment, as Sarah Jain has noted, is saturated by social discourses of gender and racial value.[51]

But even a lesser compensation payment would be a windfall for indigenous men and women. What surprise, then, that when a group of women and I read the article during a break from turtle hunting it prompted one of the women to note, "When that mob boy fight like today they say 'hey mate no more fight for chin, poke out the eye one way then everyone split the money.'" In the carnal conditions of contemporary indigenous life, an eye, a limb, or a death caused by "bumping" (being hit by a car) has immense monetary value—and so there are jokes about hanging a limb out into traffic as a way of generating money for a washing machine, or a car, or a coffin. One of the woman said, "that mob kill imself enough cash for one's funeral." These conversations often prompt laughter, but it is laughter of the abnormal camped within the normal.[52]

Baldwin reminds us, however, that subjects who can live in and experiment with environments of numbing harm must be made, nurtured, and grown out of the very environments that are poisoning them. The women and men I know constantly reflect on just this fact, how to provide their children with the self-discipline necessary to survive the "hard facts" of poverty in the context of what they call "hard Aboriginal law." Some of these elements of self-discipline were caught in the rendition of pain and mercy that I provided various doctors in Chicago and Montreal. Often, as part of my standard sore narrative, I describe the proper personal stance toward the pain of treating a sore. "Dig as deep as possible and don't feel sorry for me if it hurts." This short narrative fragment is a truncated version of what actually happened right before I left Belyuen for the conference. A few days before I was set to leave Australia for the United States and Canada, I asked one of my mothers, Binbin, to take a look at my shoulder.

> 'What's this on shoulder mine, sore?" I asked.
>
> "That nothing, what do white people call them, pimple," she answered.
>
> "Well killim pimple wulgamen," me.

She did, with her fingernail. But the pimple did not go away, and I was soon pretty sick. So I walked to the house of my cousin, a health clinic worker, and asked her to diagnose my pimple.

> "That's not pimple, menggen, that sore."
>
> "Cutimim then. . . . Don't feel sorry for me menggen you cut right down."

And she did. Pus was soon running down my back. My niece (*ngambin*), the health care worker's daughter, finger painted with the pus on my back. "What this auntie?" "X." "What this?" "O."

My decision to have minor surgery on my shoulder engaged the law of autology on its own terms. I was an adult choosing the best possible medical options available to me. No one held me down. I held myself down. I was in pain but the pain was not sovereign, I was. But this adult had a childhood that allowed her to say later, "cut as deep as possible and don't feel sorry for me." This is the question, then, for them and for me: Why can some people hold themselves down sufficiently to get the care they need? What gives someone this discipline? How should parents fashion their children so that they will be capable of taking care of their bodies, not simply in the context of traditional custom and ritual, but in the context of liberal corrosions?

A few years before this event, a twelve-year-old daughter of mine, Bronwyn Bianamu, had an aggressive sore on her left knee that had spread so deeply she was having trouble bending her leg. Scared of needles, she had run away whenever a doctor visited the community. She was camping at a site called Keldjelwik, a remote outstation with little by way of medical care beyond the bandages and antiseptic her aunt, a nurse, had brought with her. One evening, as her grandmother Binbin, her mother Diane, and I sat by a fire, Binbin told me to entice Bronwyn over with the promise of lollies (candies).

> Me: "But I got no lollie, wulgow."
> Binbin: "Nuku, then grabbim arm, head."
> Diane: "Bronwyn, Bet got lollie!"
> Bronwyn: "True, Bet, you got lollie?"
> Me: "Might be."

When Bronwyn came over to get the phantom lollies, Diane grabbed her legs and stretched them straight. I grabbed her arms, which were stronger than I thought. Bronwyn tried to scratch my face to get away. Binbin ripped open the sore on her knee with a sharpened twig, pus and blood bursting everywhere. Diane carried Bronwyn over to her aunt, a nurse, who was also camping at Kedjelwik, to be bandaged. Later, her mother led her to the salt water to soak her leg. In a few days, Bronwyn could straighten her leg and run around with the other kids. When she came into camp for some tea and chips, Binbin said to her, "See Bronwyn, that leg im straight today. You gana think hard. You gana cut that sore yourself next time. Today you run around. Not like yesterday. You're not going to be scared. You gana take care of that sore. You gana cut yourself so that you can walk."

This redemptive narrative—a child crippled by the canalized carnalities of capital's failure to trickle down is healed by the traditional knowledge of her grandmother—can determine the meaning of this scene only if other textures of revulsion and violation are kept outside. These other affective textures include my own panic as I held Bronwyn down, terrified that I was reenacting violent scenes from my own childhood, wondering what is the difference between being held and being held down, between physical pedagogies whose telos is self-discipline and physical pedagogies whose telos is the disorganization of the self. And these other discursive textures include community and public debates about sex and child abuse in indigenous communities. In these debates, all intense physicality, especially practiced on a minor's body, quickly collapses into physical abuse.

This method of disciplining subjects is not the only method that people practice within and across indigenous communities. Many people decide that the right way to nurture and protect their children, siblings, parents, and grandparents is not to constitute them as the kind of subjects who can cut themselves, but to remove them from the conditions that make cutting such an attractive option. They heed the warnings of health care professionals that sores, scabies, and endless flu should not be dismissed as "nothing." They are convinced that they have placed too much trust in their families. They decide that they will never be able to forge a middle-class life within these worlds. They take their children and close relatives away from rural and urban communities and the economic and social demands of kin. They decide that many of the moral and social practices within these worlds are repugnant, and they work for a different life in another kind of world. But when they do this, they must still teach themselves and their children to be able to bear the pain of a different kind of severing, the pain of separation. They must learn to depend on stranger sociality in their everyday lives, to look forward to the pleasures and pains of understanding *ngamaparrking*, and to reflect on their lives in terms of their own individual progress. This, too, takes discipline. It takes a person who can cut herself in a different way.

One

A pair of conch shells sits on my desk. Beside them sits a carved and decorated gourd. The shells are painted in the vibrant dot style most people associate with the Aboriginal aesthetic of the Central Desert and with Aboriginal art more generally. The carved gourd is decorated with costume jewelry, a rodent head, a golden figure affixed to a red seed, and a cheap plastic tiara clasped around the base. It is a piece that few people know how to classify when they see it.

I bought the conch shells from a small shop just outside Darwin. According to my indigenous friends who live nearby, the shells are "nothing." They are "ordinary" things, meaning that neither the designs on the shells nor the shells themselves manifest or represent any existential link to a ritual, ceremonial, or geontological event. Nothing about these shells joins the membranes of the given human world and the always-present ancestral world. They are simply pretty or beautiful or kitsch, depending on your particular aesthetic point of view. I do, however, have a relation of kinship to the artist who painted the shell. He is a son of an uncle of mine; both men usually live at Wadeye, a large Aboriginal community in the Northern Territory on the western coast near the Western Australian border. I only know this kinship connection because, while looking at the shells, one of my indigenous mothers, Nuki, told me so. I do not know exactly which "son," of all the possible sons of my uncle, was the painter (the number of candidates is large, given the system of kinship in the region). Neither did my mother. The lack of an authorial specificity, beyond his general kinship relationship to me, was

not the result of the famous co-production and co-ownership of Aboriginal designs and objects.[1] It resulted more simply from my mother's and my satisfaction that, in this case, knowing the general kinship category of "husband" that connected me to the object was enough information for this particular kind of social exchange. Because the shells were "nothing" it was enough that I liked them. It was also nice that they were connected to me by kinship. But these kinds of connections did not make the shells and their designs a membrane between human ontologies and geontologies.

I bought the gourd from a white American friend, Jai, out of the back of his car as he was traveling through upstate New York. I would call Jai my friend. We are not close, but nor are we simply acquaintances. According to Jai, the gourd is a spiritual object. This may seem odd given that, at the time I purchased it, his car constituted a little market stall, rather than a sacred site; and we seemed to be engaged in a market exchange—cash for art—rather than in a ritual event. For Jai, however, what made the gourd something more than a mere decorative object, more than the subject of commercial exchange, was how it materially articulated various personally transformative events of his life. The day I bought the gourd, Jai was traveling from an artist commune in Vermont to a radical faerie sanctuary in central Tennessee, where he lived and about which I will say more later. The gourd was composed of symbolic and material elements of these other social worlds—the lotus design refers to a pond in the Vermont commune, the bead comes from an ayahuasca ceremony in the Amazon, the rodent head and gourd are from the Radical Faerie Short Mountain Sanctuary. I added the plastic tiara, taken from my girlfriend's fortieth birthday party.

What makes the gourd spiritual for Jai—something rather than nothing—is not what it represents. The gourd is just one of many artifacts of his "journey." Among radical faeries I know, as among members of many other self-expressive counter-cultural movements in the United States and Western Europe, the term "journey" glosses self-reflexive autobiography as spiritual exercise.[2] Its sense and meaning refer to a loose set of normative propositions about what constitutes a good life and what motivates human action—in this case, constant self-elaboration through shared experiences as a mode of spiritual exercise. What makes the gourd spiritual is its status as an actual material manifestation of Jai's commitment to a practice of continual self-elaboration oriented to building an alternative, progressive way of living and of the movement of people across various kinds of places and relationships—acquaintance, lover, friend.

A journey is intentional in this sense: it is a self-conscious commitment to self-elaboration. But a journey is not intentional in another sense; the agent is not the monological author of his life. The gourd reflects the conjunctural aspects of Jai's life, what has happened to him and how these accidental happenings affected the course of his life, as much as it represents what he himself caused to happen. Though in a world of stranger sociality, Jai is as dependent on others for a social context as my friends in Australia. Thus, as well as being a durable sign of his life, the gourd acts as a kind of ontological bracket, a drawing together of existing but unconnected backdropped practices and affectivities of social life through the process of selecting the objects (elements) that will compose it. In this sense, autobiography is in its very nature spiritual, even as the writing of the self becomes a material practice that leaves behind material, if at times ephemeral and transitory, objects.

Two objects, worlds apart, would seem to have nothing more to do with each other than that they reflect my "journey" across two very different social worlds. But concluding this would be wrong. Despite the fact that they sit on my shelf in my home, the proximity of the shells and the gourd is not simply the material outcome of my particular journey or my particular approach to ethnography. I certainly move back and forth between a longstanding relationship with people in Australia and an incipient relationship with people living as or alongside radical faeries, but the road that connects these two groups had been built before I set foot on it. The gourd was carved out of the curved space of the shells, the shells inflected by the shadow of the gourd, long before I picked them up. The borders, qualities, and social effects of each of these seemingly free-standing objects are deeply entangled in one or the other, whether their authors intend them to be or not, whether I do or don't. Thus, rather than asserting that these objects and, more precisely, the social worlds from which they emerge, have no relation to each other, or have their relationship merely through me, or are utterly different or are ultimately the same thing, this essay examines the kinds of entanglements in which these social worlds find themselves, place themselves, and are placed by others. Of particular importance to these entanglements are discourses about the absolute difference between the descending object of proper culture and the immanent object of deliberative freedom, of worlds of kin and worlds of strangers, of families of birth and families of choice.[3] Why does it matter, and to whom, that certain communities and their economic, ritual, and social practices be apprehended as "free" and others as "constrained"? What work does this dichotomy do in defining the social and political exceptionality of liberal forms of constitutional democracies? How does this dichotomy allow democratic institutions to exercise disciplinary force as if they were advancing freedom and protecting the good? What socialities and politics emerge in places addressed by the violence of democratic exceptionalism?

In the previous essay I weighted the discussion toward how, through a politics of cultural recognition and sensitivity, discourses of genealogy make and unmake the voices and bodies of my indigenous friends and family even though these discourses do not describe the contours of their actual social worlds and relations *even where these relations can be described as relations of kinship*. Neither genealogical nor autological, they are nevertheless called on by state law and administrative bureaucracies and public reason to appear as now the one and now the other. In this essay the weight lies on the other side of the disciplines of individual freedom and social constraint. I track the disciplinary effects of discourses of autology and genealogy in the experimental social worlds of friends of mine who identify as radical faeries and their allies. And I try to show how intimacy is made there, an intimacy that is neither free nor constrained, but something else.

Though by different ends, radical faeries and indigenous Australians are caught in the grip of the same discursive vise. The disciplines of freedom and constraint present these people with shared problems: How do they constitute social relations that are neither autological nor genealogical? How do they build material and emotional interdependencies diagonally to the disciplinary norms of these discourses? How do they do so when state regulatory and administrative bureaucracies, jurisprudence, and quotidian life treat these discursive options as either self-evident truths or life-enhancing goods? How do they constitute a subjectivity and sociality that not only absorbs the poison of a vicious pervasive racism and homophobia, a monolithic money-oriented capitalism, and an otherworld-oriented, often apocalyptic, spiritualism, but also produce from these repressive social fields a viable antidote to them?

But though they are in the same vise, radical faeries and indigenous Australians face its two very different ends. If genealogy is the covertly negative social condition through which positive state values are distributed to indigenous subjects in settler colonies—such that indigenous Australians must remove themselves from the destiny of a hyper-valued freedom in order to obtain state resources—freedom is the overtly positive social condition through which negative state disciplines are exacted on people like Jai. They are continually characterized as being unencumbered by real families or real traditions or real dependencies. At times they appear as the nightmare version of the modern unattached self. The different ways that these discourses face these groups present a real challenge to a project of the sort I am proposing. On the one hand, one must find and refuse the differences produced by discourses of personal freedom and social constraint. Are radical faeries "free"? Are their journeys of self-discovery and self-elaboration initialized by or oriented to the autological imaginary of democratic constitutionalism any more than the kinship practices of indigenous people along the northwest coast of Australia are initialized by or oriented to the genealogical imaginary of the multicultural state? On the other hand, one must resist the temptation to flatten out the social differences between these worlds. To say that there is no difference between the social worlds of indigenous people and radical faeries is as misguided as to say that their forms of difference are reducible to the dichotomy of autology and genealogy.

With this difficult double writing in mind, three broad rhetorical movements define this essay. I first sketch some of the practices and imaginaries that cluster around the identity and aspirational horizon of radical faeries, which run the gamut from a more or less rigid adherence to doctrine to a more or less celebratory refusal of all doctrines. "Radical faeries" are in this sense a social genre, a social identity coordinated to and made sensible by an entire field of possible social positions and practices. At one and the same time, people claim and assert this identity to make sense of the self within a complexly unfolding social field, to assert or contest a position vis-à-vis others, and to designate a point of departure for the elaboration of new forms of social being. But I do not treat the immanent practice of this social genre as merely discursive, if by discursive we mean the play of signs outside their material inhabitations. My radical faerie friends and I are not merely creatively coordinating a regime of signs. We are finding ourselves made by these social regimes in such a way that as we move across social space the social space itself comes to be haunted by these makings. As discourses become hardened into the subject it becomes something other than mere discourse, it becomes affect, stance, and morality—independent vectors within social life.

Next, I examine how some people within the critical indigenous public and the jurisprudence of religious certification and cultural copyright apprehend these practices. I will suggest that these publics and jurisprudences often read experiments in sociality such as the radical faeries as mere ideological cover for illicit sex acts, as mere appropriation of other people's culture, or as seriously intended but legally dubious modes of religiosity. Many practitioners of law as well as many indigenous critics are clearly unsettled by what radical faeries are doing and claiming. They are apprehensive in the double sense that they wish to impose an epistemological discipline on the radical faeries and that they experience a sense of imminent harm in the vicinity of their practices. It is in these critical and juridical domains that the absolute difference between the descending object of proper culture and the immanent object of deliberative freedom, of worlds of kin and worlds of friends and strangers, of families of birth and families of choice are deployed to discipline and steer social groups to their proper homes. Why?

The essay ends by trying to understand how the disciplining of radical faeries through a discourse of freedom paradoxically reanimates the self-evident good of liberal democratic forms of freedom and how, in this context, a politics of espionage emerges as the foil to the cunning of recognition.

103

Two

The radical faerie movement emerged as a philosophy of life associated with Harry Hay. By philosophy of life, I am referring to the argument of the French historian of ancient philosophy Pierre Hadot that the ancient Greeks saw philosophy as a lived experience, a mode of being in the world, rather than as a scrutiny of doctrines or an exercise in hermeneutics.[4] Hay may never have read Hadot but his life can be read as dedicated to just this form of philosophy, a claim that enters the dense, multivocal, and highly contested mytho-poetics that surround him.

The emotional nature and volume of these mytho-poetics

are not surprising given Hay's role in the founding of the modern gay movement in the United States.[5] In the 1950s, along with Chuck Rowland, Bob Hull, Dale Jennings, Konrad Stevens, and John Gruber, Hay founded the Mattachine Society as a social vehicle for promoting gay-positive attitudes and civil rights in the United States, drawing significant theoretical and organizational principles from leftist and Marxist politics in Los Angeles. The Mattachine Society, as David Churchill has shown, was itself part of a larger transnational homophilic movement. This transnational movement, fostered by the print media circulating across it, pursued two significantly different strategies for state recognition—one based on the human civil rights of all men and women and another based on an anthropological study of homosexual cultural relativity.[6]

In some ways these two strategies complemented each other. The civil rights strategy argued that respectable homosexuals were no different than respectable heterosexuals, dissolute homosexuals no different than dissolute heterosexuals. The anthropological strategy argued that homosexuality was a ubiquitous feature of all known cultures, even if the ways that so-called primitive societies expressed homosexuality differed. The anthropological currents rippling through these transnational discussions provided a rich archive for Hay and the radical faerie movement he would help found, and continue to provide fodder for a number of anthropologists making sense of the worlds of Native and gay Native Americans, especially Will Roscoe and Walter L. Williams.[7] As an editor and contributor to the Mattachine Review, Hay mobilized both strategies, advocating for the civil and human rights of homosexuals and researching what he considered to be the homosexual traditions of Native Americans, then called the institution of "berdache" and now better known as "two-spirit."[8] Hay's relation to berdache was not merely academic. He claimed that as a young man he had been given the blessing of Wovoka, the Washoe founder of the Ghost Dance, to help native peoples.

Hay resigned from the Mattachine Society in 1953, during the McCarthy era, which placed heightened scrutiny not only on homosexuals but also on those who, like Hay, combined a Marxist perspective on class with a gay liberation politics. For the next ten years he researched Native American "berdache" practices, seeking to understand them as a different way of conceptualizing the history of homosexuality. He described his study as focused on the centrality of the institution of berdache in the spiritual life of Native Americans and other tribal people; its origin in the ancient Near East and Mediterranean where it developed into a priesthood; its history allowing the male takeover of matrifocal institutions; the distinction between "state" and "folk" berdache that resulted; and the continuing manifestations of these patterns up to the eve of the modern era in Europe.[9] From 1970 to 1979, Hay lived in northern New Mexico, where he pursued his studies of Native American two-spirit and developed a post-Hegelian understanding of gay spirituality. According to Hay, "spirituality" would come to "represent the accumulation of all experiential consciousness from the division of the first cells in the primeval slime, down through all biological-political social evolution" to the moment-to-moment development of gay consciousness.[10] He publicly inaugurated the radical faeries in 1979 at the "Spiritual Conference for Radical Faeries." "Offering invocations to the spirits, Hay called on the crowd to 'throw off the ugly green frog skin of hetero-imitation to find the shining Faerie prince beneath.' The intense air of celebration in a natural setting precipitated all manner of pagan practices, circle castings, Wiccan-inspired rituals, ecstatic dancing, communal feasting and Nature-based religious offerings."[11]

John Harry Bonck has argued that the radical faerie movement emerged from the thinking of several leaders in the gay consciousness movement in the 1970s, among them the psychologist Mitch Walker and the philosopher Arthur Evans.[12] For many social historians and activists, however, Hay stands out because of his assertion that gay men had been cut off from their spiritual natures, and that this spirituality could still be glimpsed and reclaimed by re-enacting pre-Judaic, pre-Christian forms of ritual practice.

For Hay and other early members of the movement, the spiritual practices they were elaborating were not merely something borrowed from other cultures. They were *their* heritage. Because the old ways of faerie transformation were obliterated during "the nightmarish centuries of Judeo-Christian oppression," radical faeries were "free to invent new ones."[13] The anthropological arguments of the 1950s, 1960s, and 1970s were redeployed. Homosexuality was not merely culturally ubiquitous. Homosexual culture was this ubiquity. This continues to be the position of some voices within the movement. For instance, Scott Treleaven has argued that "although the Faeries still don't subscribe to any particular set of dogmas or religious structures" and although they draw eclectically from a wide range of cultural forms, they are "nonetheless a distinct tradition."

> It is generally accepted as a henotheistic system, meaning that there is one specific force or deity from which all others precipitate; a God, usually associated with Cernunos, Pan or another horned, priapic male deity; and a Goddess, recognized as a Divine Mother, a gender-variant male, a warrior or a Kali-like destroyer. This seemingly hetero-binary pantheon is actually considered to reflect both sides of every human's psyche, with gender and sexuality being fluidic. Appropriately, Faerie Gatherings often involve ritualistic dismantling of gender barriers, gender transformation and celebrations of both the hyper-masculine and hyper-feminine.[14]

The radical faeries are certainly not the only counter-cultural movement that has turned decisively away from normative Judeo-Christian theologies and embraced, as antidote, a pan-pagan/indigenous spirituality. Symbolic rebirth through one or another indigenous/pagan/animist spiritual body was a central feature of certain U.S.-based eco-cultural feminisms of the 1970s and 1980s, and that is still the case for environmentally oriented self-expressive members of counter-cultures.[15] For instance, the biocentric philosophy of Earth First! and other radical green groups, or green faeries, draws heavily on a distillation of indigenous eco-philosophy. Bron Taylor has argued that, as with many radical greens, the founder of Earth First!, Dave Foreman, "blamed the advent of agriculture . . . , and Christianity as well, for environmental decline."[16] Not surprisingly, then, "the early Earth First! journal included language in its masthead about not accepting the authority of the state. Its pages expressed enthusiasm for anarchism, on the one hand, and paganism, indigenous religions, and sometimes religions originating in Asia, especially Daoism and Buddhism, on the other."[17]

Historians have debated various parts of the history of the radical faeries. Why did Hay leave Mattachine? How central was he to the inauguration of the radical faeries? Did Wovoka really give Hay his blessing? Did Hay travel through the Southwest looking for a shaman? Whom did he meet there? Whatever the facts, the social life of this history in the contemporary practices and imaginaries of self-identified radical faeries runs the gamut from inspirational horizon to embarrassing hagiography. Understanding when this history is relevant and for whom plunges us into the array of social projects, aspirations, and aesthetic styles that cluster under and around the sign "radical faerie." Like all social identities "radical faerie" can be a longstanding, deeply presupposed, resource of the self, continually reflected back onto the self by surrounding social institutions; or it can be a momentary allegiance that is taken up, cast aside, or invaginated with other available social forms. Radical faeries can be articulated to gender, politics, environmentalism, and anti-imperialism resulting in female faeries, radical elves, and postcolonial queers. As a result, to understand what radical faeries are we should not define the term and then find those who satisfy its criteria. Instead, we need to understand the modes of life across which this social genre is dispersed, contested, and made sensible.

This social genre is elaborated in part on various faerie sanctuaries and communities in the United States, Canada, Australia, and Europe.[18] Sanctuaries and communities have different legal standings vis-à-vis the state—some communities own their land as not-for-profit organizations; some own it as federally recognized not-for-profit religious organizations; some rent. They also have different ways of framing what kind of community they are—Wolf Creek in Oregon, for instance, presents itself as an "intentional community" whose goal is to "create, preserve and manage places of spiritual and cultural sanctuary, for Radical Faeries and their friends" and "to gather in harmony with nature, for renewal, growth and shared learning."[19]

What "intentional" and "spiritual" refer to is a point of some contention, no matter Hay's definitions. Indeed, the very residential principles of many of these communities foster such contestation. Some sanctuaries and communities have a core set of permanent residents, some don't. Permanent residents and visitors are welcomed to these sanctuaries for a host of reasons. Some people, after pursuing mainstream politics or being shaken by a dramatic event in their lives, are looking for a deeper and more meaningful way of living their lives. Some people grew up in alternative communities—rainbow tribes, organic communes, or urban squats—so the radical faeries are a continuation rather than a rupture of their way of life.

Many sanctuaries host annual gatherings and rituals open to anyone who feels called to participate, though some gatherings are restricted to men. During these gatherings, small residential communities of a dozen or so men and women are dramatically transformed as hundreds of people flock to them. Some of the people who come to these gatherings have come for years; for some it is their first time. Some are full-time faeries; others are not. Some are men; some are not.

Some are fixated on Harry Hay; some see Walt Whitman or the Cockettes as more relevant to the world they wish to build. Some visitors are founders of alternative presses or alternative housing movements, while some are just seeking a space for making sense of their alternative gender identity. Some come to have sex. These visitors and tourists return to homes and work rhythms that may or may not reflect a radical faerie philosophy, although most of the people with whom I have spoken at these gatherings say their life is given a new intensity and dimension by participating in them—the ordinariness of their "outside lives" is invested with a new quality of spirituality.

The further we move inside these gatherings the richer becomes the mélange of self-presentational styles and their citational and corporeal anchors. During these gatherings some men and women seek to re-enchant sociality by fostering forms of magical realism. Others have no interest in re-enchantment, but rather see these spaces as a place for changing their attitudes, desires, and aspirations through an orientation to nature's spirituality, material interdependencies, and progressive politics of self-exploration. Indigene, pagan, Wicca, clown, s/m, psychedelic, and hippie: these stylizations and others stretch across the surface of gatherings and across any one person's individual body. They may remain on the surface, or they may be etched deeper within the social skin.

Take, for instance, a ritual I attended during an annual Beltane gathering at a Southern radical faerie sanctuary.[20] The ritual center of the Beltane gathering is the raising of a maypole. Surrounding this event, visitors perform a host of other rituals that they invent on the spot or have carefully prepared to perform on what they consider to be sacred land. These rituals occur within a landscape spotted with faerie shrines, biodegradable art installations, memory stones of lost lovers, and a biochemical space of drug-enhanced self-discovery. One afternoon, a white man, Antler, a didjeridoo player, led one of his posse of much younger white men through a ritual branding. It was an amazing event—the brand was of a blazing sun and the burnt area covered the young man's entire midriff. The sheer physicality was intensified by the sounds of the drone pipes played by other members of Antler's group. Wrapped in the arms of another, surrounded by the sounds and swirling of bodies, the young man was considered, in some deep sense, to be alone on his journey. This alignment of radical individual experience within a dense collection of witnessing intimates and strangers in many ways defines the ritual activity of these gatherings. As the branding was going on, various Wicca conjurings, Celtic chanting, and astrological readings were also occurring. Some people were high, some quite high. Some were not high at all. Some people engaged in spontaneous, interpretive dancing around the event, while others drifted off into the woods to engage in their own spirit quests. People were learning how to cook a range of vegetarian dishes, how to make mud-based houses, circulating literature about other alternative gatherings, or working a social connection that might provide a place to stay after the gathering. Throughout, many of the people watching the ritual repeated, with equal parts irony and seriousness, a specific, highly formalized aspect of discourse that can be heard within these gatherings—that, although they themselves thought such practices went "too far," the young man was on his own journey and this journey should be respected, or at least be provided the space to be conducted safely.

To intern radical faeries in their sanctuaries and rituals would, however, artificially constrain the sources and trajectories of their cultural makings. This is a social movement that is explicitly oriented to circulation. As the composition of Jai's gourd and even these few vignettes suggest, the circulation of people, knowledge, and practices plays an important role in the world-making practices of this movement. And objects like Jai's gourd do not just travel. They may also be transformed in order to travel in a different culture of circulation. Jai took images of some of his gourds and turned them into a tarot deck. In other words, self-elaboration as a shared practice works in, through, and across a wide range of other intentional or accidental communities, including faerie sanctuaries, Peruvian villages, indigenous settlements,

hippie gatherings, and urban squats. People trade information or surf the Web about where knowledgeable shamans
lead ayahuasca or peyote rituals. They travel there, and elsewhere, looking for something that will expand their epistemological and moral horizon and that will provide them with
new languages and ways of thinking about self-expansion. All
of these diverse life experiences inflect what everyone is doing
together at these gatherings. In other words, the social variation within this counter-public is not merely or most substantially found in the surface register of sartorial styles. It is the
very nature of this counter-public to move and vary.

I, too, am a part of this world, insofar as I cart all sorts
of ideas, objects, and social relations back and forth, bring-
ing indigenous perspectives to faerie gatherings and faerie
perspectives to indigenous communities, sometimes accidentally, sometimes because this is what I have to contribute.
During a particularly tedious moment during a radical faerie
heart circle—the communal means by which information is
shared and conflicts resolved—a young man got hold of the
talking stick and was clearly going to speak for a very long
time. I turned to Hush, a permanent member of the community, and quipped that all "true cultures" had mechanisms of
discipline and closure. Hush ran out and tackled the speaker.

On the other side of the world, one day I recounted the
branding scene to a group of older indigenous women during a drive from Belyuen to Wadeye. They listened with an
intense focus in marked contrast with the banter that charac-
terizes these trips. When I was done, one of the women, in-
dicating her seriousness by saying, "Now you listen hard,"

urged me to find Antler and explain to him that branding was for cattle—real indigenous rituals did not brand people. But I did not know where Antler was at the time. Even if I had found him, he might not consider himself to be doing an Aboriginal ritual. And even if I did persuade him to stop, he and I are not the only, or even the most important, couple in the global circulation of New Age, freak, and alternative cultures that move through places like Belyuen and that refigure the commonsense view of what Aboriginal culture is.[21] In 1989, on a beach road, Belyuen women and I met one such traveler. He was from Turin, Italy, and he was pushing a bicycle, dressed in nothing but his underwear. He had come to learn the Aboriginal way, he said, and according to my companions, some of the young men from the area had taken him around the coast showing him Dreaming sites in exchange for cigarettes and beer.

I don't know where the man from Turin went after he left us, but I'm sure he took the encounter with us as a personal citational resource. Again—as I do. After all, I'm not merely spectator and translator between these communities. I'm called on to participate in ways that make my encounters as awkward as anyone else's. A particularly painful example of this awkwardness occurred around the death of a younger indigenous sister of mine in 2004. She was born and raised at Belyuen, but was living in Darwin when she was hit by a car and left for dead. She spent a few weeks in the intensive care ward in a coma at Darwin Royal Hospital, during which time her family was given false hope that she might recover. She did not. With her daughter's death, her mother, Ruby

Yarrowin, had lost four of her children. Angry and grieving, she declared that she was not going to wait the usual year for her daughter's *kapug*, a mortuary ceremony in which the personal possessions of the deceased are ritually burned. Instead she asked her *menggen*, Alice Wainbirri, the sister of her late husband; a few other female age-mates; the *menggen* closest to her daughter, Diane Bianamu; her youngest daughter; and I to take her daughter's clothes to a nearby coastal outstation and burn them immediately. Ruby's family had lived at the outstation when her husband, Roy Yarrowin, was alive. His *nyuidj*, spirit, still resides there, playing games with his extended family whenever they visit. Two troop carriers went to the burning, loaded with extended family. During the burning Ruby Yarrowin insisted that I help Diane burn the clothes. I hesitated, and the other older women lightly objected, but on Ruby's insistence I went ahead. At a certain point the clothes touched me.

After we were done, some of the older women asked me to take them home, and then others insisted that I drive them back so they could fish for the rest of the day. Right when we reached the beach, the gearbox of my troop carrier broke. The short version of the story is that, until three in the morning, I pushed, tugged, and begged the truck, inch by sandy inch, back to the main road with the help of people from Belyuen and two men from the truck rental agency. The next morning, earlier than I would have liked, I was awakened by a delegation of elder women. They wanted to make sure that I knew that Roy Yarrowin had punished me for touching my dead sister's clothes. "That old lady know that. Bet you know that." Which was true—I do know that the cousin (*menggen*) or aunt of the deceased is the only person who can safely burn personal items during these ceremonies. I knew that, but I couldn't refuse Ruby Yarrowin, no matter why she might have asked me to violate this law.

Though I know this, I do not know other things. I do not know, for instance, how far these mortuary rituals can be, or should be, extended. Should these ways of mediating between the living and the dead stop for me when I drive out of Belyuen? They don't. How could they, after so many years?

I would have to be made out of concrete for this to be the case. And yet, although the forms and modes of my grieving are now deeply informed by Belyuen ways of grieving, this simple fact does not provide any guidance on how these forms and modes, or *how I, as an artifact of them,* make any sense outside of the social fields that make up "Belyuen." How can these forms of mourning, and other ritually mediated modes of life, move across social worlds whose social presuppositions are significantly different? In other words, the form and mode of mourning sensibly regiment, and are made sensible by, all the social characteristics of the worlds in which they arise. How can a *kapug* be held in the United States if everyone there is related by stranger sociality? Are families of choice good enough? Who would be the *menggen* in such a family? And yet, the lack of these social roles and the social practices that support them does not change the fact that I am also, in this lack, *still* mourning as if they were there. This haunting is not merely, or perhaps primarily, a challenge of translation—not about what these practices *mean*—but about the fact that material, subjective, and social conditions are imposed on and necessary for forms to circulate across always already informed social space.

Men and women from the coastal region in northwest Australia face a similar sort of problem when they decide to move away from the thick kinship-inflected communities of their birth to places such as Darwin, Elcho Island, Katherine, or Broome. They may do so for jobs or to get away from the low-level infections rife on rural communities, the constant demand-sharing, or a fight. If I listen to my sister Diane Bianamu, who has made such a choice, these cities provide the excitement and relief of stranger sociality. Demand-sharing is not as all-consuming as it is in small indigenous communities, and day-to-day health and health care is often better. There are movie theaters and video stores, twenty-four hour food and liquor markets, casinos, public transportation, and the rich languages and styles of the region. The positive benefits of suburban dwelling do not, however, evacuate a person's social history. How does one hold a *kapug* in a suburban backyard surrounded by friendly, or not so friendly, neighbors? Some of these neighbors might be indigenous, but from significantly different social backgrounds and cultural practices; some might be non-indigenous Christians, Confucians, or Muslims. Many urban-dwelling indigenous men and women return to their natal communities to hold such rituals. But this simply creates other kinds of problems. How does someone living in Darwin or its suburban hinterland maintain the emotional and social connections necessary for organizing a mourning ritual? Sometimes the impossibility of constituting these rituals of grief or any of the other informal rituals of interaction is exactly what binds people to local worlds. To move too far away from them is to move too far away from the self that has been constituted by them.

These embodied disturbances are hardly limited to indigenous people. They constitute, in some critical sense, human existence. Wicker, who lives at the Short Mountain Sanctuary, describes his journey into the radical faeries as initiated by this same kind of subjective haunting. Drafted into the U.S. Army from a moderate-sized Midwestern town, he returned from his tour of duty in Vietnam to find the town in which he was once happy and comfortable now too culturally and socially homogeneous. No matter how traumatic his stay in Southeast Asia, it sensitized him to other ways of being, and this sensitivity made him uncomfortable at home. There is nothing particularly unusual about Wicker's experience. People who leave a sleepy town for college in the big city are often affected in the same way. It is a cliché: "You can't go home again." Moreover, what caused Wicker to leave his hometown is, no doubt, more complicated than his retrospective suggests. *Bildungsromans* often condense, reorder, and sweep clean parts of a life that fall outside the narrative emplotment. What particularized Wicker's experience was his encounter with a set of homophobic institutions including the Army and the early medical establishment around HIV/AIDS. A variety of consciousness-raising and self-realization sessions in the 1970s led him to ask what was possible once one saw the self-deforming effects of commercial, social, and political conformity. The magic of the radical faeries was one answer.

Two objects, three scenes, and multiplying forms and modes of connectivity: What differentiates these modes of social life, mine from faeries' from indigenous people's? Where are the boundaries separating one mode of producing "something" and designating "nothing" from another mode? Who and what is interested in producing these separations, their meanings, dynamics, qualities, and destinations? Some people might wonder why they should care whether or not nonindigenous people engage in practices of self-elaboration that sometimes use indigenous and pagan symbols and sometimes do not. How does caring capture, constrain, or control the play of social life?

Not all indigenous people are critical of New Age spiritualities such as those practiced by the radical faeries. The men who took the man from Turin around the coast, showing him camping and sacred sites and telling him public stories about these sites, didn't mind whether he wore a feather, played the didjeridoo, or shared with them stories he had collected from other indigenous communities. But others are bothered. Their reactions range from a barely disguised homophobia to a sustained critique in terms of cultural property rights. In his blog essay, "An Innovative Affair of Genocide," the Indigenist commentator, educator, and activist Reverend Sequoyah Ade reflects on some of the defining legends of the radical faerie movement and their political impact on his own struggle to articulate an "indigenist political ideology."[22]

While supporting the emancipation claims of gays and lesbians, Ade considers the symbolic appropriations of indigenous traditions by radical faeries to be at best insensitive and at worst a form of cultural genocide.

According to legend, in 1970, Hay (who also claimed to have had an Apostolic encounter with spiritual leader Wovoka, the prophet of the Ghost Dance in his youth in Nevada) journeyed to New Mexico in an attempt to make this connection by finding a real living Berdache, since "real" Indians are primarily seen as phantasms of the American past. While I could not find any evidence of Hay actually locating his Berdache among the Pueblos, in 1979 the first official gathering called the "Spiritual Conference of Radical Faeries" took place in Arizona headed by Hay, John Burnside, Don Kilhefner, Mitch Walker and openly gay writer Will Roscoe. More than 200 men took part in the meeting conducting what they felt to be "authentic" Native American spiritual rituals sprinkled with various bits and pieces from other European traditions, mostly Pagan. Euroamerican Gay males stood about in the desert dressed for the occasion. Scottish kilts combined with fringed buckskin boots and Southeast Asian body markings of warrior clans past were displayed alongside others dancing to Indian hand drums buck naked with feathers tied to their "Indian" braids and other appendages. Initially this hodgepodge of confused Wasi'chu pseudo-religious theology seems harmless and fun for those involved. Practicing bewildering rituals comprised of two parts of what they think is Sioux religion, Celtic sun worship, a dash of the I-Ching and three-eighths of revisionist sex-positive Christianity curiously appears to arrive at a sort of Gay version of the neo-Nazi World Church of the Creator.[23]

It is important to note that Ade does not dismiss the structures of power and discrimination that gays and lesbians face. He seems to believe, more or less, that if gay people would just remain *gay* that would be o.k. What he criticizes is what he considers to be the helter-skelter appropriative religiosity of the radical faeries. What initially seems harmless, even fun, when gay men are just being gay men, becomes fascist and genocidal for Ade when they *express* this gayness through ritual appropriation.

Why this emphasis on ritual invention and on gay sexuality? Why do the appropriation of indigenous identity and the invention of religious rituals become the key tropes through which the eclectic worlds of this and other counter-cultural movements are artifactualized and critically apprehended?

Three

Ade's emphasis on the appropriation of indigenous identity and the invention of ritual is due, at least in part, to claims by Hay and his hagiographers that his encounter with Wovoka, the founder of the Ghost Dance, constituted an indigenous authorization of the movement. This emphasis is also due, in part, to the centrality of ritual in defining cultural difference

in a post-anthropological imaginary and the absolute difference this imaginary draws between cosmological meanings
and sexual practices.

Ritual is arguably the heart of culture and cosmology in
the classical anthropological imaginary as well as in mass
media accounts of cultural difference. If you want to understand a culture, study its rituals. And anthropologists did,
tracking, mapping, comparing, and theorizing ritual differences throughout empire. From this point of view, ritual
is where culture symbolically expresses itself most densely,
most unconsciously, most self-referentially and with breath-
taking virtuosity, even as "culture," as a shared normative orientation, is re-constituted. Ritual reanimates and re-presents
social normativity through the refracted mirror of another
ontic realm—another more powerful world enters this world
by means of ritual—and ritual manages this entry in such a
way that the given world is reproduced rather than shattered.

In other words, many anthropologists have viewed ritual
as the primary means by which a culture's clock is continually reset, remaking the present in the affective, symbolic, and
practical form of the past.[24] In this literature, the real point
of ritual—its telos—is the generation and reconstitution of
community by stimulating desires and feelings toward components of the moral and social orders through concentrated
references to symbolic phenomena and processes.[25] The task
of cultural theory has been to answer how ritual achieves
this multi-worldliness and how in achieving it social norms
are iterated. How does ritual signal the presence of another
world? How does it signal the break between this new onto-

nomic realm and ordinary time and space? How does it signal its singular ability to reanimate and manage this multi-worldliness?

So, how do faerie rituals sit within this anthropological imaginary of culture? The symbolic center of a Beltane gathering, held annually on May Day at a faerie sanctuary in the rural South, is the ritual raising of a maypole. The commune of about twenty people swells to several hundred visitors who camp throughout sanctuary grounds. The first thing to note about this ritual, as with many faerie rituals, is the enormous innovation around the key symbolic events—what kind of dress people wear, the choreography of the maypole dance, and the shape of the maypole—and the sub-rituals that precede and follow the pole-raising ceremony. This said, a basic diagram of the ritual can easily be discerned. In the weeks leading up to the event, elder members of the commune choose, cut, and prepare the maypole, which is usually about twenty feet, and prepare the hole on the central knoll into which it is inserted. After breakfast, participants are encouraged to go to their tents and prepare their bodies for the ritual. In the late morning, community elders call the group to the knoll and assemble them into a large heart circle in which everyone present holds hands. Then, members and friends of the sanctuary are called on to open the ritual with their own, often quickly inspired, sub-rituals, such as lamentations to Earth, water, and fire. The maypole is raised. A dance around it commences, its end marking the end of the formal phase of the ritual. Participants are then released into a day of general and multiple activities—dancing, sex, drumming, food preparation, sun-bathing, tarot reading, sweats, and massage. It is during these post-ritual meanderings that the ritual is ratified, and where a general consensus emerges that the ritual did, or did not, effectively reanimate an ontic realm always already within the quotidian world.

Although it's left to members to decide how to prepare their bodies for the event, bodily preparation and discourses about bodily preparation are elaborate and intense. They include the construction of a wide range of costumes from the sideshow "carny" to witch and warlock motifs, and the consumption of drugs. Usually, a consensus emerges over the course of the week, guided by those responsible for the ritual, about which kind of drugs would best enhance the activities. Individuals are free to do other drugs, or no drugs at all. But the ritual is conceptualized in part through the way that ordinary space-time can be bent on the basis of well-known and well-practiced understandings of the typical psychological states of a man or a woman on ecstasy, LSD, psychedelic mushrooms, Ketamine, GHB, and other homebrews. The experience of space and time is not bent merely by drugs but also by the opening and closing of ritual events, the kind of music played, natural or artificial lighting, the color and shape of costumes. All these elements are coordinated to intensify the biospace-time. Nevertheless, the ingestion of drugs and the constitution of biospace is not merely functional. Many faeries have participated in indigenous organized rituals that utilize the hallucinatory powers of ayahuasca, psychedelic mushrooms, and peyote to conjoin the ordinary and geontological worlds. Drugs act as medium, index, and certification of the authenticity of the ritual nature of the event because they are already discursively linked to drug-inflected ritual techniques of indigenous Southwestern U.S. and Amazonian groups.

The way I have just described the raising of the maypole would fit neatly within most anthropological views of ritual. The ritual draws on and creates a rigid separation between the supra-ordinary and the ordinary world, its typical rhythms, values, and styles of the self. Careful thought goes into the construction of this biospace, drawing a far-flung network of human and material resources into its central axis, much in the way that indigenous women and men I know recruit their neighbors into rituals in order to expand, consolidate, or initiate claims to places, people, and things. Poetically reflexive, fractually recursive practices consolidate the internal coherence of particular ritual as well as linking it to the larger arc of the gathering. Throughout the week, for instance, visitors are encouraged to participate in small heart circles, which are consensually organized spaces for the expression of feelings about the gathering, how it has or has not changed them, and thoughts about how it could be better organized. These formally construed informal spaces cultivate and direct feelings, providing them with a shape, procedure, and language. These small heart circles provide the affectively and semiotically reflexive ground from which the large heart circle moving around the maypole at the main event draws its semiotic energy.

Other radical faerie rituals might stretch the classic anthropological imaginary and public patience about the legitimacy of the claim that faerie rituals are rituals in any serious sense. For instance, a dance party might lie at the far end of the kind of event that qualifies as a ritual for many anthropologists, as well as for many ordinary people. And yet some local commune members described a dance party, held during one Beltane week, as a ritual. The party was held in the sanctuary temple, a three-story wooden building with a central open atrium, a second-story balcony, and several bedrooms on the third floor. A group of New Yorkers who had come to the mountain for the gathering hosted the party. They took responsibility for the community dinner before the event, designing it around the theme of an exclusive New York restaurant. A number of men and I acted as status police, allowing some people to enter the exclusive section of the dinner, turning back others. When the Statue of Liberty showed up drunk, homeless, and lacking an invitation, he was beaten and thrown out. The dinner thematic of rigid social status was then contrasted to the dance aesthetic of radical social blurring.

A consensus emerged that what made the party great was this blurring of social identities, its attempt to push beyond the notion of social heterogeneity, not merely by promoting a density of the "kinds of people" participating (men, women, and transgenders; straight, gay/lesbian, and bisexual; locals, out-of-towners, and residents) but also interrogating the desirability of "kinds of people" on which liberal heterogeneity depends—the rigidly preserved Bantustans of identity politics. After the event, people noted that at certain points they did not know who was a token of which type of person. De facto, partyers tended to sexualize in a way that did not appear to break sharply the token/type relations that preceded the party, no matter how they socialized. Men who liked men sexualized with men though they socialized in erotic ways with women and transgendered persons. The same can be said about the women and transgendered persons at the party. But for many of these same people the ideal of "openness," an orientation to new affective, sexual, and carnal opportunities and the way that this orientation placed typical life under suspicion, mattered corporeally. The very fact of this normative shift changed the materiality of normative sexuality no matter who had sex with whom.

However, the value of the party hardly escaped the play of contestation. The shape, scope, and outcome of a range of chemical enhancements and public sex acts were debated the next day, especially as they concerned practices of safe sex. People argued about: whether the sanctuary should take a harm reduction or abstinence approach to sex and drugs; whether people should disclose their HIV status; what kinds of sex should take place on sanctuary land; how and which drugs and chemicals should be used; if there should be a consensus about these things or if it was the point of radical faerie sociality and spirituality that each person was on his or her own journey of exploration. But then again, was the use of the ambiguous notion of "journey" just a way people avoided their ethical responsibilities in an epidemic?[26]

These questions certainly suggested why many participants thought this was a great, or not so great, *party*, but it hardly tells us why it was considered by some to have been a *ritual*. The answer has several parts. In some sense, the ritual nature of the party was the result of nothing more than an assertion that the party was a ritual. This assertion was supported by the narrative coordination of the place and time of the party to the context of the May Day gathering and the coincidence of a lunar eclipse the night of the party. In other words, the illocutionary force of the assertion that the party was a ritual drew its baptismal energy from its performative association with these other events. These externally oriented narrative coordinations were anchored to other internally co-referential practices—for instance, the opening and closing of the party, which marked it off from the ordinary ebb and flow of the gathering. All of these semiotic anchors were carefully coordinated to the anticipated biophysical reactions that participants would have to certain forms of music, lighting, rhythms, and chemicals. Finally, as with the pole-raising, the party was retroactively ratified as a ritual—some people claimed this status for the party because it had produced spiritual effects. Throughout the following day, discussions centered on a dragon that some people said they saw flying across the full moon, in the post-eclipse sky, and on a certain vibration that the temple seemed to give off long after the party had ended. Of course, all these assertions and interpretations existed amid competing points of view. Some questioned whether the temple was actually vibrating, countering that these vibrations were the result of the sound system or the "racked" perceptual systems of post-partyers. Some questioned the status of the dragon; clearly, it could have been a cloud. They offered these alternative possibilities with a good dose of scorn, saying that other people didn't know the difference between real magical events and their own addled minds and that such naiveté was what led to unsafe sexual and chemical practices. Others responded with humor. But the possibility that magic *could* happen, not whether it did in this instance, is one of the deep presuppositions animating these ritual events, and what makes them, for some of these men, not merely a circuit party.

Demonstrating that these practices meet certain popular and anthropological criteria of ritual would not quell evaluations, such as those by Ade, that these are really just a bunch of white guys, with smatterings from other social groups, making up spirituality as they go along, mystifying what is really just a drug-addled sex party. To think Ade would be satisfied with this analysis is to miss the broader historical and social conditions out of which his specific indigenous critique of the intersection of ritual and sexuality emerges. To understand these historical and social contexts we need to shift from an abstract analysis of the formal properties of ritual and from a focus on gay sexuality and spirituality to the historical uses of indigenous spirituality and sexuality in the making of anthropological discourses concerning ritual sex.

Christopher Herbert has detailed some of the broad outlines of this history. He has, for instance, shown how, during the late eighteenth and early nineteenth centuries, "a broad reversal of assumptions [occurs] in which 'savage' society is transformed from a void of institutional control where desire is rampant to a spectacle of controls exerted systemically upon the smallest details of daily life."[27] Indeed, the emergence of anthropology as a modern science pivoted on ethnopornographic portraits of saturnalian rituals of savages giving way to ethnographic analyses of the cosmological meanings of colonial ritual. Where sex was thought to or did exist in ritual form, anthropologists argued that its primary purpose was to express, represent, and transact a symbolic order—a cosmology. Professional anthropology increasingly insisted, contra older ethnopornographers—sexologists such as Havelock Ellis and novelists and amateur ethnographers such as Richard Burton—that the secret of ritual carnality was not human sexuality but human culture, the rule of law animating the social order. What were initially perceived as indexes of the primitive corporeality of savage life—passions unregulated by any real cultural logic—came to be understood as the material manifestations of a profoundly cosmological system that integrated social realms. Professional anthropologists argued that to apprehend this law lurking beyond the flesh of ritual, one needed to look past, not more closely into, the actual corporeality of ritual. This transfiguration of carnal acts into symbolic acts provided the discursive grounds for domesticating the difference between the sacred and profane, religious and secular, private and public. For instance, the coastal and inland region from which the two shells sitting on my desk were collected was the scene of exactly these kinds of scientific disciplines. And lest anyone forget, the print media in the far north of Australia periodically circulated the "true" and "scandalous" history of ritual sexuality.[28]

In the shadow of this history, Ade's insistence on the separation between ritual acts and sex acts, between homosexuality as a sexual identity and indigeneity as a cultural identity, makes a certain sense. Ade is struggling to pull a way of being out of the grip of the Western opposition between sexuality and spirituality. As some radical faeries attempt to build a form of religiosity out of a mode of indigenous sexuality, indigenous people like Ade are struggling to separate an actual indigenous history from the cultural imaginary of settler history. He is criticizing radical faeries for parroting rather than critically deconstructing this history. The gourd housing itself like a hermit crab within the shells finds itself in a property struggle or, perhaps, in a propriety struggle about the proper elements that must be in place for a ritual to be a true ritual, for a spirituality to be a true spirituality, culture a true culture, because all of these truths are the condition of recognition of indigenous people within the framework of state cultural difference. The conditions of recognition for radical faeries aren't the same.

The separation of ritual acts and sex acts is one of the foundations for establishing the difference between gourd and shells. But it is not the only separation. The charge that radical faeries are having sex seems less charged at times than the claim that they are making up their culture. Creativity is often cast as the Achilles heel of the New Age. On its Web site, one gallery of Aboriginal art proclaimed:

> Contemporary Australian Aboriginal Art derives its worldwide acclaim from the very roots of Australian Aboriginal Culture and Tradition. It is not NEW—it is not ORCHESTRATED—it is not DEVISED—it is not DESIGNED —it is not and never can be a NEW AGE "CREATED" WONDER. . . .

No whiteman could ever be so clever as to propagate, negotiate, advertise and launch such an undertaking — no other people — other than our Australian Indigenous people — could be capable of such a feat.

Of course, it is relevantly new in the history of collectable art — of course Aboriginal Painters and Aboriginal Communities are employing curators to exhibit their art — but DEVISED and NEW AGE are not relevant adjectives.

The best team of writers in the Walt Disney Enterprise could never, never, create the stories, characters, charm, situations, mystique and authenticity of the works which our Indigenous people have in the past and still are, offering to the world.

It is inherent in our Aboriginal peoples' culture to observe, to endure, to live in harmony with their Mother land, to use the gifts she offers, to share them amongst the family, to guard the land on which they depend, to abide by the beliefs and tradition passed on to them, to obey the wisdom of their elders and the stories of their Dreaming — all this is what we are privileged to perceive in Contemporary Aboriginal Painting and Artefacts.[29]

Custom and creativity, inheritance and innovation, past and future orientations: the shells I bought at a shop in Australia might be nothing. But for people like Ade and the authors of this Web page on Aboriginal art, the shell derives its status as nothing from a source that is very different from the source from which the gourd derives its status as something.

The shells could have been something, could have been tethered to an authentic spiritual tradition, because something
sits behind the shells—as Charles Taylor once put it, a human
culture that has "animated whole societies over some con-
siderable stretch of time."[30] Not so with the gourd. No matter
how exactly it may replicate an indigenous artifact (note, not
a claim that Jai makes for it), no authentic long-standing culture is seen to subtend it on which a politics of recognition
can or should be built. Because the gourd is created freely, as,
supposedly, are the radical faeries themselves, no presumption of cultural value need be extended to them. Certainly,
Hay may have considered the radical faeries to be a part of a
long cultural tradition viciously destroyed and now freely re-
invented. And given the weight that the law of cultural recognition places on the genealogical conditions of tolerance and
worth, it is not surprising that Hay and others would seek a
genealogical solution. But for many outside this movement,
the faeries remain at most a "partial cultural milieu within a
society" and, given their blurring of sex and religion, no more
than a phase of "decadence."[31]

The bald claim of the Web site quoted above may be true
enough in many instances. The problem, however, is not that
members of various New Age movements, such as the radical faeries, aren't all that creative, although, to be sure, particular people may *in fact* be more or less creative, more or
less predictable, in how they sample and assemble diverse elements of social life, elements scavenged from junk heaps, gar-
bage cans, and thrift stores as well as from other people's traditions. The problem is the discursive emphasis that radical

faeries place on individual creativity, that *in expressed ideology* the orientation is toward sampling, selecting, and assembling one's own life as a self-expressive artifact in a context in which true indigenous culture is characterized, in the ideology of law and society, as iterative, as disciplined by the descending object. If the radical faeries have a "culture," then its discursive grounding seems to rest firmly on the backbone of the *parvenu*—discourses and practices that measure the worth of a life, and a society, relative to its capacity to constitute and vest sovereignty in the individual—even if this is not strictly true.

This is what I mean when I say that there is a certain truth to Ade's claim. If members of the radical faeries are not "making up" their culture, they are certainly oriented to explicit contestation about what lies within the borders of the radical faerie movement and what lies outside them— what is and is not "something." We can simply listen to the multivocality and multifunctionality of the term "journey" to see this. As well as referring to a certain onto-theology of self-reflexive autobiography, the term "journey" provides a discursive pivot around which a person can elaborate his own identity, allegiances, and self-reflexive capacities against and across the full spectrum of permanent, part-time, and occasionally identified radical faeries who constitute this particular counter-public. Relying on cascading orders of inference, the term "journey" can be used seriously, and ironically, as onto-theological insight, doctrine, and self-delusion, in such a way that the location of the center, edge, and heart of "the radical faeries" is continually disturbed, divided, and debated. For instance, Jai may invest spiritual value in the gourd because of how it draws together and manifests an important set of events in his life. And he may attribute my attraction to and selection of it as evidence of this spiritual investment. But I can decide that the gourd contains no such spiritual qualities without breaking any of the discursive protocols of the onto-theological discourse of autobiography as spiritual exercise. My journey may well be that I am not in touch with the energy of the gourd or, more interestingly, that in my presence the gourd does not have this energy—that with me, it is nothing.

These exercises of doctrinal discourse, irony, and self/other-deprecation are mobilized not merely for the sake of identity formation but also for the sake of the economic health of self-identified faeries and the self-identified faerie sanctuaries that dot North America, Australia, and Western Europe. Living for the most part in national and international grey economies, committed radical faeries (for whatever duration) often support themselves through a mixture of welfare, occasional work, small organic food markets, and small "suitcase" markets such as the one that Jai and I constituted out of the back of his car.[32] Faerie sanctuaries, for the most part nonprofit land trusts, must generate income for taxes, building expansion, travel, and food. Gatherings—communal events drawing into these communes members of the counter-public and other interested or allied groups—on the land or benefits held off the land provide one means by which cash is generated. Particular styles of identity-as-difference emerge in part from this economic need to draw people's resources and identifications to one place and away from other possible places. Just as one person may quash another person's assertion that a magical event has happened, or that some object is in fact generating spiritual energy, so members of one community may charge another with becoming too commercial—tourist-oriented—and with having lost sight of the spiritual orientation of the movement. Visitors to gatherings sometimes voice criticisms of what are perceived as non-progressive aspects of gatherings. Permanent members of sanctuaries sometimes address, sometimes dismiss these criticisms, helping to generate the divergent personal and community styles that are then drawn into debates about what makes a radical faerie a "true" radical faerie—that is, the qualities that hinge token to type, and constitute type as such.

But how different is this kind and level of contestation from what we see in the ordinary lives of my friends along the northwest coast? What is and is not "something," for instance, in the sense that Nuki and I were using this term to refer to the shells, can be a matter of serious dispute in indigenous worlds, animating heated debates not only about the status of a thing (song, picture, object) but also about what should be the evidential grounds for assessing competing claims about the status of a thing. Among indigenous people I know, special emphasis is placed on the personal experience of the power of a geontological site or thing as this experience is mediated by the opinion of knowledgeable elders.[33] The importance of this mode of knowledge acquisition in authorizing truth claims is signaled by such common statements as, "That one sebi properly, im been there got that wulgamen"

(She really understands. She learned it from that old lady). In other words, seeing for oneself under the tutelage of knowledgeable elders is the firmest ground on which an assertion of truth about something can be made. Second to this mode of knowledge acquisition and truth assertion is the personal experience of the power of a geontological event during ordinary everyday interactions, as in "I never believed properly, but I been look myself today."

These evidential grounds do not hold for all indigenous Australians, whose social experience and life-courses vary widely, and certainly do not hold across the global terrain of indigenous worlds. Disinherited by the forces of settler colonialism from anything that could be regarded as a pre-settlement song, language, object, or land, many urban indigenous people individually select and sample from a variety of public sources to constitute their own personalized, often marketable, version of indigenous symbolic life.[34] In these spaces, the differences between indigenous and non-indigenous can begin to blur. Take, for instance, the reaction of a young white man at a faerie gathering to the spotting of a red-tailed hawk circling the communal kitchen. He pointed to the bird, telling a couple of us sitting nearby that it was his spirit totem. I asked him how he had acquired this particular bird as his totem. He replied that he had just always felt a strong personal attachment to the red-tailed hawk. He then described an encounter with another hawk that figured this personal attachment as ultimately authored by the bird itself. He said that he was standing in an abandoned field when a red-tailed hawk swooped down and caught a snake. Instead of flying off with it, the hawk just stood there eating it. Soon a crow came by and the hawk leapt into the air with the snake in its talons, passing with outstretched wings just inches from his body. This young white man's story was not so different in its surface elements from those I have heard from indigenous men and women in and around Darwin. These stories of an individual's spiritual encounter with a specific animal species sutures together, if awkwardly, the skin of these men and women as each absorbs and refigures the mytho-poetics of indigeneity available to them.

However, even where urban indigenous people lack text artifacts that signal the presence of the descending object, they can evoke the presence of the genealogical society through the notion of race. Since the 1980s, urban indigenous groups have marked their distinct social standing in the heteroglossic settler nations through their racial heritage as figured by a human descent group. A sociocentric genealogical chart can be used to designate membership in a social group even in the absence of any shared knowledge, symbolic substance, or social practice. The political effectiveness of this strategy depends on the compelling nature of a distinction between aggregated individuals of choice and the mass subject of genealogical determination. It was just these questions—what makes a group a "group" and what constitutes the differences between kinds of groups—that fascinated, fastened, and gripped the attention of lawyers and anthropologists in an exchange during a land claim as they tried to articulate why a large, thousand-plus, urban-oriented Aboriginal claimant group, many of whom did not know each other and did not share common activities or beliefs, fit the legal definition of a local descent group:

> His Honour: It's a bit of a nebulous concept, isn't it? I mean if you take the members of the Melbourne Cricket Club, of which there are tens of thousands, I certainly, being one, don't know all of the others. I know how to ascertain who all of the others are in the sense that I know that somewhere there's a register on which the names all appear. Are we a group or are we a category or how do you describe us?

> His Honour: There's some— you have to have, you would say, some kind of cohesive element before you become a group?
> Dr. Rose: Some kind of shared project together, perhaps. Some kind of mutual understanding of why you belong together.

> His Honour: That's not really what I'm putting [*sic*]. If you go back to the Melbourne Cricket Club, you say that for some purpose, at least, the Melbourne Cricket Club would constitute a group and that, notwithstanding that we're not watching sport together at the same time, only some of us are from time to time, but we are all descended from people, are we a descent group?
> Dr. Rose: No.
> His Honour: No. And why not, because there has to be some, presumably, some relevant connection between the ancestors and the cohesive factor?

Dr. Rose: Well, no, because the Melbourne Cricket Club
is not constituted on a principle of descent. You become
a member — well I don't know, but you would know how
you become a member.

His Honour: The criteria for joining is not descent.[35]

In this exchange, indigenous groups, as opposed to cricket-
ers and, for that matter, radical faeries, are not families of
choice any more than they are cultures of invention, because
a status of common descent stands in the background. And
this difference provides social traction for people like the land
comissioner who need some distinction to operate the legal
machinery of the politics of cultural difference. Individuals
may choose to *identify* as indigenous, but the *fact* of their
descent transforms this choice of identification into merely
the question of whether or not someone wishes to activate
what is always already there. The lack of choice in the domain
of genealogical classification effectively mirrors thick public
presumptions about culture as determination.[36]

The land commissioner and Rose were discussing a situation in which the only aspect of mutuality defining the group
was descent. But, even when thick ties of social and cultural
cohesion are clearly present within a descent group, disputes
about what is or is not something do not end. The social cohesion merely helps to shape how disputes will proceed. After
all, who is a knowledgeable elder and on what grounds is the
assessment being made? What was the mode of tutelage —
ritual? Ritual of what sort? Hunting? Song acquisition? These
questions and others continually shape the center and edges,
the content and form, of what is considered to be properly

indigenous; i.e., just as with the radical faeries, the category emerges retroactively, an artifact of these social struggles over genre.

Particularly heated disputes can arise when a person claims to have been given access, through ancestral mediation, to sacred sites, narratives, and designs previously unknown. Fred Myers, for instance, has described how, among the Pintupi he worked with in central Australia, dreams about ancestral beings offer "enormous interpretive possibilities."[37] The setting, components, and texts of the dream may provide new important insight into the geontology, but they may also be "nothing." They may be "just a dream." These interpretive possibilities can then be mobilized for political and social gain within a community.[38] In the northwest coast where I have lived, part of this struggle pivots around individual skills and capacities: the reputation for "cleverness" that a person can acquire by discerning actual, but as yet not cognitively or visually articulated patterns of kinship and geontology.[39] "Cleverness" in this context refers not to the creative capacity to pull into the plane of existence new forms—it is not an existential form of freedom—but to pull into the plane of human epistemology forms and patterns not yet known but already existing.[40] Rather than its abrogation, human ingenuity is deeply integrated into the ways that humans encounter the geontology. Indeed, the absence of a clever person and his or her ability to discern the immanent patterns of the geontological world is a source of much anxiety for small indigenous communities which, without such a person, are blind to the forces of this geontological world.

Radical faeries find themselves on the opposite side of this discursively constructed difference between aggregated individuals of choice and the mass subject of genealogical determination, and not simply because members of this group do not always physically reproduce. Insofar as they constitute a counter-public, radical faeries seem to be an epiphenomenon of the social imaginary of a public, rather than the social imaginary of kinship, race, and the reproductive family. What exactly "a public" is, where it is, or how it emerged historically is, of course, a matter of much, and strenuous, debate. If we narrow our focus to this particular public, then I think the description that Michael Warner gives of public and counterpublic is quite useful. The counter-public of radical faeries exists by virtue of members feeling addressed by a set of circulating media that explicitly posit this public as an alternative to the normative dimensions of public life. It would cease to exist as a living body the moment no one felt addressed.[41]

In other words, radical faeries constitute themselves as a social group by identifying with a specific kind and set of circulating texts and practices. These circulating media never address anyone in his or her particularity. On the contrary, the texts are constructed to address a wide range of strangers, even though many people writing and reading them may be close friends and lovers and even though many members of this counter-public are more than happy to restrict access to specific public events to those members of this counter-public whom they consider "just so." (The theme of an exclusive dinner party during the May Day party ironically signaled just this.) For all this, the counter-public of radical faeries, even if it is restricted to this mode of address, is not necessarily built out of an exercise of freedom in the liberal sense—agents choosing what to call home. It is a modern prince, a "concrete phantasy which acts on a dispersed and shattered people to arouse and organize its collective will."[42] However, these counter-publics are not organized simply by the articulatory power of addressivity. In some permanent radical faerie sanctuaries, housing is determined by the longevity of residence, a material sense of commitment and belonging. People often spend years living in a tent before a room opens in a more permanent structure. Other people may move more quickly into such permanent structures if they become lovers with someone already living there.

At this point the semantic distinction between contestation and creativity seems extremely relevant to the difference attributed to radical faeries and indigenous Australians, at least at the extremes of their social types. Why does contesting whether someone has in fact encountered a Dreaming, when sharing a presupposition about the truth of Dreaming, seem distinct from contesting whether someone is in fact progressive or magical, when sharing a presupposition about the truth of progress and magic? Both are instances of contestation, but whether they are instances of creativity depends on the framework one brings to bear on time, form, and destination. They depend on the relevance of questions such as: Do the forms stay consistent over time? Are innovations in producing these forms oriented toward changing them or keeping them consistent? Are some indigenous men and women changing certain aspects of their ritual practice in order to maintain them in a changing colonial context? Are some radical faeries maintaining certain aspects of their general ideology of spirituality in order to allow for self-transformative practices?

Four

Even if the interpretive and material status of a text artifact in indigenous communities may never be closed, this does not stop the law and public from demanding textual closure and a genealogical difference as the basis not merely for the recognition of the worth of a culture (note, not necessarily for the people within that culture) but for the granting of legal rights to engage in certain kinds of social, cultural, corporeal, and religious practices. No matter the actual dynamic between the form of an artifact and the norms for producing it, law and public may well demand that a text artifact appear stable, unified, and essential and past-oriented rather than future-oriented, for specific kinds of rights and values to accumulate around them.[43] This seems especially true in cases of sexual and religious difference.

The first thing to note is that, no matter the truth of Janet Jakobsen and Ann Pellegrini's argument that "specifically Christian ideas about sexual morality" inform most Supreme Court cases touching on sexuality, *Reynolds v. the United States* (1878) is the only case that the United States Supreme Court has heard in which plaintiffs were seeking to establish their constitutional rights to engage in nonnormative sex acts under the Free Exercise Clause of the First

Amendment ("Congress shall make no law respecting an establishment of religion, or prohibiting the free exercise thereof").[44] In *Reynolds*, the United States Supreme Court found that the government could regulate marriage forms —by implication, sex acts—even though it also stated that marriage was sacred "from its very nature" in "most civilized nations." Subsequent cases before the Supreme Court that probed the relationship between religious beliefs and actions and government regulation did not focus on sex or sexuality per se. In *Sherbert v. Verner* (1963), the Supreme Court heard the case of a Seventh-day Adventist who was denied unemployment benefits because she refused to work on Saturdays, the Sabbath of the Seventh-day Adventist Church. The Supreme Court held that, although the government did not have the constitutional right to punish religious beliefs, it did have the right to regulate "overt acts." But this regulation was conditioned. The Supreme Court also found that the government had to show a "compelling state interest" in legislation that accidentally or purposely adversely affected a specific religion.

In the landmark decision *Employment Division v. Smith* (1990), the U.S. Supreme Court ruled that it would no longer hold the government to the standard of heightened scrutiny if a law only accidentally affected a religious practice. In *Smith*, the court reviewed whether or not two Native Americans, Alfred Smith and Galen Black, could be denied unemployment benefits after testing positive for the Schedule 1 drug peyote they used during a Native American Church service.[45] While iterating the constitutional distinction between belief and action, Justice Antonin Scalia's majority decision stated, "We have never held that an individual's religious beliefs excuse him from compliance with an otherwise valid law prohibiting conduct that the State is free to regulate. . . . The mere possession of religious convictions which contradict the relevant concerns of a political society does not relieve the citizen from the discharge of political responsibilities." Citing *Reynolds*, Scalia argued that a person could not excuse a criminal practice on the basis of religion. "To permit this would be to make the professed doctrines of religious belief superior to the law of the land, and in effect to permit every citizen to become a law unto himself." The threat of anarchy, Scalia argued, must at times expose democracy to the prejudice of the majority. "The Court today suggests that the disfavoring of minority religions is an 'unavoidable consequence' under our system of government and that accommodation of such religions must be left to the political process." It is no little irony that, in cases pertaining to homosexuality and abortion rights, Scalia has foregrounded the religious roots of his opinions.

Smith led to the creation of a coalition to lobby for the Religious Freedom Restoration Act in 1993, which, when signed by President Clinton on 17 November 1993, restored the compelling-interest test and ensured its application in all cases where religious exercise was substantially burdened. On 25 June 1997, the U.S. Supreme Court declared the law unconstitutional because it forced states to go beyond the religious protections guaranteed by the First Amendment as these had been interpreted in *Smith*.[46]

The struggle to protect the religious use of peyote and aya-huasca from criminalization does not merely pivot on the difference between belief and action, but on the differences between the people acting—a mass or cultural subject; a free or constrained subject. The establishment of the religious exemption for peyote use in the Native American Church and later for marijuana use in the Rastafarian religion rested on the understanding that these practices were essential components of long-standing, stable, and distinctive religious cultural traditions. These religions were not recently invented, individually authored, or under constant revision. They were genealogical. Not surprisingly, a penumbra of race hovers over these religious practices and their belief structures. The descent of persons and the descent of beliefs are tightly articulated.

In *U.S. v. Robert Lawrence Boyll* (1991), the U.S. District Court for the District of New Mexico was asked to decide whether Boyll should have been indicted for unlawfully importing and distributing peyote for use in the Native American Church. Chief Federal Judge Juan Burciaga began with an observation that the "war on drugs" had tattered the "Fourth Amendment right to be free from unreasonable searches and seizures and the now frail Fifth Amendment right against self-incrimination or deprivation of liberty without due process" and threatened "the First Amendment right to freely exercise one's religion." He then signaled his view of the spirit of the law in the context of a multicultural society: "To us in the Southwest, this freedom of religion has singular significance because it affects diverse cultures. . . . To the Government, peyote is a dangerous hallucinogen. To Robert Boyll, peyote is both a sacrament and a deity essential to his religion." The federal government argued that religious protection did not apply to Boyll—that peyote use could not be considered religious from a legal point of view—because the Uniformed Control Substance Act (1990) relied on a racial designation. Only federally recognized Native Americans were exempted. Because neither Boyll nor his wife was 25 percent Native American or a member of a federally recognized tribe, the exemption did not apply to them.[47] Burciaga rejected this argument. "Church" for him referred "to a body of believers and their shared practices, rather than the existence of a formal structure or a membership roll." Membership in the Native American Church derived from the sincerity of one's beliefs and participation in rituals, not from a federally recognized blood quantum. The federal government appealed Burciaga's ruling in the 10th Federal Circuit Court, but a panel of three judges upheld his decision.

The Utah Supreme Court heard the *State of Utah v. Mooney* in 2004. By that time the legislative climate regarding the religious use of peyote had changed. Amendments to the American Indian Religious Freedom Act had been added in 1994 that, on the one hand, made lawful the use, possession, and transportation of peyote by an Indian for "bona fide traditional ceremonial purposes in connection with the practice of a traditional Indian religion" and, on the other hand, defined an Indian as a member of "any tribe, band, nation, pueblo, or other organized group or community of Indians . . . which is recognized for the special programs and services provided by the United States to Indians because of their status as Indians." This congressional act did not, however, clarify how an earlier regulatory exemption should be interpreted. In 1970, the Bureau of Narcotics and Dangerous Drugs, the predecessor of the Drug Enforcement Administration (DEA), had already exempted "the nondrug use of peyote in bona fide religious ceremonies of the Native American Church, and members of the Native American Church" from Schedule 1 prosecution. Judge Gary D. Stott, who heard the case of *State of Utah v. Mooney*, noted that the DEA had subsequently decided to interpret this exemption as applicable only to members of federally recognized Native American tribes. And Wilhelm Murg, writing for the *Native American Times*, noted that in December 2001, the DEA's Deputy Assistant Administration for the Office of Diversion Control, Laura Nagel, had referred to a department decision to "delete all references to the 'Native American Church' and to 'members of the Native American Church' in the regulation." The DEA "would then add language identical to the language used in AIRFA that protects the use of peyote by members of federally recognized tribes for bona fide traditional ceremonial purposes in connection with the practice of traditional Indian Religion."

These legislative and regulatory changes allowed the State of Utah to argue that Stott should defer to the interpretation of the DEA and rule that the Mooneys were not entitled to the protection of any exemption for the religious use of peyote because they lacked the government seal of recognition. The State of Utah also argued that the restriction of the exemption to federally recognized Native American tribes, rather than to members of the Native American Church, did not violate the Fourteenth Amendment Equal Protection Clause because it was a political designation rather than a racial or religious designation, "designed to preserve tribal culture, rather than a constitutionally suspect racial preference." Judge Stott rejected these arguments. Interpreting Utah's Controlled Substances Act under the two federal exemptions—those under the AIRFA Amendments and those under the regulatory exemption—Stott decided that the Mooneys had a constitutional right to use peyote in their religious services. Stott's ruling does not answer whether, under federal law, the use of peyote by persons not recognized as members of a federally recognized tribe should be permitted. Currently, the Supreme Court is being asked to decide whether the O Centro Espírita Beneficiente União do Vegetal, the U.S. branch of a Brazilian Christian group, should be allowed to import and use ayahuasca, another Schedule 1 drug, in its religious ceremonies.

In the end, the Utah court ruled that the exemption applied to all members of the Native American Church irrespective of racial identity. Several other judgments and regulatory decisions on religious practice are interesting in this regard, including the tax status of Nomenus, a radical faerie sanctuary in Oregon, as a not-for-profit religious organization. Nevertheless, under the administration of George W. Bush, the Justice Department remains committed to tightening the relationship between corporeal inheritance (race) and symbolic inheritance (religious customs) in order to restrict the scope of religious exemptions for criminally defined acts. The preservation of "tribal culture" is not intended to make this culture equal to established religions or to provide a space for social experiment and self-elaboration. The preservation of tribal culture through the exemption of members to charges under federal drug law, where drugs become "nondrugs" in a religious transubstantiation, writes into tribal culture both this catholic reading of materiality and a Protestant reading of the mature subject of salvation. Drugs cannot be adminis- tered to children or to anyone else forcefully. Such adminis- tration of drugs transfigures religion into child abuse.

These court cases do not, of course, describe what people actually do. Courts may uphold the rights of governments to regulate actions, but they do not compel the various levels of government to act. For instance, many communities in Utah and elsewhere openly practice polygamy as a manifestation of their religious belief. In many other forests, towns, and cities, men, women, and transgendered persons engage in spiritu- ally inspired practices of drug ingestion formally proscribed by law. Many of these men, women, and transgendered per- sons seek to exploit the incommensurability of state and fed- eral law, and the regulatory language that surrounds it, to further their religious practice. Nevertheless, these legally sanctioned governmental powers are part of a broader inter- national regime of recognition that apprehends religion and corporeality through the grids of the autological subject and the genealogical society.

No elaborate jurisprudence on indigenous ritual drug ingestion exists in Australia, in large part because state- regulated drugs were not and, for the most part, are not a part of "customary" practice.[48] The Australian state does, however, actively regulate other aspects of ritual practices where these practices touch the criminal code. In a series of decisions, Commonwealth, state, and Territory courts have found that many practices considered to be related to traditional ritual life, or to be a necessary correlative to cultural life, are not protected from the criminal code: classic examples are the customary marriage of pre-adolescents, ritual punishment, and honor killings.[49] At the same time, High Court decisions since *Mabo* (1992), which recognized native title, have narrowed the basis of what can be considered an example of "traditional culture." To be considered an artifact of a traditional culture, objects, people, or practices must show significant continuity in their form over time. This status includes the external form and the normative social protocols for producing this form. A social group must maintain this form even as local, state, and commonwealth statutory and common laws and regulatory regimes are evacuating the legal and social incentives for doing so.[50]

The Yorta Yorta native title application provides a good example of how restrictive the juridical imaginary of the "traditional" can be. The application was lodged in February 1994, covering an area along the Murray River in southeastern Australia. The hearing began in 1996, but concluded after the restrictive Native Title Act amendments were passed in 1998.[51] Later that same year, Justice Olney determined that native title did not exist over the land and waters claimed by the Yorta Yorta. He concluded that before the end of the nineteenth century the ancestors of the Yorta Yorta had ceased to occupy their traditional lands in accordance with their traditional laws and customs. Olney cited the very language of the *Mabo* decision that recognized native title in order to nullify its effects in this case. "The tide of history has indeed washed away any real acknowledgement of their traditional laws and any real observance of their traditional customs." The Full Federal Court upheld Olney's judgment, stating, "the Yorta Yorta community had lost its character as a traditional Aboriginal community." In his minority dissent, Blackburn argued that Justice Olney was in error for having applied too restrictive an approach to the concept of what is "traditional" and for having failed to take seriously much of the oral evidence provided by the claimants. The Yorta Yorta submitted an application to the High Court to appeal this second ruling. In December 2002, the High Court upheld Olney and the Full Federal Court.

Olney based his decision on a simple comparison of the discourses and texts of contemporary Yorta Yorta claimants and the written record of Edward Curr, a pastoralist and amateur ethnographer who lived in the region in the 1850s. Olney focused on the issue of whether the normative protocols underlying the Yorta Yorta attachment to land had fundamentally shifted.[52] His answer was yes. He argued that the language and beliefs of the claimants placed them closer to the Friends of the Earth, who put in a supporting brief, than to their own ancestors, as recorded by Curr. The Yorta Yorta had entered the New Age which meant, for Olney, that they had departed their proper Age. As Lisa Strelein has argued, Olney's reliance on the survival of a pre-contact normative system imported two additional criteria into the usual understanding of tradition: that traditions have what she calls "an age" and what I call a temporal orientation, and that society be reduced to its normative features.[53] To satisfy the criteria of native title, indigenous applicants must not merely produce text artifacts (objects, bodily habitus, songs) that resemble those documented in the history books, they must also produce them on the basis of the same normative protocols of their pre-contact ancestors. These ever-multiplying conditions of cultural subjectification sit side-by-side with other bodies of

154 law that criminalize the practices and normative attitudes that Curr described — ritual sex, gender subordination, pre-adolescent marriage — whether or not these practices actually existed or were mediated through the fevered mind of Curr himself. The Yorta Yorta are, by law, already in the New Age.

Olney did not pull his understanding of tradition from thin air. A certain representational gravity pulled him there. Within the anthropological community, much ink has been spilled in academic debates concerning the normative orientation and the actual capacity of so-called oral cultures to reproduce long ancestral texts over great expanses of time. Tzvetan Todorov famously argued, in *The Conquest of America*, that such sacred texts as the heuhuetlatolli were "learned by heart, without individual variation. . . . Even if we suppose that these informants, doubtless old men, exaggerate the importance of ritual discourse to the detriment of improvised speech, we cannot help being impressed by the number and length of such discourses [such as the Popul Vuh] and hence by the place ritual occupies at the heart of the community's verbal life."[54] Other folk theorists and linguistic anthropologists have recounted the incredible ability of Amazonian shamans to repeat without deviation poetically complex, esoteric texts. That said, not all scholars of the verbal arts examine the iterative nature of postcolonial poetics from the point of view of the domination of speech form over speech event and iteration over innovation. Many examine instead the creative interplay between text artifact and interactional norms.[55] But this point of view is loudly rejected in law as well as in popular culture.

In the shadow of this case law, what avenues are available for radical faeries to legitimate their practices where they touch a criminal code? Cast outside genealogy by critical publics and juridical rulings, faeries fall back, or are pushed, into the disciplines of freedom—but a severely qualified freedom. Read under the sign of "homosexual," radical faeries are barely equal citizens under the law. Understood as a religion, they straddle precariously the divide between the autological subject and genealogical society. Radical faeries seem to be free, but they are then refused their freedom and refused a proper "culture" in any deep (i.e., historical) or robust (socially governed) sense. Indigenous people face the opposite side of this discursive dynamic. They may be seen to have culture in the robustly genealogical sense—biologically, socially, and culturally descendent—but they're not "free." Lacking freedom, they teeter on the rim of humanity. It is not a surprise, then, that media and legal discussions revolve around how far their toes can dip into actual life before they lose whatever social, political, or economic compensations refusing actual life might provide them. Nor is it a surprise that media and legal discussions of progressive alternative social groups revolve around the ethics and legality of appropriating other cultures, given the insistence these alternative groups be culturally stillborn and indigenous groups be culturally frozen.

Five

Perhaps we should be surprised, then, that the social forma-
tions that least fit the state, legal, and public imaginary of the clean division between the autological state and the gene-alogical society, between individual freedom and social coer-cion, are ideal examples of what makes constitutional democ-racies so exceptional. It is, supposedly, exactly the freedom of the radical faeries from social constraint—even as the law criminalizes them—that makes them good to think through for those theorists interested in the exceptionalism of con-stitutional freedom. The arts of the self practiced by radical faeries and by indigenous people struggling to find a disci-pline of the self in the wake of settler colonialism are a part of what Jürgen Habermas, Michel Foucault, and Hakim Bey, for all their varying rhetorical styles, conceptual foundations, and disciplinary locations, tried to comprehend through the notions of unregulated public spheres, practices of the self, and temporary autonomous zones. A fascinating convergence of interest among theorists of such divergent perspectives, rhetorics, and disciplinary locations emerges about the poten-tial that counter-publics such as the radical faeries present for

the revitalization of social and constitutionally protected freedoms — or, for Foucault and Simone de Beauvoir, the practice of freedom as such.

The play of sexuality among the radical faeries would seem to exemplify what Foucault had in mind when he reflected on practices of freedom as practices of critical transgression. One of his favorite rallying cries, "Develop your legitimate strangeness," could, after all, have been the banner of various queer hippie communes in the Bay Area during the 1970s.[56] The Cockettes, its founder, Hibiscus, and the communal movement they helped foster seem to embody Foucault's musings on the politics of self-fashioning. And the visual legacies of these movements — films, writings, sartorial styles — provide an ongoing archive for some faerie salons. Many of the cultural and spiritual predecessors of the radical faerie movement had died, disbanded, moved, or moved on to far less transgressive lives by the time Foucault arrived in San Francisco in 1975 to lecture in the French Department at the University of California, Berkeley, and discovered the thriving s/m culture in the city.[57] To be sure, not all radical faeries, nor all queers, share the Foucauldian emphasis on self-elaboration. Some within the radical faerie movement reject outright the constructionist attitude exemplified in Foucault's genealogical method, seeking instead to find a "berdache spirituality" that defines the essential difference of gay men. For them, the orientation of radical faeries is not to an event horizon, but to the reestablishment of a severed spiritual genealogy.

Although individual radical faeries may disagree with

Foucault's approach, it was exactly the possibility of self-transformation among the gay lives he witnessed in the United States in the 1970s that influenced Foucault's late meditations on the practices of sexual freedom. Insistently driving into the thicket of social life's material and discursive conditions, he sought not a new collective bargaining agreement to extend rights to new communities and identities, but to interrogate the limits of each and every such bargain. How do we make things that are in reality, though not a part of knowledge, *actual*? How do we invest actualities that operate just outside vision with the power to change dominant bio-epistemologies? For Foucault, the answer lay in cultivating practices of freedom that orient the subject to restless experimentation with the givenness of life, with how life might be otherwise than it is—otherwise regimented, otherwise habituated, otherwise unremarkable. These "games of truth" are densely deictic, organized around specific temporal and spatial questions. Why am I governed *like this* rather than like that, here and now? Why is it *this* organization of sexual pleasure, eroticism, amour, that constitutes the relationship between myself and myself, and myself and others, rather than some other?[58]

In other words, Foucault was not interested in sexual freedom's secret *meaning*, or in sexual freedom in the abstract, or as an abstraction that represented the end of history—a state in which the self experiences a radical and ultimate break from all social determinations—or in freedom in the abstract—a state in which the self experiences the jouissance of the collective suture—or the return to the bare naked body.

He was primarily interested in a politics of endless transgression rather than in a politics of repression or translation. In this way, Foucault sounds remarkably like his contemporary, Simone de Beauvoir, who argued that freedom is the treatment of every goal as both a destination and a point of departure.[59]

Even radical faeries who would support a general Foucauldian perspective are, arguably, neither the most radical nor the most conservative among gay, lesbian, and queer publics and counter-publics. In its broader social context the world-making orientation of many faeries is quite different, for example, from the world-negating sexual experimentation of writers such as Jean Genet — or at least from Leo Bersani's reading of Genet. Bersani argues that Genet's vision refuses "relationality" in order to imagine "a form of revolt that has no relation whatsoever to the laws, categories, and values it would contest and, ideally, destroy." This nonrelational ethics allows Genet to be radically alone, and absolutely distinguishes him from "the tame demand for recognition on the part of our own gay community."[60] Of course, Genet's vision of self-shattering, accomplished through a specific organization and orientation of faceless bodies, exactly presupposed the sanctification of *entre nous* as a form of recognition that passes most profoundly and fundamentally between two people nakedly facing each other, no social status or superficiality of flesh standing between this embrace of eyes and souls.

If radical faeries stand diagonal to an anti-communal deployment of corporeality, they likewise stand awkwardly alongside a domesticating homosexuality that calls for recognition by institutions of state and civil society on the basis of the essential sameness of gay and straight people. For many self-identified heterosexuals and homosexuals, a person's sexuality does not necessitate alternative forms of spirituality found in other worlds, but can be richly accommodated and explained by the traditions of the book.[61] Hay certainly knew that many gay men and lesbians understood themselves to be Christian, Jewish, or Muslim. It was exactly this "assimilationist" tendency that putatively prompted him to establish the radical faeries in the first place. According to Hay, as well as queer feminists such as Lisa Duggan, the demand that state benefits, property rights, and social recognition be *extended* to homosexuals is seen as opposed to a demand that the very nature of these institutions be transformed by the multiple forms of desire and association that queer life makes possible. Hay and Duggan may part company over the question of identity essentialism. They share, however, a worry about the extensionalist, rather than transformative, nature of the contemporary liberal politics of recognition. I put "assimilationist" in quotes because, for many who oppose homosexuality, gays and lesbians cannot be assimilated into the dominant national culture without culture itself being radically transformed.[62]

The social implications of practices of self-elaboration, counter-publicness, and the techniques of freedom and coercion that emerge from them were not merely an interest of Foucault, but also of his intense intellectual rival, Habermas. For Habermas, unregulated public spheres—"overlapping subcultural publics having fluid temporal, social and substantial boundaries" such as faerie gatherings and the variety of sub-cultural styles such as Wiccans, radical vegans, and anarchist jugglers they draw in — provide much of the creative energy of regulated public spheres.[63] Many of the residents of radical faerie communities, for instance, travel to other alternative communities to sample arts of living otherwise, including communes of radical clowns, sites where ayahuasca can be ritually taken, ashrams, alternative housing movements, independent newspaper collectives, and organic/vegan food cooperatives. Though Habermas insists that these kinds of publics are possible only within a framework guaranteed by a democratic constitutionalism, nevertheless, unregulated public spheres "develop more or less spontaneously."[64] Insofar as they are at least semi-autonomous to the field of discipline within the regulated public sphere, unregulated public spheres provide a context for creative discovery. "New problems can be perceived more sensitively, discourses aimed at achieving self-understanding can be conducted more widely and expressively, collective identities and need interpretation can be articulated with fewer compulsions than is the case in procedurally regulated public spheres."[65]

Although Foucault foregrounded the conjunction between practices of life and the organization of power, it was Habermas who focused particular attention on the problem these kinds of publics face in the institutionally saturated thickets of deliberative democracies.[66] Some of the contours of Habermas's theory of deliberative democracy are fairly uncontroversial. For him, democratic communicative proceduralism "grounds the presumption that reasonable or fair results are obtained insofar as the flow of relevant information and its proper handling have not been obstructed."[67] In this way, practical reason can be freed both from the republican philosophy of consciousness whose hope for legitimate and just governance rests in the establishment of an ethical citizenry and from the liberal philosophy of interests whose hope for legitimation and justice rests on the establishment of an ongoing compromise between interest-oriented economic actors.[68] As opposed to both republican and liberal philosophy, deliberative democracy grounds practical truth in nothing more than a constitutionally protected procedure of communication such that all conclusions that citizens reach and that have been reached in conformity with the procedures of deliberative rationality, are reasonable, reason being the ultimate ground of legitimation.[69]

Unregulated public spheres pose a particular kind of problem to Habermas's faith in public reason and social justice. After all, unregulated public spheres do more than creatively energize the normative public sphere. Unregulated public spheres also expose constitutional democracy to the charge that openness, transparency, and non-coercion never actually hold in moments of serious difference, difference that matters—that openness and non-coercion exist only when no real challenge exists to normative public life or when the major edges of the challenge have been neutralized. Even where they are not directly opposed to democratic forms of governance, from the point of view of normative publics, unregulated public spheres may present a robust challenge to the substance and procedures of democratic constitutionalism, fostering forms of subjectivity, embodiment, and institutionality at odds with them. As a result, unregulated public spheres are often sites where the state exerts repressive, coercive power. Habermas notes just this, arguing that because of their "anarchic structures," these unregulated spaces are more "vulnerable to the repressive and exclusionary effects of unequally distributed social power, structural violence, and systematically disturbed communication."[70] Vulnerability exists not merely because of police force, but because of the force of sense and nonsense. As Kirstie McClure notes, "the appropriateness or desirabiity of toleration" of specific social groups assures a "discursive frame within which toleration makes sense." Many unregulated publics go beyond the conceptual boundaries of the frame of toleration, "beyond which toleration appears foreclosed as senseless, as non-sense, in both principle and practice."[71]

One doesn't have to travel that far into any alternative public to see what is at stake. Practitioners of social critique can exist squarely within the institutionally regulated spheres of public reason and still have to contend with the police function of the regulated public sphere. One of the founders of the Critical Art Ensemble, Steve Kurtz, an art professor at State University of New York, Buffalo, was investigated by the FBI for culturing bacterial forms as part of the CAE's performance pieces and faces possible charges under the Patriot Act for possession of biological agents. The *Washington Post* reported that Adele Henderson, chair of Kurtz's department, was among the people the FBI questioned. "On May 21, she says, the FBI asked her about Kurtz's art, his writings, his books; why his organization (the art ensemble) is listed as a collective rather than by its individual members; how it is funded."[72] Two of Kurtz's texts, "Digital Resistance: Explorations in Tactical Media" and "Electronic Civil Disobedience and Other Unpopular Ideas," were published by the same press, Automedia/Semiotext(e), that published the anarchist Hakim Bey and other avant-garde fiction and nonfiction writers and French theorists. In short, unregulated public spheres can be situated at the crosshairs of democratic coercion and creativity—the sources of creative discovery are often the sites of social conflict, and this conflict presents a potentially decisive challenge to the exceptionalism of freedom claimed by deliberative democracies.

Many counterpublics practice forms of spirituality that are a panoply of religious, cultural, and social traditions. These practices of spirituality present a robust challenge to the ideal account of the unregulated public sphere, not merely because their beliefs challenge normative beliefs but because their practices are riddled by low-level illicit, often criminal activity, the physical and social outcomes of which may not appear redemptive on the surface—high rates of HIV/AIDS infection, drug addiction, and low life expectancy. The charge that deliberative democracy is merely a liberal mode of social coercion would annul one of its differences in the competitive field of governmental forms. Democratic freedom would merely be one of a number of competing forms of social coercion. For Habermas, the possibility that social coercion may be secreted in the very heart of deliberative proceduralism, rather than merely in instances of its abuse, becomes especially acute, or at least acutely visible, when the division between the public and the private threatens to be ruptured by the disciplining of the very creativity that democracy and capital claim to foster. We can assume a robust referent for the "private," including the domain of the individual, the family, or a culture. In all of these cases, the question is whether, as Habermas puts it, the procedures of deliberative rationality are themselves neutral and impartial, or are merely misused. Does the very fact of an orientation to public reason act as a type of coercive force?

Habermas says it doesn't, and he tries to demonstrate why by introducing a difference between thematization and coercion; namely, a distinction between "procedural constraints on public discourses" and "constraints or limitations on the range of topics open to public discourse."[73] Any topic related to "ethically relevant questions of the good life, of collective identity, and of need interpretation" should be open to public discourse. Simply making something the topic of discussion, Habermas argues, does not "*yet* imply any infringement" on the individual, or, we might add, on her cultural elaborations: "To talk about something is not necessarily the same as meddling in another's affairs."[74] Many critics of Habermas's approach to deliberative democracy have focused on the problem of defining "ethically relevant questions of the good life."[75] To these critics, Habermas has replied that such definitions are the outcome of ongoing coordinating and integrating processes of public reason. I think this is true enough, and so I want to turn instead to the stakes of the distinction between thematization and coercion in the everyday worlds in which the gourd and shells were made.

To this end, let us return to the New York dance party, held during the week following the Beltane May Day celebration. Remember, what made the party interesting, even magical, to some people was the way in which it was able to remove itself from the quotidian connection between sexual tokens and types. Some partyers thought it was moving not to know who was a token of what, i.e., what was something and what was nothing. But, however much the party/ritual was able to constitute a spiritual realm by removing itself from the sexually quotidian, the quotidian nature of sexual politics was not far afield; moreover, the force of these quotidian sexual politics provided some of the critical social energy of the party itself. As the dancers danced, the country was debating the social meanings and ramifications of a county ordinance banning gays. In the weeks leading up to the gathering, commissioners in nearby Rhea County, Tennessee, had passed a resolution banning gays and lesbians from residence. The ban did not merely criminalize homosexual acts or ban homosexual marriage. It made it illegal for anyone who was identified as a homosexual to live in the county.[76] The resolution was quickly rescinded. Former county executive and clerk Jimmy Wilkey claimed the media had misrepresented the discussion, asserting that the commissioners had merely voted to ban gay marriage. The expulsion of a class of people based on their social classification and worded in such a way as to avoid judicial scrutiny raised the specter of the violently segregated Jim Crow South, if not the soft racial segregation of neighborhoods throughout the United States.

The Rhea County vote would certainly fall on the coercive side of the division Habermas posits between thematization and coercion. The commissioners went far beyond merely opening to public discourse an "ethically relevant" question "of the good life, of collective identity, and of need interpretation." Indeed, their strategy was intended to discourage public discussion. Even if the commission had gotten its way, it would have faced problems enforcing the ordinance. Before race and sexuality can be regulated, the subject must be disciplined to inhabit that race and sexuality. The immanent play of discourse around bodies and their circulations, invaginations, and refigurations must be appropriated violently or surreptitiously in such a way that a play without an essential meaning is given a direction.[77] In other words, race and sexuality need to become meaningful, vital, foci of social life.

In U.S. racial regulations, a genealogical fantasy bears much of this disciplinary weight. Discourses about the materiality of genealogy (race, ethnicity, sex) figure the truth of the body and its reproduction as simultaneously escaping and leading social and individual sovereignty.[78] In some cases, racial classification was determined by a "one drop" rule.[79] In other cases, such as recent U.S. census regulations, individuals are allowed to choose among various governmentally stipulated races, in effect opening race, if only slightly, to the agency of the autological subject. In still other cases, the racialization of populations may directly challenge the status of state sovereignty, as is the case with indigenous populations in settler nations, or challenge the moral legacy of that state, as in the case with slavery in the United States.

In sexual regulation, the disciplinary weight is split between the fantasy of the autological subject and the materiality and symbolics of genealogy, between discourses of the sexual self as the outcome of a set of sovereign acts and the sexual self as determined by some aspect of the body (desire, genes, the brain). This way of examining sexual regulation is somewhat different than Janet Halley's reading of the judicial logic of homosexual sodomy as presented in the majority opinion of *Bowers v. Hardwick*, in which, she argues, sexual regulation is maintained by an "equivocal reference to identities and/or acts."[80] Nevertheless, sexual regulation can appear to be operating on the analogy of the one-drop rule—the homosexual act substituting for the droplet of blood. Locating the truth of sexuality in the act, however, confronts another set of iterative problems. Who did it? What did they do? When? Perhaps ironically, the homosexuals easiest to regulate under the proposed Rhea County resolution may well have been those who organize their public and private lives on the basis of the normative fantasy of heterosexual monogamy—men and men, or women and women, who live in committed or proximate relationship to each other. Perhaps this was what worried some social conservatives: that these committed gay partners provided evidence that there was no moral or cultural difference between heterosexual and homosexual couples. Even so, as Halley notes, when pushed too hard, the homosexual and the heterosexual as a cluster of acts becomes merely a tendency, a probability manifesting over the long run. This fundamental psychic, physical, and practical indeterminacy constitutes sexual identity as a potentially paranoid structure. Are you or have you ever been a homosexual are questions that potentially diverge, converge, and tense up.

These practical problems open Habermas's proposal to far deeper conceptual problems. The Rhea County proposal was certainly shocking for some, and certainly aimed to mobilize the coercive and disciplinary policing function of the state *before* engaging the public in a critical rational debate. But the thematizations subtending this surprising governmental action are not extraordinary events. They are the very stuff of how we go about the day. If we treat sexuality and race as if they were the gourd and shells sitting on my desk, the prob- lem becomes quite clear. What is and is not "something" can be a matter of serious dispute, animating heated debates not only about the social status of a thing (a kind of person, object, mood), but also about what should be the evidential grounds for assessing competing claims about the status of a thing (an act, identity, heritage). But these decisions about who and what are an instance of one thing rather than another are also the covert presuppositions that allow us to go about our daily routines without much thought. In other words, thematiza- tions are not restricted to instances of extraordinary, strongly glossed, normative statements. The problem is not simply that ethically relevant questions of the good life, of collective identity, and of the interpretation of need *should* be open to public discourse, but that at every scale of interaction these questions are *actually* being asked and some response is de- manded just to know whom to ask for a cup of coffee, which pronoun to use, which adjectives might refer to a person in a crowd. In other words, the problems are not only at the level of such things as "spousal abuse" and "polygamy." Nor is the problem the manner with which a form lends itself to a translational compromise. Nor, finally, is the problem confined to determining when exactly a thematization becomes a regulation; or how large the interval between *yet* and *now* has to be before coercion can be said to enter the scene.

Not surprisingly, counter-publics, unregulated public spheres, and minority and subaltern individuals and groups have extensively reflected on how the inherently stipulative nature of intimate, state, and public thematization should be confronted. Their answers are multiple. Some people are ignorant of how images of them are being circulated regionally, nationally, and transnationally. This ignorance is not confined to remote, unplugged regions commonly imagined as existing in the undeveloped Third and Fourth worlds, but in media-savvy centers. Other people actively ignore how their lives and life-worlds are represented. They refuse to engage in such conversations, perhaps because they do not see their practices as open to discussion. They might have various reasons for this refusal, not least of which would be a profound skepticism about the relationship between the themes and aims of the conversation. They might think that, although thematized as a moral issue, debates about gay marriage in the United States have nothing to do with homosexuality but are poll-driving issues meant to get a person into office who will help radically transform the tax code and the Social Security system. For whatever reason, they absent themselves from any role in steering public discussions about their way of life. The discussion proceeds around them without any significant counter-discursive input by them. The obvious problem here is that whatever legislation emerges is based on a discursive horizon that did not include those being discussed. They will nevertheless be subjected to the police function of the state. Of course, many people may well wish to participate but cannot because the regulatory regime has closed the door on their perspectives.[81]

Some people actively engage public thematizations of their life worlds. They may think there is something demeaning about having to say why, though their practices appear repugnant to the legislative and moral majority—or at least, the legislative and moral group that holds the keys to the instruments of political legislation—they are nonetheless worthy of tolerance and recognition. But they engage in these conversations anyway in order to steer the public conversations and their refiguration of the background conditions of casual conversations and economic dispensations that result from one way of thematizing rather than another. Who counts as a homosexual, a faerie, a heterosexual, indigenous, woman, from the point of view of states' rights, interactional dynamics, and economic address? For whom do these various constructions of homosexuality, indigeneity, and femininity count? On what social grounds are these differences built? These politics of engagement often take quite seriously the manner in which unequal social and media power direct how social identities are commensurated, coordinated, and translated across the public sphere and into civil society.

Finally, many people within counter-publics, unregulated public spheres, and minority and subaltern groups neither engage nor ignore the call to thematize/translate their practices and beliefs for a normative public; they neither ignore the integrating function of stipulating thematizations nor do they engage them in the sense of translating their life-worlds for others. Instead of the dialectics of recognition and translation, we are witnessing the emergence of a practice of espionage and transfiguration and of an orientation to the re-elaboration of the self rather than self-identity. In these social fields, the point may well be to reshape habitudes ahead of recognition, to test something out rather than translate it, *not* to produce meanings that can be translated, or embodiments that can be recognized.

Bey is perhaps the best-known popular theorist of the politics of espionage within these counter-publics. Sounding much like the later Habermas, Bey, for instance celebrates what he sees as the radical nature of so-called pirate utopias of the eighteenth century — the islands and ports under control of seafaring bandits. For Bey, these utopias consisted of semi-permanent enclaves of freedom, what he calls "temporary autonomous zones." Bey claims that whereas pirate utopias existed in the seams between the emergent nation-state and the barbarian coastline, contemporary temporary autonomous zones (TAZ) now exist in the space (what he calls "the margin of error") between social "abstractions" and social "reality"; this is also what Habermas refers to as *social norms* and *social facts*. "Because the State is concerned primarily with Simulation rather than substance, the TAZ can 'occupy' these areas clandestinely and carry on its festal purposes for quite a while in relative peace. Perhaps certain small

TAZs have lasted whole lifetimes because they went unnoticed, like hillbilly enclaves—because they never intersected with the Spectral, never appeared outside that real life which is invisible to the agents of Simulation."[82]

Because TAZs are not sites of revolution but sites of insurrection and uprising, they are not oriented toward establishing new forms of permanence. They seek merely to foster social habitudes "which do not match the expected curve, the consensus approved trajectory."[83] TAZs are contingent and impermanent in their very nature: "Life festivals, uprisings cannot happen every day—otherwise they would not be 'non-ordinary.' "[84] For Bey, the question of whether to inhabit the space between fact and norm, and how one actually does this, demands being comfortable with a life of contingency and impermanence, fostering uprisings and insurrections rather than revolutions and new social permanences, and being at peace with the ebbs and tides that this mode of impermanent existence entails.

This condition of impermanence is, Bey claims, the source of the power of TAZs rather than their abrogation because the purpose of a TAZ is not to establish permanent modes of subjectivity and sociability but to foster a "quality of enhancement" that acts like a " 'peak experience' as opposed to the standard of 'ordinary' consciousness and experience . . . [these] moments of intensity give shape and meaning to the entirety of a life, the shaman returns—you cannot stay up on the roof forever—but things have changed, shifts, and integrations have occurred, a difference is made."[85]

Here again the indigenous—the shaman urging us on to

peak experiences and self-elaborations, standing in for and, perhaps, in the way of, the social and carnal complexities of actually inhabiting zones of simultaneous hyper-surveillance and utter neglect. Experiments in sociality such as those engaged in by radical faeries are not, however, always as picturesque as the image of a shaman channeling the spirit world might suggest. They are instead awkward, misfiring, malfunctioning social interactions, blurred moral lines between appropriate cultural borrowings and insensitive appropriations, all of which are sometimes, perhaps too often, deformed by accidental addictions and illnesses. They are the social strategies conceived to deal with the consequences of the party as well as the party. They are the struggles to build houses without money, to get care without health insurance, to speak a language of dependency when the broader political economy is increasingly oriented to the socially detached conjugal couple.

To excoriate Bey would be an odd way of ending this essay. We might instead pause and follow his transubstantiation more closely. Bey makes his "gourd" something by lodging it in two chambers of the shell. One chamber is carved out by the restricted set of liberal rights attached to genealogical societies. The other chamber is deeper inside, carved in turn by the first. It is more exit from, than chamber of, humanity. This exit-chamber is discipline and possibility—a site of humanism's disciplinarity and a possible exit from autological humanity.

3 The Intimate Event and Genealogical Society

One

Randall Kennedy, a legal scholar and race theorist who has written extensively on *Loving v. Virginia* and its relation to same-sex marriage, has suggested that in matters of love, the issue is the humanity of the person, not the accident of birth or forced enclosure within a social skin.[1] Thus, when asked in a *New York Times* interview what role racial, or other social statuses, should play in the organization of his own children's intimacy, Kennedy said, "I'll say, go into the world and try to find good people that feel genuine affection and love for you, and disregard everything else about their background. Love is just such a crucial, wonderful thing, and if you are lucky enough to find somebody who genuinely loves you, grab that person and hold on to that person and nothing else matters."[2] For Kennedy, love is an intimate event. It happens to you or it doesn't. If you are lucky, it happens between you and someone else simultaneously. But love is not merely an interpersonal event, nor is it merely the site at which politics has its effects. Love is a political event. It expands humanity, creating the human by exfoliating its social skin, and this expansion is critical to the liberal Enlightenment project, including the languages of many of its most progressive legacies. Echoing Kennedy, Al Sharpton insisted in the political public sphere of the 2004 Democratic presidential primaries on the connection between Richard and Mildred Loving's suit challenging the legality of Virginia's anti-miscegenation legislation and Mayor Gavin Newsom's issuing of marriage licenses to same-sex couples in San Francisco. For Sharpton, these two moments represent the same progressive edge of an ongoing struggle for human rights within the liberal diaspora, especially its rule by genetic, epidermal, and genital difference.[3] C. L. R. James noted, long before, in his study of the Haitian revolution, the profound effect that the articulation of "the aristocracy of birth and the aristocracy of religion" to "the aristocracy of the skin" had on French republicanism.[4]

But what is the difference between the "intimate event" of a love that refuses the dictates of the social skin and constitutes humanity retroactively and other kinds of intimacy? What is the proper relationship of these other forms of intimacy to state-backed forms of sexual intimacy? In *Loving*, the Supreme Court found for the plaintiffs under the Equal Protection and Due Process clauses of the Fourteenth Amendment, which they argued placed a "very heavy burden of justification" on any "state statutes drawn according to race." At the end of his majority opinion, Chief Justice Earl Warren argued that the right to marry could not be tied to the accident of ancestry without shattering the doctrine of equality, a doctrine foundational, and fundamental, to the American notion of freedom — except in the case of the immediate family, a social collectivity whose referent he saw no need to define. But what happens to the foundation of equality when it touches non-normative sex and sexuality? What were the U.S. sodomy cases, *Bowers v. Hardwick* and *Lawrence v. Texas*, really about: sexuality, sex, or intimacy? Did *Lawrence* domesticate the aberrant sexuality of *Bowers* by reading it through the penumbra of humanity-making love?[5] Did *Lawrence* allow the love that dare not speak its name to become audible and claim its accidental birth in the same way that race was able to do? Or were both cases fundamentally about sexual privacy, about the notion that with or without love, people can do what they want with their bodies as long as they are consenting adults?

Kennedy's reflections on love take us to the heart of the promise and problem that the "intimate event" holds for those who put some store in it as a liberal mode of self-abstraction and social unity. For these people, the intimate event is not merely a substantive good in and of itself; it *opposes* all other modes of organizing intimacy. In this Manichean universe, those multitudinous others who don't organize their intimacies on the basis of socially exfoliating love, but on the basis of lust, tribalism, race, kinship, or religion, do not have true love. Love can accidentally happen in these other kinds of socialities — it can happen *in spite of* their constraints on and distortions of the subject. But true love works against the social as such even as it figures the social as a set of constraining surfaces, encrusting and deforming the true destination of the self.

At least that's what we hear. We hear that love creates a

higher civilizational form even though it happens only between two people. We hear that love changes history even though its own history stretches no further than its own performative duration and even though it has no social anchor beyond its own self-positing. And yet the line between this form of intimacy and other kinds of affective attachments—desire, lust, and social duty—is remarkably thin. Sometimes the difference is said to be dependent on the duration of the affective attachment. Sometimes the difference is said to be inseparable from these other modes of attachment. Love is sometimes described as a loss of self in another, even though love is often opposed to lust because in lust the self dissolves into the body. And yet without a little lust, love may be nothing more than friendship. Freud noted early on love's promiscuity as a concept: "People give the name 'love' to the relation between a man and a woman whose genital needs have led them to found a family; but they also give the name 'love' to the positive feelings between parents and children, and between brothers and sisters of a family, although *we* are obliged to describe this as 'aim-inhibited love' or 'affection.' "[6] Why are we obliged to do this? What obliges us?

After all some people don't feel this sense of obligation. Nor do they share Kennedy's sense of the self-evident good of social exfoliation in the field of intimacy. Even if we separate the intimate event from sexual desire and lust, Kennedy's vision of love is still very different from that of many of my indigenous and radical faerie friends, or, for that matter, from that of some fundamentalist Christians.[7] At the same table with Kennedy and Sharpton might be Phyllis Burke. Burke, a lesbian mother, claims in her autobiography, *Family Values: Two Mothers and Their Son*, that what makes a family and a nation is the intimate recognition of human worth lying beyond the social skin. Love, not the epidermal or genital components of the lovers, makes a family; more — love makes these components irrelevant. But at another table might be others who would beg to differ, who would do everything within their power to make this bit of flesh matter, to attach it to a reproductive imperative or an imperative of sin. Debates within and across these tables arise not merely because participants cannot agree about what they are referring to when they refer to families, values, bodies, and sexualities. They also arise because people still dream of a form of equality that would hegemonize the entire social field, solving once and for all the difference of difference.[8]

For all of these people, intimacy is, among other things: an intensification of enduring social relations of kinship, geontology, and ritual, themselves anchoring and anchored by institutions of everyday life; a means of building collectively oriented and materially anchored socialities; and a manner of securing the self-evident social roles of men and women. And at least some of these people are neither seeking to exfoliate the social skin of public life nor wrap themselves away in the winding cloth of the conjugal bed. For some progressives, the point of loving is to thicken rather than thin out the social world. Richard and Mildred Loving were married in Washington, D.C., which did not have an anti-miscegenation statute on its books. But they lived and wished to continue living in their hometown of Central Point, Virginia. When they returned to Virginia, they were arrested, charged, and found guilty of breaking the anti-miscegenation statute, and they were sentenced to a year's imprisonment unless they agreed to leave the state and not return for twenty-five years (a number whose practical and symbolic logic bears its own separate reflection). Rather than primarily pursuing the isolating chamber of the socially deracinated bed or the nowhereness of stranger intimacy, perhaps the Lovings wished a return from exile, a reentry, for all its complexity, to the rich interracial kin and friendship public that made up the rural community of Central Point, Virginia.[9]

It is certainly the particular experience of social exile that results from gays and lesbians being abandoned by family and friends when they express what they believe to be a true version of themselves that motivates some to push for marriage rights. Didier Eribon suggested exactly this in his meditation on gayness, the family, and melancholia.[10] Not surprisingly, progressive critics of gay marriage, such as Lisa Duggan, have insisted that we remember not only that decisions about whom we marry are inextricably about a larger network of social kinship and friendship, but also that many people are seeking to organize and capture public resources and legal rights on the basis of a multiplicity of forms of social desire stretching beyond the conjugal couple.[11] These forms of social desire may be akin to what my two great-uncles from Carisol, Italy, Justy and Benny, shared. On immigrating to the United States in the 1920s, they lived together until Justy died in his 70s, whereupon Benny got married. My great-uncles were not particularly progressive, nor were they gay, to my knowledge.

But experiments in progressive loving seek to imagine the kinds of mutual benefit programs that would provide state-backed worlds for them. As Judith Butler notes, these experiments would not reject kinship per se but move it "beyond patrilineality, compulsory heterosexuality, and the symbolic overdetermination of biology," and, I might add, beyond the two-by-two of the Biblical flood, a sanctification of a conjugal couplet rather than, say, a group.[12]

It was exactly in this mixing and thickening of intimate and public space by networks of kinship, friendship, nationality, race, and sexuality that the Virginia trial judge who first heard 181 *Loving* in March 1966 saw the threat of interracial marriage: "Almighty God created the races white, black, yellow, malay and red, and he placed them on separate continents. And but for the interference with his arrangement there would be no cause for such marriages. The fact that he separated the races shows that he did not intend for the races to mix."[13]

For all this, the intimate event of modern love has an odd status in the liberal diaspora. It is more a phantom of liberalism — now you see it, now you don't — than an actual necessity of it. The spectral nature of the intimate event is exactly what interests me. The intimate event seems so self-evidently different from other kinds of social affect within liberal democratic orders and from other kinds of non-liberal socialities and their modes of governmentality. And yet, these differences often vanish when we focus on them too carefully — and with them go liberalism's exceptionalism. No less than liberalism, the intimate event and the genealogical society are not things, but rather moving targets developed in Empire and used to secure power in the contemporary world. The intimate event is thought to be a mode of the self-other relation that links together a number of key institutional orders of modern social life, themselves said to be a condition and reflection of this mode of affective and ethical self-positing. And yet what is also clear is that the intimate event is only incoherently linked to these institutional orders and is, at best, an indeterminate form of self-other relation.

One of the purposes of this essay, therefore, is to understand how the intimate event continues to hold such a grip on liberal social and psychic life, given all the contradictory discourses that cluster around it, threatening the magical qualities invested in it. If discourses of the intimate event — and the genealogical society — are citations and disciplines rather than social truths or actual facts, as the two previous essays have demonstrated, then how are they able to secure their truth and burnish their reputations in spite of this? What role have scholarly disciplines played in securing this fantasy? How would we need to reread classic debates about liberalism's emergence in light of these maneuvers of intimacy? It is my contention that the phantom nature of the intimate event is a critical mechanism by which the history of the liberal present is written, liberal life constituted and distributed, liberal forms of evil apportioned and punished, the good figured; and against which experiments in progressive mutual obligation beyond the conjugal couple and biological family are formulated. It is equally my contention that if the magical features of the intimate event are to be animated socially and

psychically, then others must be trapped in liberal intimacy's
nightmare—the genealogically determined collective. So let
me begin by elaborating on what I mean by the intimate event,
how it is related to the sovereign subject, and how it secures
its legitimacy vis-à-vis the negative image of the genealogical
society.

Two

The play of distinctions that seem visible in liberal discourses
of love, such as those articulated by Kennedy, are projected
out of a set of relatively stable discourses and practices that
measure the worth of a life, and a society, relative to its capacity to constitute and vest sovereignty in the individual. "I"
must be the citation and the site of enunciation and address.
What do I want, desire, and aspire to? With whom do I wish to
share, not merely the materials and rights that I have accumu-
lated as I have passed through the world, but the narratives of
who I think I am, what I discover that I am, that I am desiring
to be? In its ideal form this mode of sovereignty functions as
a *foundational event*—also known as an *explicit performative*
and a *bootstrap performative*—in which the act of referring to
the event or thing creates the event or thing. Many names have
been given to this form of subjectivity across many languages:
the autological subject, the *parvenu*, the self-made man, *die
Autonomie*. Each of these terms signals at once the dissemi-
nation of this form across the liberal diaspora—across, for instance, French republicanism, American pluralism, Austra-

lian multiculturalism, and Turkish secularism—and at the same time the reunification of this dissembled form into a coherent singularity called Enlightenment freedom.

For a foundational event to bear the full weight of Enlightenment exceptionalism a set of conditions must be in play: the constitution of the subject via the *fantasy* of self-referential enclosure; the characterization of this *fantastic* self as the origin and basis of true freedom; and the reduction of Right and Truth to this form of freedom. Etienne Balibar has made a similar argument, noting that in Augustine's discussion of how a man "subjects himself to himself," Europeans glimpsed for the first time a form of obedience—self-obedience—that was not "an inferior degree of humanity, but on the contrary a superior destination, whether terrestrial or celestial, real or fictitious."[14] Foucault likewise noted that the price Europeans paid to free themselves from the external social constraints of familial, aristocratic, and religious power was to assume their own self-management and to constitute the government as its disciplinary apparatus. At this moment, self-discipline emerged not only as a viable but also as a necessary practice of human freedom—the telic and ontic truth of this man is not in his *essence* but in his obedience to a specific semiotic practice of self-performativity.

How self-obedience came to be understood as self-autonomy and freedom is, of course, the subject of no little controversy both within and across disciplinary fields. One of the projects of the academic left has been to detail the transformation of radical social projects into liberal individual contracts. Scholars have sought to understand how struggles for *freedom from* specific forms of social oppression were transformed into institutions of *individual* liberty. But whom one cites and how they read history becomes an immediate source of acrimony. Marxist historians like E. P. Thompson and Eric Hobsbawm have located the origins of self-subjectification as a liberatory project not in the canonical texts of traditional philosophy, such as Augustine, but in the historical, revolutionary struggles of specific persons and groups. Though disagreeing over the causes and locations of these struggles, scholars of the Enlightenment, in all of its divergent forms, often argue that contests over the meaning and direction of social revolutions in the seventeenth and eighteenth centuries spawned a new form of human being from the ashes of aristocratic society: the *parvenu*, i.e., the self-made man. Aristocratic trappings might have remained in the self-stylizations of titles and manners that the emergent bourgeois society adopted. The actual personages of king and court resurfaced during the Restoration (1660–1689) and various stages of European revolution and counter-revolution (1789–1848), as did radically delicious crackpots such as Charles Fourier and the Icarians, and less dreamy social reform movements like the Anti-Corn League. And yet, underneath these restoration costumes and utopian visions emerged a decisive new presupposition, an expectation that the course of a man's life should be determined by *his* life, the life *he* made, rather than from his placement before his birth in a genealogical, or any other socially defined, grid.

A number of scholars have challenged this Enlightenment narrative of freedom and individualism. Alan Macfarlane is perhaps best known for arguing, in *The Origins of English Individualism*, that, with regard to marriage and property, an English person's freedom from the family existed long before the age of revolution.[15] In this sense, England was "diametrically opposed" to the rest of the continent. In England, the great constitutional compromise of the Glorious Revolution of 1689 certainly foregrounded the liberty and freedom of the subject from the tyranny of the crown in ways quite distinct from Europe. But, the individual was "not merely an eighteenth-century difference." It can be seen as

far back as the fifteenth century, before the supposed dramatic changes caused by Protestantism and the rise of a new capitalist economy.[16] Macfarlane is not alone in considering England the oddball of Europe, and arguing that the spirit of "liberty" predated the Protestant Reformation. De Tocqueville also noted the intractability of English individualism. And Montesquieu famously quipped that the English were too busy amassing wealth to develop a taste for social refinements. According to Macfarlane, the reasons for this oddity are clear: from the perspective of law and custom, the household seemed relatively unimportant to matters of property, residence, or marriage; by and large children made their own choices about marriage, employment, and household location; and the relations between the sexes and the classes were fairly relaxed. Little wonder that capitalism took root so quickly and extensively there. And little wonder that when it did, many English workers experienced its demands as a violation of their status as self-motivated men.[17]

The discovery that English men and women had great

flexibility in their choice of marriage, work, and residence is a fascinating historical correction. But it does not discount the revolutionary form of social detachment that emerged alongside the notion of self-authorization in the seventeenth and eighteenth centuries. Reviewing in detail the record on English exceptionalism, the early American historian Gordon S. Wood concluded that no matter the great, national chauvinism regarding liberty, inequality was presupposed and was based on a monarchical necessity. "In the eighteenth century, as in the time of John Winthrop, it was nearly impossible to imagine a civilized society being anything but a hierarchy of some kind" based on "a long train of dependence . . . that linked everyone from the king at the top down to the bonded laborers and black slaves at the bottom."[18] In other words, what social theorists such as Balibar, Thompson, and Hobsbawm are tracking is not individual choice per se, but the seemingly subtle though socially significant normative shift that begins with struggles aimed at freeing persons from some *specifiable form of social organization or social injustice* within a field of tactical power but ends with a devotion to freedom as a radical and ultimate break *from all social conditions/horizons*.[19] History was inverted—man would be measured by his end rather than by his beginning. And, as Charles Taylor has observed, this shift to contractual freedom would come to characterize all of the major institutions of the modern social imaginary—the market contract, popular sovereignty, and the public sphere.[20]

The subject-in-love is like the self-governing subject insofar as both are ideologically oriented to the fantasy of the foundational event. Both self-sovereignty and intimate recognition establish a new subject out of the husk of the old and reset the clock of the subject at zero. But the foundational event of the subject-in-love is thought to happen through a relay with another subject, who is likewise oriented to sovereignty as a contractually driven foundational event. In your gaze I become a new person, as do you in mine. This becoming anew is not by way of conversion, not by exposure to law or reason, not by persuasion or formal contract. Who can persuade us into love? Because the intimate event is hinged to nothing but itself, merely by happening to us, by striking us, it happens. The truth of intimacy is that *we* know it happened because it happened to both of us, and the sign that it happened is that *we* have been transformed. Its happening made *us*; it made one out of two (note that it does not make one out of three or four or out of an unknown number). A good sign that the intimate event has occurred is the collapse of the sex object and intimate subject. Where this collapse has not occurred, love is qualified. Where social experiments are oriented to unhinging and multiplying this collapse, love is foreclosed.

Social theorists have repeatedly trumpeted the social dynamic that the subject-in-love inaugurated as the singular achievement of the Western Enlightenment. Without the intimate couple, the national mass subject (We the People) and its forms of critical reason and public debate would not have been possible. No less dominant a social theorist than Habermas has argued that this new form of intimate sovereignty provided the conceptual foundations for the democratic revolution and its models of freedom, public reason, and equality-based schemes of justice; and for direct and representational democracy. For Habermas, the humanist break was not achieved by new forms of sexuality or by self-isolation —as Descartes would have it, a man locking himself in a candle-lit room before a book-strewn desk, "raz[ing] everything to the ground and begin[ning] again from the original foundations," his own act of thinking.[21] Instead, the humanist subject was forged out of the intimate recognition that passed between two people in the conjugal household—a form of recognition that itself depended on the emergence of new organizations of markets and their textual mediations.[22] Authentic self-naming, through another person's point of view, came to be opposed to all forms of critical social attachment. "Experiments with the subjectivity discovered in the close relations of the conjugal family" rife in the eighteenth century were revolutionary exactly insofar as they considered other sources of self-opinion and thought illegitimate.[23] Do we orient our opinions and actions based on our relationship to our spouse, our kin, or our social group? Is this form of kin-based self-heteronomy opposed to self-autonomy? What about other social forms, such as the demands of religion or custom? Are these religious or custom-based forms of self-heteronomy opposed to self-autonomy?

Intimate recognition, according to Habermas, uniquely transformed socially thick people into purely human subjects. Socially deracinated, inter-subjective dependence would slowly become opposed to and conceived as absolutely other than displacements of the self through social being. For

Habermas, the relay of intimate recognition stripped the social attributes from a person even as it locked this socially deracinated self into a higher-order couplet and, vis-à-vis such couplets, into still higher orders of abstract collectivity such as the democratic state. This social strip-down and interpersonal lock-up would provide the basis of the "saturated and free interiority" of the modern subject and its rhythms.[24] And, as Yunxiang Yan has suggested, it would come to be seen in places like rural China in the 1980s and 1990s as a specifically modern, Western, and desirable form of "love" *opposed to* traditional, pre-modern forms of marriage.[25] Indeed, one of the key dimensions of the fantasy of intimate love is its stated opposition to all other forms of social determination even as it claims to produce a new form of social glue.[26] The intimate event holds together what economic and political self-sovereignty threaten to pull apart, and it does so while providing an ethical foundation to a specific form of sex; stitching the rhythms of politics and the market to the rhythms of the intimate subject; and conserving the civilizational distinction between metropole and colony.

Because this kind of self-transformation leans on the openness of other people to the same type of self-transformation, autological intimacy functions as a proselytizing religion. Like capital, intimacy demands an ever-expanding market; and, like capital, intimacy expands through macro-institutions and micro-practices. Subjects in the liberal diaspora constantly urge one another to be open to the possibility that in recognizing each other in intimate love they will experience each other as different than they were before—they will experience a break, a rupture from their prior selves and experience a purer, truer form of self, a form that they have always truly been.[27] We literally reform the social by believing in and demanding this form of love. Every time we are in this form of love, or wish to be, or are frustrated because we are not, we make social status appear as a form of bondage, mere surface or impasse, perhaps the vital frisson that lets us feel it as a resistance. In this sense, love has become the sign of a new liberal mystery, a secular religion. Love leaves people as they were in the Garden of Eden, merely men and women, not dukes or duchesses, not heirs to a title or office, not wealthy or poor. I may be a bourgeois at work, but at home I am simply, and fundamentally, the man she loves. I may be merely I, but this is all I need to be to have human worth, and this is, in the beginning and the end, no more than any of us are at core. Unless you happen to be, or are considered to be, a woman, a homosexual, not white. I will come back to this point in a moment.

In sum, whether terrestrial or celestial, for social theorists of the Western Enlightenment the power of the intimate event of self-sovereignty lay in its ability to connect the micro-practices of certain forms of love to the macro-practices of certain forms of state governance and certain forms of capital production, circulation, and consumption — to make a personal event a normative mission and a civilizational break. The semiotic operation of the intimate event so saturates the horizon of everyday life that it no longer seems a "semiotic operation" but just the way people do things — how they decide which newspaper to buy or television show to watch, candidate to vote for, product to consume, job to labor at, and person to love. All of these choices set up complex relays between self-determination and social identifications and desire: who I am, or want to be, vis-à-vis my purchase, vis-à-vis what I can do with my life, and vis-à-vis whom I end up loving. In other words, the intimate event is a semiotic operation that creates a subject, produces multiple linkages between that subject, its economy, and government, and governs the operation of these linkages. This discursive operation forms a pyramid, at the top of which is a self-governed "I," followed by the self-governing couplet of "I-thou" and the unity of "we" that unfolds out of this couplet, followed in turn by various levels of social organization — say, our "family," "nation," "race," "culture," "religion." The truth and right of self-reflexive sovereignty means that social value runs in a specific direction along this pyramid of self determination: I should determine I, We determine Ourselves, Races themselves, Cultures themselves, Religions themselves, but Religions should not determine cultures, cultures should not determine us, and we should not determine I. Herein lies the semiotics of liberal freedom that allows liberal subjects to hinge the most personal of feelings to the broadest currents of world history. To assert a bond of love was to be world-historical.

Except, of course, where it did not — the world before *Loving v. Virginia*, and the world as it is under *Reynolds v. United States*, and *Bowers v. Hardwick* and its incommensurate counter-currents in *Lawrence v. Texas*, and the Defense of Marriage Act. The imaginary of the intimate event is always disrupted and secured by the logic of the exception — "except, of course, in the case of . . ." The "nothing more than" of deracinating intimacy always projects the question of "what about this, then" — the color of skin or the fold of flesh. If we are to understand the hold that fantasies of the intimate event have on social life in the liberal diaspora, then we must first examine all the ways in which they are secured at the very moment these fantasies seem thoroughly disseminated and referentially untrue.

One way in which these fantasies are both referentially un- 193 true and ideologically robust is that the very semiotic com-position of the foundational event is internally disruptive to the foundational subject of love. Positing oneself as addresser and addressee creates a new "I," a type of first person "you." This internal "you" is not the subject who asks the question "What do I think?" but the "I" who is entailed as the object of the question, and placed in the role of the potential subject of response. "Hey you! What do you think?" Object and sub-ject of enunciation appear to collapse into one another, form-ing a new plural subject of thought. "Hey you, yes, you-who-are-I/me, what do we think?" This discursive form creates neither the Freudian split subject nor the Deleuzian subject of surplus. It creates them both. The more I ask myself to speak my own truth, the richer and more multi-dimensional the interior terrain of "I" becomes, literally the more of my-self there is. But, at the same time, the more I query (produce) myself — thematizing the different aspects of myself that I am interested in (thinking me, inner me, wounded me, spiritual me, sexual me) — the more I build my own removal from myself. In short, self-elaboration and self-alienation are born at the exact same moment because they are the dynamic consequences of this type of self-referentiality. As a result, if the *parvenu* emerged in the seventeenth century, it emerged as a split and a surplus. We might say it was born with an *agitated detachment* from any and all forms of social attachment, including the subject's attachment to its own foundation. It is no surprise, then, that the intimate event is where I find myself and where I lose myself, where reason is subverted by desire rather than installed, where I am compelled more than compelling, where there is always more of me than I know what to do with. The very form itself absorbs me, swallows me up, and overwhelms me even as it agitates and detaches me. And the compelling fiction of the foundational event creates an anxiety as plural as it is incommensurate: Will I be isolated if this event does not strike me? Is my social world formed in such a way as to preclude it striking me? If it does not strike me will I be left alone without social support or renewal? Will I be cast out?

A related problem with viewing the intimate event as an actual event is that sovereignty is just another form of obedience. I mentioned this above, but it bears repeating. The liberal subject is said to become sovereign at the moment she projects herself as her own authentic ground. This foundational self is necessarily phantasmagorical for the simple reason that no one can pick herself up by her own bootstraps. The felicity of this foundational event depends on an entire host of conditioning social institutions and relations. Jacques Donzelot showed in his study of the emergence of the bourgeois family and social welfare in France how the contract between power and self-authorization insinuated itself into the very tissues and membranes of practices of state disciplinary care. And, as Ann Stoler has written, this insinuation may well have had its origins in colonial practices of child care.[28] In short, the sovereign and intimate subject of recognition was anything but free, in the sense of undetermined and stabilized—it was very much a social determination.[29] Even Kant recognized this. Marx certainly did. Hannah Arendt made this point precisely in *The Human Condition* where she argued that the classical distinctions between the private as a realm of necessity and the public as the realm of agonistic play would be entirely blurred when "the body of peoples and political communities" came to be seen in the "image of the family whose everyday affairs have to be taken care of by a gigantic nationwide administration of housekeeping."[30] For Arendt, the decisive turn is not from an older form of sovereignty into biopolitics but from an older form of biopolitics into a new form of oikopolitics. Whatever we call it, this self-management would later, especially under the pressure of the psychoanalytic mandate, become re-thematized as anxiety, the price of becoming a subject as such rather than the effect of a specific type of subjectivity and its institutional supports.

A third problem with viewing the intimate event as an actual event is that all intimacies stretch between the actual and the possible, the long duration and the punctual, the singular and the general. What are the criteria by which we assess whether the event has happened to us or to others? How do we decide what is what—what is love; what is lust; what is a passing fancy? On the other hand, what kind of bargain do we get ourselves into when we fall in love, when the event of intimacy strikes us? This question has been of particular concern for contract law. No matter how closely the intimate event is aligned to other kinds of economic and political contracts, it is also continually distinguished from them. Indeed, the intimate contract is often represented as if it were in imminent harm of collapsing into the political and economic contract. After all, if all these contracts are based on the same kind of subject, then what is the difference between buying and selling a car, marrying and divorcing a spouse, choosing and rejecting a state representative? As early as Locke and as recently as the California Supreme Court's 1948 decision in *Perez v. Sharp*, some difference between these kinds of contracts has, nevertheless, been asserted. In *Perez*, the court struck down California's miscegenation legislation nineteen years before *Loving v. Virginia*, arguing that "the fungibility that was arguably present with respect to some goods and services was absent with respect to marriage" because "human beings would be diminished 'by a doctrine that would make them as interchangeable as trains.' "[31] But, the potential that all aspects of intimate human life may become fungible has intensified in court cases concerning new reproductive technologies.[32] The importance of the dense hermeneutic and institutional mirroring between economic, political, and intimate contracts is not that it shows how these contractual forms have collapsed into each other in some absolute way, but how their possible implosion created widespread anxiety.

Finally, liberal forms of constitutionally backed democratic state governance did not move from social status to the intimate contract—the genealogical to the autological—as the foundation of liberal government, but merely reorganized how social status was deployed in governmental logics. Self-sovereignty is itself undermined in the liberal democratic states that claim to have produced, and to be the product of, this form of subjectivity. Certainly, it is easy enough to show that they have not freed themselves from the "external" constraints of family, class, and religious power. Count-less feminist scholars of Western Europe, the United States, and Australia including Amy Dru Stanley, Amy Kaplan, Lora Romero, Carol Pateman, Nancy Cott, Hester Eisenstein, Diane Bell, and Helen Garner have demonstrated that the foundational event is phantasmagorical in the simple sense that liberal societies are not, in fact, structured in a manner consistent with the ideological fantasy of the intimate event. The very conceptual form of state citizenship, insinuated into the deep tissues of economic, state, and national life, is based on birth from a human body or a territorial body and thus is inflected by the governing metaphors of flesh—race, gen-der, and sexuality. Moreover, while the formal practices of the family may have narrowed over the past thousand years, the heterosexual family has become more explicitly theorized and politicized as the core institution of the nation-state. In the United States, immigration policy is skewed to a narrow reading of the heterosexual family, as is most inheritance legislation, tax codes, health benefits, and family and repro-ductive law. Debates in France and the United States over gay adoption and recent restrictions on new reproductive technologies in Italy and the United Kingdom suggest how, even across such different state and national contexts, heteronormativity and its genealogical underbelly continue to play a role in determining the intimate event.

How, then, do these discourses deepen their grip on social life though they are internally unstable and referentially untrue? The maintenance of intimate sovereignty as a truth of liberal empire depends on a method of constituting three kinds of truth about the subjects and objects of empire: the truth of intimacy's proper domain, the truth of its normative ideals, and the truth of contrasting evils that surround it.

The first method, the proper domain of the genealogical, works by casting some of the liberal dependencies on genealogical principles as "private" matters. Nancy Fraser noted a related point in her essay, "Rethinking the Public Sphere," where she pointed out that the rhetoric of privacy excludes certain interests and issues by casting them as "private, domestic or personal, familial matters in contradistinction to public, political matters."[33] Other dependencies on genealogical principles, such as the inheritance of citizenship, of state-backed property, of legal-backed forms of care, are cast as public goods and bureaucratic matters.

Second, the language of normative ideals provides a way for freedom-loving, self-governing people to distance themselves from their own practices by describing internal incoherencies as mistakes and aberrations of a well-intentioned system; a sidetrack on the general march to freedom; or necessary compromises in an imperfect world. These mistakes, alleyways, and compromises do not, so the story goes, negate the fact that freedom from social bondage is an ideal of the North/West.

Third, the language of contrasting evils mitigates the volume of autological intimacy's own internal incoherence by situating the intimate event beside a contrasting evil. The incoherence of discourses of the intimate event is continually cast against some other societal form that supposedly staunchly opposes the intimate event as the true and right basis of personal and state government. To get traction on these questions we need to understand that the productivity of the intimate event derives much of its ideological force from something that co-emerged with it—discourses about the genealogical society. So we must start our inquiry anew and note that the distinctions that appear visible in scenes of liberal adult love—including their incoherencies and undecidability—do not merely arise from an internal tension within discourses about the intimate event, but rather from how these discourses interact with another phantom of liberal passion and reason: the genealogical subject and the genealogical society. The intimate event is itself captured and conjured by way of a set of relatively stable contrastive discourses about the determination of individual choice, mystery, and discovery by some type of social custom or convention. The terrain of genealogical discourses is as complex as those of the intimate event and autological subject. Kinship and the family, tribalism, and patriarchy are obvious examples of discourses of genealogical inheritances. But the law of genealogical inheritances also encompasses the complex exchanges of race and ethnicity; the nation and its historical legacies; and the capture of the subject by hegemony and by the processes of the unconscious. In all these instances, genealogy is a specific reckoning of time and the human(ist) subject of reason; genealogical inheritances threaten to determine the present by the past, and reason and the conscious by unreason and the unconscious.

In sum, the power of the modern intimate event lies not merely in its ability to employ the social order, nor merely in its ability to anchor itself to other like-structured institutions, nor merely in its ability to invest itself with magical qualities and ethical purpose. Its power derives equally from a mirror image that supposedly marks its geographical and civilizational difference. In other words, the intimate event does not merely characterize some truth about liberal desire—it asserts its difference by reference to the differential truths of social geographies and its own social hsitory.

The cunning of those promoting Enlightenment exceptionalism is that they claim the Enlightenment as a European heritage and as an event that shattered this heritage, and that they claim this shattering absolutely differentiated the Enlightenment subject from all others. The Enlightenment and intimacy are bootstrap performatives, ruptural foundations, events that happened in a place but, because they broke with that place, therefore can be universalized.[34] This is why arguments by Islamic scholars, African philosophers and state theorists, and indigenous leaders that their customs, traditions, and histories already include elaborate discourses and practices of freedom, agency, and individualism do not dislodge this Enlightenment exceptionalism. It is not freedom as such, but the performative break with its own tradition that signals to the adherents of the Western Enlightenment its own singularity, its world significance, its revolutionary advance out of custom. But this insistence that the Enlightenment had broken with its past and shattered its relation to all others, even if it had not, let to an intense anxiety over how to consider the collectivity and collective goods in relation to it. From Hobbes to de Beauvoir, from Rousseau to Fanon, social theory pivoted around a set of central questions. If man is securely enclosed within himself, how can he get out? If man is the foundation of his own desire, what of the collective good that may well counter his desire? What was the source of the collective good if not some sort of amalgamated set of individuals or collective mind, the General Will, the People?

Before looking at how the scholarly disciplines have answered these questions and, in the effort to ground these answers in historical and anthropological facts, secured an Enlightenment fantasy, let me outline three major topographical spaces within liberal discourses of the genealogical society: the materiality of genealogy, the symbolics of genealogy, and the economy of genealogy. By tracking these discourses, we can begin to see how the intimate event and the genealogical society function not as isolated discourses and practices, but as co-constitutive fields, riveted together in such a way that they secure and distribute power and wealth in the liberal diaspora.

First, discourses about the materiality of genealogy figure the truth of the body and its reproduction as simultaneously escaping and leading social and individual sovereignty. The materiality of genealogy is what is behind, or before, the individual and the social—what material they inherit to work with and what can be given life or death by the sovereign. This is what I refer to as *corporeality*. Corporeality is not so different from what Giorgio Agamben has called "naked life," the separation "of some simple fact of living common to all living beings" from "the form or manner of living particular to a single individual or group" and especially to a human community that constitutes the modern political subject.[35]

Agamben notes, and I would agree, that the division between naked life (what I am calling corporeality) and political life is the result of a social division. It is a "biopolitical fracture" that has a specific history and path of circulation in capitalism and empire. Carl Schmitt's definition of sovereignty is fundamental to Agamben's notion of bare life—the sovereign is she who can establish the state of exception. The rule of law suspends itself; it is not suspended. And this suspension creates the difference between sovereign life and bare life, transforming the human into meat, reducing the person to her body. The biopolitical capture of sores, discussed in the first essay of this book, suggests exactly how the state of exception in which my indigenous friends in Australia are placed creates a population that can continually suffer death without evoking mourning.

The discursive play of the materiality of genealogy is captured in such ordinary phrases as, "I cannot choose who my biological parents were." Here grammar mimics ideology: the present tense of the subject's negated choice ("I cannot choose") is barricaded by the past tense of its conditioning ("who my biological parents were"). The materiality of inheritance is, in short, a metaphysics of substance that posits a material legacy beyond the control of a person or society. This metaphysical stance on corporeality does not necessitate any agreement about where this truly deracinated materiality lies: within the thin skin of the individual body, in the hormonal systems coursing through it, in the DNA that provides a code for it, or in the particular manner in which that DNA is wound and unwound.[36] Rather, this metaphysics merely projects a space beyond the dialectic of social determination and individual freedom, and in projecting this space, it incites a certain hope that we might transcend the division between flesh and discourse, along with a certain despair that flesh can ever be extracted from its discursive conditions. This metaphysical stance does not preclude the present deployment of corporeality for disciplinary ends. Indeed, rather than precluding these ends, the metaphysics of substances helps to legitimate certain disciplinary regimes. Biometrics, for instance, has emerged as a means of surveillance since September 11, 2001: the United States has begun requiring biometric identifiers on the passports of people coming from nations without visa requirements.[37] New reproductive technologies are also riddled with social regulation, as are First World multinational thefts of the genetic material of the second, third, and fourth worlds.

If, however, we are interested in the maintenance of the truth of intimate sovereignty as a means of liberal empire, then we need to confront the question of whether the flesh should be seen merely as a juridical and political maneuver, merely as a social tactic, or also as a physical mattering. What I am claiming, and have tried to show throughout this book, is that the uneven constitution of the flesh is a key way in which the dynamic between autology and genealogy is secured, maintained, and reproduced. What interests me, and what I am trying to get at through the notion of *carnality*, as distinct from *corporeality*, is what is enabled—what becomes possible physically—at the moment when people are so reduced and how these actual and possible carnal worlds help secure the fiction of the intimate event and its genealogical other. A biopolitical fracture may indeed have separated bare life from sovereign life, casting the exception into a social and psychic camp. But once separated in this way, a certain meatiness, a certain benign brutality, becomes available for politics, certain relations of capital become possible, acceptable, and even inevitable. The trouble with Agamben's model is that the clean division it projects, or that sovereign power projects, between life and death is a wish-fantasy. As I tried to show in the very first essay of this book, the temporality of life for many at the edge of liberal capital's promise is the temporality of diarrhea—slow, debilitating, and blurred. The uneven speed with which people die, the distribution of violence attached to these deaths, or the slowness of their decay, all present different temporalities for how power is invested through local biospaces. If we are interested in the relationship between intimacy and the liberal diaspora, then we need to understand carnality as not merely a juridical and political maneuver, nor merely as a social tactic, but as a physical mattering, just as the intimate event and the genealogical society are also *physical* matters, facts of carnality as well as of discourse.

Second, the symbolics of genealogy include discursive practices that organize corporeality and meta-discursive practices about the relative value of these different discursive practices. Symbolics of genealogy include actual practices of kinship, race, and nationalism along with theoretical and political discourses about the meaning, shape, and value of these kinship, race, and national practices to the health of the nation, the people, and an ethical way of life. Symbolics of genealogy are dispersed across bureaucratic space in such a way that different social classes within the same social group have, or are denied, access to different languages and styles of genealogy. This bureaucratic dispersion continually fractures and fragments already fractured social groups. Sarah Barringer Gordon has shown, for instance, the ways in which nineteenth-century sentimental novels about Mormon polygamy made people in the Northeast feel that their moral values were threatened — that if polygamy were allowed in the territories, then all women would potentially be not a man's wife but merely his first wife.[38] According to Gordon, the U.S. Supreme Court may have decided in 1878, in *Reynolds v. United States*, that monogamy was foundational to civilized democratic states, but it was the production and circulation of texts like these sentimental novels that moved people to make laws and inscribe themselves in these laws. Similarly, Françoise Verges has built on Lynn Hunt's groundbreaking study of the function of the family romance in the making of the French Revolution by arguing that the relationship between the French Antilles and Continental France was enunciated and imagined in terms of gender and kinship that figured France as the elder, paternalistic brother addressing his brown and black island brothers, excluding in the process the black sister, mother, and lover from the halls of government.[39]

In sum, symbolics of genealogy encompass all the conventions and languages of the body, its reproduction, and the means by which goods and materials, rights and obligations, move through these corporealities as markers of inheritance. As a result, symbolics of genealogy run the ideological gamut from biological essentialism to cultural relativism to radical (de)construction. In the latter case, the semi-autonomous materiality of the body itself disappears under the deferred scribbling of discourse.[40] Although they might differ as to which conventions are seen as opportunities and which as threats, all these ways of figuring the meaning, shape, and value of inheritances figure them as specters, the ghostly remains of the past still imprinting the present.

Third, the economy of genealogy includes all the ways that these genealogical inheritances are called on to circulate wealth and power. Again, this is an extraordinarily complex field that includes discourses about how societies organize personal and communal wealth on the basis of descent along with discourses about the obligations that the past places on the present, such as reparations for slavery, colonialism, and war. In other words, the economy of genealogy encompasses not only the family inheritances of individuals, but also the historical inheritances of empire, such as debates about taxing the financial markets in order to redistribute wealth from the North to the South.

The complexity of state policy regarding the economy of genealogy in democratic states is apparent in U.S. debates about affirmative action in public universities' admissions practices. These debates are not merely about whether the history of slavery should determine, or does determine, contemporary life, but whether race as a social status and social history should have a privileged relationship to other types of social statuses and histories. In the wake of *Grutter v. Bollinger et al.* (2003), public debate focused for a while on the difference between race-based admissions and legacy-based admissions. Legacy admissions are those that favor the sons and daughters of alumni. What was the difference and dynamic between taking a person's race into consideration in the admissions process and taking a person's immediate family history into consideration? During these debates, social conservatives tried to disarticulate these preferences by claiming that legacy admissions were color-blind and thus not about what happened in the past, but about what a person made of him- or herself. To some people it seemed to make little difference that the person who made something of him- or herself was not the student receiving the preference, but his or her parent or grandparent.

> To the Editor: Your April 22 front-page article regarding the rising numbers of students from higher-income families at American colleges and universities misses a very basic point. Sure, the children of the wealthy have advantages. But the children of successful parents are more likely to be successful not simply because their parents were wealthy but because their parents

had the skills necessary to create that wealth. The parents did not inherit doctors' degrees; they earned them because they possessed intelligence and drive. Thus the odds that the children possess the same qualities and therefore are admitted to institutions of higher learning should be neither a surprise nor a negative.[41]

In sum, apologists of intimacy argue that the point is not whether intimate sovereignty is a true or false description of actual liberal life. Those who claim intimate freedom as the singular achievement of the West insist that the shift from social status to intimate contract, from social determination to individual freedom, is a true description of an emergent norm. It is a method of constituting two kinds of truth about the subject and her social world, one reduced to mere fact and the other raised to a normative end, and it creates two kinds of worlds, starkly separated and morally opposed. One is autological; the other is genealogical. Each is said to have its contrasting modes of intimacy. Those enthralled by the intimate event say that in matters of the heart and the labors of a life, attitudinal and discursive practices *should* be based on foundational events, at least most of the time, at least in the context in which this social form is being advanced as the end of history. They do not say that they always are. In other words, the intimacy grid is normative politics, not actual politics. This incredibly thin but incredibly resilient regulatory ideal renders actual life irrelevant. Actual life is like the object of Lacanian desire, that away from which we should move, that with which we should be disappointed. Sure, we fail. History is littered with examples of these failures, not the least of which was the longstanding fact that only men of certain races, privileges, and property had the right of contract and that these same men held the property of their wives and their enslaved or colonized subjects under the legal principle of coverture.

Let me return to two questions I asked at the beginning of this essay: How do we reread classic debates about liberal exceptionalism in light of these apologies of intimacy? And how is the liberal present written by reference to its own and others' phantom genealogical past?

Three

We can begin by asking which of the many debates are relevant. These debates include how transformations of the intimate event and the genealogical society were affected by the long struggle for independence in the colonial world and how the languages and attitudes that emerged from these struggles were translated into the social movements of the 1960s — feminists, diasporic peoples, indigenous people, homosexuals, the non-aligned, and many others.[42] The cultural meanings of these struggles could themselves be situated in an even older history in which the primary civilizational difference was not metropole and colony but medieval Europe and various competing Islamic empires. Finally, a treatment of these topographies would need to bring together historical studies of inheritance and gender, exemplified in the work of Martha Howell, Amy Dru Stanley, and Ann Kaplan, with theories of the subject as the effect of the inheritance of gendered and sexual positions, such as those of Jacqueline Rose, Joan Cop-jec, and Liz Grosz. After all, the problem of genealogy does not merely encompass issues of social property and gover-nance, but also includes the question of how the problems of the conscious and the unconscious, culture and hegemony, language and metalanguage became problems of subjective governance and inheritance.

When we bring together these strands of scholarship, new questions about the intimate event and genealogical society emerge, changing how we read the history of intimacy. How did the difference between the intimate event and the gene-alogical society emerge in such a way that they appeared to represent the difference between civilizations and epistemic cultures? How was this putative difference absorbed into the governance of peoples at home and abroad? The immediate trouble we face asking and answering questions like these is that most of the literature we read on intimacy and geneal-ogy has presupposed the difference between the autological subject and genealogical society and the kinds of intimacies they produce. This becomes quite clear when we examine two bodies of literature on intimacy and its autological and gene-alogical foundations: on the one hand, literature examining when, where, and why the modern intimate subject emerged and, on the other, literature examining how genealogical soci-eties govern themselves in the absence of a formal domain of politics.

The critical questions of when, where, and why modern forms of intimacy and marriage emerged in Europe and its settler colonies have primarily focused on individual consent in the domain of marriage. Take, for example, debates about the impact of twelfth-century Gregorian reforms in the Catholic Church around the family, property, and sexuality. The reforms are usually described as a reaction by conservative theologians to the excess of the Carolingian period, especially the increasing penetration of the church by the laity as the aristocracy, the church, and commoners maneuvered to gain, or keep, control of land and wealth.[43] A vital part of this struggle was the refashioning of two arenas of sexuality.[44] The Church instituted new restrictions on the clergy and new demands on the laity. Clerical celibacy became the sign and tactic of a separation between these two social domains even as marriage and reproduction became a sacred duty of the laity. Within this new field of sexuality, the Church attempted to out-maneuver the aristocracy by insisting that individuals rather than households be the locus of the felicity and fidelity of the marriage contract. Arranged marriages continued, but their validity increasingly depended on the consent of the two individuals concerned rather than on the marriage ceremony itself.[45] However, though it was easy to demand "consent" as the condition of marital legitimacy, what signaled consent was not always clear. What "consent" referred to was itself a site of conflict, although, over time, one discursive form became dominant over others.[46]

The question of what signaled consent in the context of intimacy was soon colliding with other contractual forms and problems. At one and the same time, these contractual forms seemed to have a deep affinity and continually disrupted one another. For instance, according to Charles Taylor, Grotius understood political authority to be legitimate only insofar as individuals consented to be so ruled. But they assumed this initial consent created a binding contractual obligation that could not be broken.[47] Locke, by contrast, insisted the government should be set to a more regular clock of consent between individuals and society; revolution was justified only when this clock was upset. Individual political consent became something that needed to be continually re-theatricalized in the form of the franchise. Alongside the emergence of this new form of political and economic consent came new understandings of intimate contracts and *mutatis mutandis* new differences within Christendom.[48] Expectations and fantasies about what marriage can and should do changed. Did the original consent create a binding obligation between two people, or were they continually required to re-affirm their commitment? What exactly needed to be said, in what tense and pronominal form? Did it need to be witnessed or authorized by some (disinterested) person outside the conjugal couple? Who should that be?

These new contractual possibilities opened lines of socially possible and subjectively sensible questions. An approach to marriage that necessitated continual consent as opposed to a first and final consent changed the orientation of the self to itself. Present-tense feelings become socially relevant in a new way. "What am I feeling now?" or "Do I still love her?" Who is the "I" asking and answering these questions? If a husband provided materially for his wife, did her happiness matter? Did his? It is not surprising, then, that many studies examining the emergence of the intimate event focus on the subject-in-love in relation to contractual events. They look at how the betrothal became a proto-contract, a public, first-person, present-tense announcement, and they note that this proto-contract predated the Hobbesian contract by four hundred years.[49]

At the same time that the Gregorian reforms focused on individual consent in the marriage ritual, they vastly expanded the sphere of kinship in which individuals maneuvered. The Church doubled, in an extremely short period, the number of kin prohibited from marriage by substituting Roman law for German law as the basis for reckoning kinship degrees and by instituting new sexually restricted kinship categories such as godparent, widow, and spiritual parent. British social anthropologist Jack Goody has argued that the reforms were not merely aimed at aristocratic control of social life but at the control of property by collateral kin at all levels of society.[50] Even if we remain agnostic about whether these reforms were primarily in the service of property accumulation or doctrinal purity, there seems little disagreement that the tension between the contractual conjugal couple and the expansion of the genealogical grid instigated a struggle across all orders of society over these new disciplines of sexuality and kinship. The genealogical grid became a pervasive constraint at the very moment that the individual seemed to be freed from its dictates. Everyone was suddenly in real or potential danger of a dangerous liaison. The Roman Catholic Church increasingly claimed the role of arbiter, verifying licit unions, dissolving or dispensing absolution for illicit marriages where it saw them as appropriate (or lucrative). It was not until the

Protestant Reformation that the genealogical grid slowly contracted around the conjugal couple and their immediate filial relations, although strong regional variations remained.

Though the political relevance of family trees was slowly narrowed and relocated after the Protestant Reformation, their social relevance was in fact democratized and dispersed into the life-worlds of ordinary people and into the seams of homogeneous national space-time. We could argue that, in being democratized, the genealogical grid has become more vital and real to the political order, whether it is attacked or defended. Certainly it ceased to function as a broadcast model in which concentric circles of genealogical ranks and associations radiated from the apical crown. The polity no longer unfolded out of the (fictive) ranked affiliations of the people from the point of view of the sovereign family. Now everyone could have a little heritage of his or her own—diagrammed as a personal tree—a stake in some plot that tracked generationally.

As a result, the genealogical grid that operates as the presupposition of national life in the present is not the same grid that operated before the seventeenth century. And yet, what operated prior to the seventeenth century did not lack the space of maneuver and tactic any more than autological intimacy operates outside the space of genealogy. Here Jacques Le Goff's discussion of the king's body and Habermas's discussion of intimacy—"saturated and free interiority"—are crucial.[51] The aristocratic genealogy was rich in distinctions of rank, role, and kinship that both ordered people and allowed them multiple avenues for contestation, elaboration, and negotiation. The genealogical grid inherited by market society was only unevenly deracinated from social status and rearticulated to *humanity*, a term intended to suggest equivalence. Questions about the internal dynamic of hierarchy within the new bourgeois family arose almost immediately, as did questions about the grounds for building these new families. What forms of subordination should extend out of the reduced differences among men and women, parents and children? What could — and should — be the presuppositional grounds for forming these petite genealogies if not the social or religious status of the contracting members? Who should be included and excluded from the ranks of blood and money, property and inheritance, love and affection, and sex? All these questions inserted genealogical relations into intimate relations even though many scholars continue to portray "pre-modern" society as subject to the constraints of a genealogical imaginary. In other words, they take the ideological side of the autological subject, representing modern intimacy as if it were actually other than genealogy, outside it, opposed to it.[52]

The rigid separation between pre-modern and modern Europe was projected onto the relation between Europe and its colonial subjects, the metropole and colony, the West and East, the North and South, the Christian and Islamic. Even as scholars of the liberal and radical Enlightenments debate the timing and location of the emergence of the intimate event and the ways it floated free from fixed matrixes of social status, they and other scholars project a rigid form of genealogical determination onto the social organization of pre-modern Europeans and colonized peoples. Sociological scholarship on Europe revolved around the problem of social degeneracy and women and men's liberation from home economies, while anthropological scholarship revolved around what Michel-Rolph Trouillot has described as the savage slot.[53] The British anthropologist Marilyn Strathern has argued that it was Lewis Henry Morgan who provided the conceptual foundation on which many of these debates about savagery and intimacy would take place. "Morgan conceived the contrast as between those closer to and more distant from nature . . . Indeed the draft opening chapter of *Systems of Consanguinity* referred to family relationships existing in nature independently of human creation."[54] Strathern is referring to a text that Morgan published in 1871 that presented an account of how colonial societies ordered and reproduced every aspect of their lives on the basis of modes of kinship. Morgan began with the foundational subject, the socially deracinated subject of the Enlightenment, and the ego as an event: "Around every person there is a circle of kindred of which such person is the centre, the Ego, from which the degree of the relationship is reckoned, and to whom the relationship itself returns."[55]

According to Morgan there were "but two radically distinct forms of consanguinity." On the one hand were descriptive systems, such as "the Aryan, Semitic, and Uralian families." This system recognized only the "primary terms of relationship . . . which are those for husband and wife, father and mother, brother and sister, and son and daughter, to which must be added, in such languages as possess them,

grandfather, grandmother, and grandson and granddaughter
. . . Each relationship is thus made independent and distinct
from every other." On the other hand were the classificatory
systems of consanguinity such as the Turanian, American
Indian, and Malayan families. These rejected "descriptive
phrase in every instance, and reducing consanguinity to great
classes by a series of apparently arbitrary generalizations, [ap-
plied] the same terms to all the members of the same class.
[Such a system] thus confounds relationships, which, under
the descriptive system, are distinct, and enlarges the signifi-
cation both of the primary and secondary terms beyond their
seemingly appropriate sense."[56]

Morgan's research and writing were directed at an already
heated discursive environment in which Victorian society and
Victorian anthropologists were struggling to square themes
of the evolution of marriage with the struggle for female
suffrage and the protection of "aboriginal" populations.[57]
Johann Bachofen, Sir John Lubbock, John McLellan, and
others debated the evolution of marriage types — matriarchy,
patriarchy, communal marriage, monogamy — as well as the
relationship between kinship and marriage. Famously, they
debated whether the kinship terms that colonized peoples
used were actual kinship relations or merely strategic modes
of address meant to normalize what were at root savage passions. Over the course of debates about the meaning of marriage in the metropole and colonies, the state of nature and
the savage slot shifted from being the empty backdrop against
which seventeenth-century legal theorists could abstract people from all social relations of superiority and inferiority,

to, during the Victorian period and beyond, being flooded with images of real and phantasmagorical social practices.[58] Rather than all freedom and excess, the passions of primitives were all control and coercion. For Emile Durkheim and his student-nephew, Marcel Mauss, "this logical order" was "so rigid, the power of constraint of these categories on the mind" was "so strong" that all "ideas seem to the primitive to be subject to a logical necessity by which they are entailed."[59] In short, if in Freudian psychoanalysis the unconscious became "the dark continent" of the autological subject, it became so as sub-Saharan Africa, Aboriginal Australia, and other colonial spaces were being enclosed within an anthropological discourse of tribalism and colonial paternalism. Soon pharmaceutical companies could mobilize tribal ritual as a "basic tool of primitive psychiatry" in advertising campaigns for such drugs for schizophrenia as Stelazine.[60]

For a while, the topic of primitive religion rather than primitive kinship and marriage was thought to provide more fertile grounds for a comparative sociology.[61] But in 1901, the British psychologist W. H. R. Rivers revitalized the study of kinship by announcing a major methodological breakthrough in the study of savage societies. Shortly after returning from a collaborative study of the Torres Strait Islanders, Rivers announced new procedures for collecting and analyzing data that moved the study of man beyond conjectural history and onto hard scientific grounds.[62] Rivers recommended the genealogical method to the emergent anthropological community on the basis of its simplicity and its proven ability to collect huge amounts of social data in short amounts of time.

A couple of assumptions about human beings, sex difference and heterosexual reproduction—assumptions that could be claimed to be the universal preconditions of human life—provided just enough structure for the maximal comparison among societies. The comparative reach, the territorial possibilities of this new demographic method, stretched as far as the British Empire.

What was originally a research method very quickly became a full-fledged social theory, as Rivers's student A. R. Radcliffe-Brown transformed a tool for generating social data into a theory of the generative structure of social systems. Harking back to Morgan, Radcliffe-Brown posited that genealogy (kinship and affinity) provided the structural principle out of which all social systems unfolded, operated, and were reproduced. Radcliffe-Brown left little doubt about what social relations composed the "elemental family"—"that between parent and child, that between children of the same parents (siblings), and that between the husband and wife as parents of the same child or children."[63] All the great and small societies of Africa, Australia, and the Americas provided clear demonstrations for Radcliffe-Brown and his teams of students of the "elemental family," a structure so parsimonious that just two principles, sex difference and heterosexual descent, provided the minimal dual pairs out of which all other social differences, such as rank, status, and duty, could be built. Both principles had to be in existence for a "family" to exist. Thus, the childless heterosexual couple, and others, fell off the genealogical grid for Radcliffe-Brown —just as they sometimes do in contemporary land claims in

Australia, where consanguineous ancestors who did not re-produce are often left off genealogies for clarity's sake, and in contemporary debates in the United States about homosexual marriage when proper marriage is based on the reproductive couple.

In the *Elementary Structures of Kinship* (1949), dedicated to Morgan, Claude Lévi-Strauss simultaneously decapitated the sovereign subject from the logic of kinship and tethered the advent of marriage to the advent of culture. (In what must truly be called a footnote, it should be noted that when Lévi-Strauss was fleeing France in 1941 with André Breton and others, he stopped at Martinique. There, Breton discovered and read the first issue of *Tropiques*, edited by Aime Cesaire. The revolutionary poetics of Cesaire's *Tropiques* would be something quite different in Lévi-Strauss's *Triste Tropiques*.[64]) Kinship was no longer a projection out of the deracinated ego, or out of the elemental family, but out of a deeper structural semantics of binary exchange. This binary logic determined not merely the primitive mind, primitive religion, and primitive kinship, but modern versions of the same. Indeed, Lévi-Strauss transformed the possibility of associating the human being and the natural being (the state of nature) by arguing that the human and his kinship structures existed not prior to but posterior to a law of culture. Humanity and kinship, culture and nature, emerged as such in the transition marked by the advent of the first rule of exchange, first announced in a marriage prohibition, the incest taboo. This rule of rules is dependent on another: a "deep polygamous tendency, which exists in all men," which "always makes the number of available women seem insufficient."[65] Homosexuality, polyandry, and wife-swapping were immediately transformed into solutions for the seeming scarcity of women, an illusion created by the incest prohibition. More social forms and relations fell off the genealogical grid or were recast as a mere by-product of its logic, as the atom of kinship and the very nature of culture emerged as the dialectic of binary exchanges that consisted of I and thou; man and woman; parent and child; wife-givers and takers. During national debates over the *pacte civil de solidarité* (a civil union open to both heterosexual and homosexual couples) in France, those who wished to deny gays and lesbians adoption rights relied on structural principles first proposed by Lévi-Strauss and subsequently elaborated by Lacanian psychoanalysis (it is notable that Lévi-Strauss refused to testify before the National Assembly on behalf of this conservative position). Those in favor of the *pacte* struggled to rethink the nature of filiation outside this anthropological history.[66]

The complexity and controversy of these positions were critical to the establishment of the discipline of anthropology. The French schools argued with the British over generality and comparison. In the United States, a generation squabbled over whether kinship was a cultural construct or a universal category. With every new argument, the interior complexity of the intimate event and the genealogical grid intensified. Careers were built or destroyed. New discursive contours, possibilities, and lines of flight emerged. And, insofar as scholars struggled to characterize the essential properties that determined the applicability of the genealogical grid, they cast the grid itself into the background. Finally, genealogy as such became the means by which language and thought worked.

But debates about the genealogical society were not merely academic. They crisscrossed governmental bureaucracies, print publics, and commercial practices. They were truly international debates. They did not just draw together the educated classes, but those Europeans living on the margins of the British Empire. The debates circulated by means of newspapers, government legislation, court decisions, and memos to pastoralists, missionaries, and police administrators from the Kakhalins of Siberia to the Aboriginal Australians to the Pacific Islands and Native North America. And because people reading these newspapers, facing state officials and courts, or answering queries from anthropologists had to conform to their language, not only were the administrating classes brought into a certain discursive space, so were those they administered. For instance, Morgan's ideas circulated first as inquiries to pastoralists, missionaries, and government officials, then as books and pamphlets, and finally as government policy as administrators in the Soviet Union and later Maoist China used Engel's interpretation of them as a blueprint for managing the transition from feudal to modern society.[67]

Four

The two social ends of these struggles over genealogy met spatially, if not literally, in Manchester in 1945 at the Fifth Pan-African Congress (the meeting was timed to coincide with the Communist-led World Trade Union Meetings).[68] At this meeting the leadership of the Pan-African movement shifted, Africa-based Africans taking over from their diasporic colleagues. With this change came a shift in ideology — the Pan-African movement stopped focusing on how indirect rule in Africa could be organized justly to how to install self-rule in Africa. Manchester was also the site of one of the most influential, progressive, and left-leaning anthropological schools of tribalism.[69] Max Gluckman, the chairman of the anthropology department at the University of Manchester, received major grants in 1945 from the British Colonial Development and Welfare Fund as well as from other organizations to organize a collaborative and comparative study of tribal forms in South Africa.

By the time the Fifth Pan-African Congress met, a very different history of empire, marriage, and tribalism had emerged to counter the Manichean dualism of the intimate event and the genealogical society. Take, for example, some features of debates on interracial marriage within progressive movements in Australia and the United States during the mid-twentieth century. Members of the Pan-African movement raised very specific kinds of questions about love, governance, and social deracination. Should race and other forms of ancestry decide love, labor, and national governance in the African diaspora? How did colonial powers variously deploy an ideology of social deracination across the landscape of empire? This latter question was focused in particular on how the white metropolis was able to exfoliate from its ideological commitment to wealth and freedom the actual conditions of colonial totalitarianism, rape, and genocide and how this representation was able to stage this exploitation as civilization, transforming the act of theft into the generosity of the gift. For many, a powerful example of this type of ideologically conservative social deracination was written into the landscape of Belgium and its capital, Brussels. David Levering Lewis reflects on how this landscape appeared to W. E. B. Du Bois.

> With its outsized public squares, monumental governmental palaces, and florid architecture, the capital had served as the unnamed city in *Heart of Darkness* that always reminded Conrad's hero of a "white sepulcher." In novel and in reality, Brussels was headquarters to one of imperialism's most malefic cartels, a rapacious entity using quasi-slave labor to strip an area half the size of Europe of its seemingly bottomless wealth in copper, rubber, and ivory. As Du Bois and the others had to know, the construction of King Leopold's new Brussels—the city within the hexagonal belt of sweeping, broad boulevards beyond the ancient center—depended upon the grinding exploitation of the people and minerals of the Congo.[70]

Of course, there were important differences among those participating at the center and periphery of this movement. In the United States, Du Bois and Marcus Garvey battled over the meaning and legitimacy of interracial marriage and its relation to the shape and direction of the international Pan-African movement.[71] For all their personal and ideological intensity, these debates focused on such issues as formal and social equality and firmly presupposed the colonial origin of the problem of the color line — Garvey proposing at one point that all diasporic Africans return to Africa, Du Bois that Africans living on the continent and in the diaspora be elevated to the highest levels of human civilization. For neither of these men was the color line a national problem. It was not a problem of the United States that began and ended at its borders, but an international, colonial problem that stretched the territoriality of the United States and Europe into Empire and across time.[72] The legacy of U.S. and European empire tied together natal and international forms of racialized love, labor, and national governance. They were tied together because they arose from (and continue to ramify across) the nervous system of the liberal diaspora. Over time, the McCarthy purges in the 1950s, including the departures of Paul Robeson and heightened scrutiny of C. L. R. James and Du Bois, helped to deflect the international orientation of the U.S. civil rights movements.[73] But by the time the Supreme Court heard *Loving v. Virginia* in 1967, a vibrant radical black movement, epitomized by the Black Panthers, had reconnected natal racial oppression and neo-colonialism, this time mainly through the writings of Frantz Fanon.[74] The separate "races" had, indeed, mixed and with them were mixed competing imaginaries and practices of intimacy and genealogy.

Understanding genealogy as a discipline rather than as a recognition of the other allows a history, focused on a specific asymmetry between the intimate event and genealogical society, to emerge more clearly.[75] The exfoliation of the social skin in one place is now seen as the demand for the foliation of the social skin in another place. The self-evident value of liberal adult love depends on instantiating as its opposite a particular kind of illiberal, tribal, customary, and ancestral love. Where it exercises control over life, these discourses of the intimate event and the genealogical society do not merely represent people as located in one or another of these discourses, nor does it merely find them there. It demands that they occupy a location in the assemblage on the pain of death, life, and rot.

After all, while Du Bois and Garvey were debating the virtues of interracial marriage in the United States, indigenous men and women were being classified as wards of the state in large parts of Australia; interracial marriage was prohibited between legally designated "whites" and "blacks"; and marriages between "whites" and "half-castes" were tightly regulated, all toward the end of "breeding" out black racial and cultural difference. But in the colonial context, race was inflected by cultural designata—to be a "real black" was to maintain the appearance of a "tribal black."[76] In Australia, as elsewhere in the British Empire, intimate interracial regulations emerged side-by-side with discourses of tribal custom. The social valences of custom have changed, some would say radically, over the course of Australian federation, moving across state policies of genocide, assimilation, self-determination, reconciliation, and now, "shared responsibility agreements." The government's official propaganda sheet describes these agreements as new arrangements in indigenous affairs linked to wider indigenous reforms. In practice, these agreements condition government funding on behavioral changes within indigenous communities, changes focused on labor discipline and cultural uniformity. In the long run, these agreements are calibrated in such a way as to create the conditions for the evacuation of rural culturally sustainable forms of life in so far as these forms of life do not correspond to the labor market. What has remained across these shifts in the state and public (e)valuation of indigenous custom is a sense of the subject of custom and the genealogical society—the overwhelming sense that individual choice, mystery, and discovery are determined by social custom or convention, or by what I am calling a genealogical discourse. When culture/custom is considered to have positive social or moral values, then *demanding* this *determination* is seen as merely recognizing facts on the ground.

A good example comes by way of recent laws of recognition in settler nations such as Australia and Canada. There, indigenous people are granted special legal status on condition that they show a genealogical relation to their customs and their bodies. The state and public demand that indigenous people demonstrate that they come from a lineage associated with a particular territory and that a cultural genealogy connects their present beliefs, desires, and hopes to the beliefs, desires, and hopes of their pre-colonial ancestors.[77] Unlike in *Loving v. Virginia*, where ancestry was ruled out as the legitimate grounds for prohibiting forms of adult marriage, in contemporary laws of indigenous cultural recognition a demand is placed on the subject of cultural rights to demonstrate the determination of individual choice, mystery, and discovery by cultural and racial inheritance. The *cunning* of recognition, as opposed to the *law* of recognition, is that, given the dense relationship between intimate sovereignty and liberal humanism, the demand that indigenous people demonstrate their rule by custom within the field of racial difference is also a practice of dehumanization. Dehumanization is the price they must pay for even the most remedial forms of recognition. In short, they are presented with a mirror that is actually a double-bind—either love through liberal ideals of self-sovereignty and de-culture yourself, or love according to the fantasy of the unchanging dictates of your tradition and dehumanize yourself.

Courts and publics have come to accept the fact that indigenous subjects are not frozen in time and that, as a result, some degree of change will always exist between present indigenous people and their long deceased relatives. Accepting a small degree of difference between indigenous pasts and presents is held up as demonstrable proof of the tolerant attitude of multicultural recognition, of the enlightened law's good will. And so we should not lose sight of the fact that diversifying the content of a demand does not negate the demand itself. Nor should we lose sight of the fact that in demanding that indigenous subjects place themselves under a genealogical inheritance, the state and public are also demanding that indigenous people dehumanize themselves relative to a discourse of intimate freedom and self-elaboration. The emergence of the discourse of rule by culture goes hand-in-hand with its disciplinary opposite, the "liquidation of tradition and its substitution by a 'culture of indifference' and 'restlessness' that nourishes 'self-stylization,'" as Achille Mbembe has put it.[78] Discourses of

cultural retention and loss and cultural recognition and de-
mocratization are key means through which the uglier aspects
of liberal empire are exfoliated.

These juridically organized demands, and the disciplinary
discourses of cultural retention and loss that they lean on,
have little to do with the actual experience and experiments
of life within the liberal diaspora. There, cultural loss and retention are not the only relevant values in play—and rarely
the most immediate. They are displaced by the dynamics of
social elaboration and contestation, values with very different
logics from the law of recognition. Discourses of the intimate
event and the genealogical society function as genres that
make sense—make sense of and make matter into sense—of
the long history of liberal dominance even as they are contested. The fact that the Pan-African Congress met in Manchester the same year that the anthropology department of
the University of Manchester received funding to study tribalism in Africa suggests the entanglement of these practices
and imaginaries of the self in empire.

This meeting reminds us that the enclosure of empire into
the genealogical grid occurred alongside the struggle of new
social groups to reinsert themselves into the family order and
the struggle of the colonial world not to be enclosed within
tribalism or not within tribalism *like that*. It would be wrong
to say that Europeans simply juxtaposed or imposed their way
of life on colonized people. The genealogical matrix laid into
the social life of colonized people is not simply a wrong description. That would be simple enough to denounce, to turn
away from. Instead genealogical discourses, like intimacy, are

diagonal to local worlds, slightly off center, a sort of funhouse mirror of the self and its social world.

This struggle to define collectivities in languages and practices other than the dialectic of the intimate event and the genealogical society was not merely an indigenous struggle, nor was it merely a struggle within settler colonies. Take for instance, kinship and friendship as Fanon posed them in his difficult essay, "Concerning Violence." Less than one-third of the way into this essay, Fanon posits what a "genuine eradication" of the colonial order would consist of after a "real struggle for freedom" had taken place. "Individualism is the first to disappear," Fanon argues, describing what he means by individualism — "the idea of a society of individuals where each person shuts himself up in his own subjectivity." [79] This disappearance responds to a social and a philosophical field — to the Algerian struggle as well as to the existential struggle described by de Beauvoir: if man is once enclosed within himself, how can he get out? [80] Fanon's answer on both fronts is equally, if deceptively, clear. "The very form of organization of the struggle will suggest [to the native intellectual] a different vocabulary. Brother, sister, friend — ." [81] These forms remind the native intellectual of the positivities of social embeddedness and mutual obligation. Lest he be mistaken as an anthropologist of naïve communalism, Fanon insists that "self-criticism" and "analysis" are immanent in and to the relational terms he evokes. [82] If group criticism is not to degenerate into a form of social subjection, how might an orientation to a critical social embeddedness solve the problem of the individual's self-encasement without triggering the specter of his or her oppression? Put another way, why doesn't a real struggle for freedom oppose social re-absorption? If I am irreducibly in, of, and through my *sister*, what of *my* freedom?

Brother, sister, friend: Such an unobtrusive series of social addresses. And yet the hail of a friend is in this assemblage a form of stranger sociality made intimate. To be a friend is to go beyond kinship into a self-reflexive, chosen relation. Friendship opens kinship into a relation between individuals, into a variant of intimate love. We say, she is not simply my sister, she is more: she is my best friend. Yet the exit from kinship as the condition of becoming a friend is exactly the kind of work discourses of the intimate event and the genealogical society do, inserting European history into an indigenous social imaginary. It inserts a difference where none existed before. It is not that indigenous worlds had no term analogous to *friend* or had nothing that could be called *intimacy*, but this local kind of intimacy may well be derived from an intensification of kinship rather than its negation. Aboriginal friends of mine indicate the closeness of their kin by intensifying the social relation, saying they are "sister-sister," rather than by negating it.

In other words, African theorists such as Fanon and Kwame Nkrumah, and more contemporary writers such as Anthony Appiah, as well as Indian and Australian scholars and activists, were not merely encouraging a clash between European commitments to contractually based mutual benefit and pre-colonial commitments to dependent reciprocal relations—the one based on the intimate event and the other on the genealogical society. They were also struggling to pull a way of being out of the grip of the Western dialectic of individualism and tribalism, contract and status. They insisted that this dialectic of individual freedom and social determination was Europe's history of itself and its brutal exploitation of the colonial world, rather than History, rather than pre-colonial history. These debates were inflected locally by the different social contexts within the uneven terrain of the colonial landscape—in great transnational debates over Negritude, Consciencism, the African Way, the Red Power movement, and indigenous rights movements.[83] As the rule of difference became a colonial-wide method of governance, it was diversified by a range of national and international social struggles having nothing to do with the colonies per se as well as by social stances toward the meaning and sources of the genealogical. For instance, in *The Devil's Handwriting*, George Steinmetz demonstrates how the heterogeneity of the rule of difference in the German colonies reflected and affected struggles for power at home.[84] These debates were pulled into how colonized and colonizers, settlers and indigenous, came to think about themselves *and to think*.[85]

In the wake of these disseminated histories, numerous international women's conferences and NGOs have tried to extract questions of family, culture, and self from the stifling dialectic of Occidental freedom and Oriental bondage. The struggle against this dialectic continues to be reflected with great subtlety by contemporary African writers and politicians, such as Nuruddin Farah in his recent novel *Links* and a host of Iranian film directors, who in recent films such as "Leila," "The Cow," "The Hidden Half," and "Two Women" have explored the dynamic of the self, kinship, and desire from the point of view of Islamic piety. But the very fact of these long-standing efforts to pull local histories out of the grip of the dialectic of autology and genealogy suggests the deep insinuation of this dialectic in the South as well as in the North. These Iranian films remind us once again that the great colonial anthropological discourses of self and custom, reason and passion, emerged from an even older set of discourses about the dissolute unfreedom of the Islamic Other.[86]

The multiple trajectories of the intimate event, the genealogical society, and the carnalities on which they depend within any regime of power and knowledge seem to be precisely what Foucault was trying to work out in his late essays. I have always been somewhat confused by a claim he made in one of his late interviews that people were not disturbed by the fact that a man wanted to be in another man's ass, but by the fact that he wanted to be in another man's life. Surely this is wrong. Surely this contradicts everything I have just written. What could be troubling about affection, tenderness, friendship, fidelity, camaraderie, and companionship between men and between women who also, even often, have sex with one another? Surely my neighbors are more at ease with me if they can reflect on my deep and abiding love for my female lover than if they are simply confronted with the frequency and form of our sex lives? Doesn't my love for her humanize me irrespective of our sexual difference? Isn't that why a strand of the contemporary gay and lesbian rights movement in the United States argues loudly that we feel love just like anyone else—in twos not threes—not anonymous groups, that our capacity to be struck by the intimate event makes us human, makes my family a human family, worthy of tolerance, even respect, even though in many states in the United States and in many nation-states across the world we are precisely against the law? I think this is why my mother said to me that if I had to have sex "that way" she hoped I would at least find love and settle down with one person. The couplet of the intimate event and humanity seems even more secure if by "people" I take Foucault to have meant not my or anyone's specific mother, not men as opposed to women, but the fabric of modern humanist discourse—that modern humanist discourse is upset more by gay men wishing to be in each other's lives than up their asses. And so my dilemma: Foucault sensed that human being is tied tightly to our capacity to be intimate with each other, and yet he insisted that homosexual love upset people more than homosexual sex.

Yet the mystery vanishes if I remember that Foucault was writing in the late 1970s and early 1980s, when the publicity of the carnal regimes of gay sex was cutting raggedly across an advancing, increasingly humanist, politics of a gay liberation. He was listening to a particular strain of this liberation front, whose form of refusal would have greatly interested him. Foucault continually rejected the discursive oppositions that history presented him—reason and madness, truth and falsity—seeing them as systems of exclusion, as methods of disciplining subjects and distributing properties across populations, rather than as contradictions. What Foucault was hearing, seeing, and tasting in the gay life he saw was not the choice between sex and love, but the refusal of the choice that the assemblage of sexuality I have outlined above presented to him. Which will you have, stranger promiscuity (carnality) or intimate love? What, by contrast, might the practices of, say, an intimate promiscuity be? What new forms of freedom would be attached to such a thing? What if sexual promiscuity were seen as the best means toward an intimate end rather than what gets in the way of intimacy? Experimenting with new relationships between anonymous sex and intimate friendship would indeed upset the fabric of humanist discourse because it cut diagonally across carnality and intimacy, it refused their constitutive differences, or made use of them to increase the frisson of a sexual encounter and an intimate bed.

Here I might repeat what I noted in the introduction: if the history of the colonies is a fold of the history of Europe, the history of Europe is no less a fold of the colonial world. In short, for Europeans, tribalism and other genealogical discourses ramified at home and away, recalibrating the possibilities, aspirations, repugnance, and anxieties of Europeans as well as Africans, Melanesians, indigenous Australians, and South Asians. Several of these ramifications are worth mentioning. First, the projection of the elementary family into the state of colonial society, as if it were the state of nature, powerfully constituted and conserved sexual difference and heterosexual reproduction as the *sine qua non* of human culture. Tribalism and its cognate discourses — clan and caste — recalibrated epistemological and deontological foundations of Europe's own genealogical systems. If the real family was the restricted family of Morgan, Rivers, Radcliffe-Brown,

Lévi-Strauss, and all others were primitive accumulations or evolutionary pathways, this normative frame held as tightly for Europeans as for anyone else. Second, the anxiety over the maintenance of a distinction between the intimate event and the genealogical society as a key way of differentiating Western and non-Western civilization inflected the notion of culture with the quality of hysteria. Durkheim and Mauss would report the special quality of primitive cultural hysteria.[87] But as all societies came to be seen to have a culture and a metalanguage of that culture, soon modern subjects were as caught in cultural inheritance as their pre-modern projections. The state of European dependency became a problem in part because it eliminated the difference between home and away. The more scholars tried to free the modern subject from inheritance and from the state of nature-empire, the more they dragged inheritance deeper into the body — unconscious, habitus, doxa. As Deleuze and Guattari have noted, Europeans became absorbed in genealogical trees from kinship to cognition, from the evolution of species to the grammar of language.[88] The real difference between the West and the rest no longer lay in Morgan's famous descriptive and classificatory distinctions, but in the stance people took in relation to their capture by culture. The liberal difference may be little more than an agitated reflexivity, a worry, and an anxiety of influence. In short, in the wake of the law of genealogy, he may find himself neither fully free nor fully constrained, but instead forced to focus his gaze over his shoulder as he gazes simultaneously into the deep recesses of his soul.

Notes

Introduction: Empires of Love

1   For other approaches to the intersection of intimacy and liberalism see Giddens, *The Transformation of Intimacy*; Berlant, *Intimacy*; Wiegman, "Intimate Publics"; Duggan, *Twilight of Equality*; and Gal, "A Semiotics of the Public/Private Distinction."

2   Wittgenstein, *On Certainty*, 22.

3   E. Wilson, *Psychosomatic*, 21.

4   Ibid., 22.

5   Ibid., 23.

6   Brian Massumi makes a compatible point in *A User's Guide to Capital and Schizophrenia*.

7   For different trajectories of this legacy, see Halperin, *How to Do the History of Homosexuality*; Eribon, *Michel Foucault*; Sawicki, *Disciplining Foucault*; Martin, "Feminism, Criticism, and Foucault."

8   Butler, "Against Proper Objects."

9   See, for instance, Navarro, "Experts in Sex Field" and Goode, "Certain Words."

10 For example, see Pateman, *The Sexual Contract*; Parker et al., *Nationalisms and Sexualities*; Berlant, *The Queen of America*; Warner, *The Trouble with Normal*; Alexander, "Not Just Anyone Can be a Citizen"; Stoler, *Carnal Knowledge and Imperial Power*; Mahmood, *Politics of Piety*; and Arondekar, "Border/Line Sex."

11   This said, there have been a number of excellent studies of sexuality and transnationalism. See for instance, A. Wilson, *The Intimate Economies of Bangkok*; Manalansan, *Global Divas*; Rafael, *White Love*; Babb, "Out in Nicaragua"; Patton et al., *Queer Diasporas*; Quiroga, *Tropics of Desire*; and Boellstorff, *The Gay Archipelago*.

12   See Lewis, "W. E. B. Du Bois," especially 41–44 and 496–553, and Kaplan, "The Anarchy of Empire." especially 171–212.

13   Recent studies in diaspora have emphasized exactly the origin-less, or origin-obscuring, nature of diaspora. See, for instance, Axel, "The Diasporic Imaginary"; Roy, "Discovering India"; Edwards, *Morocco Bound*, especially 1–28; and Sharpe, "Is the United States Postcolonial?"

14   Social scientists are now examining the methodological implications of the shift from a comparative to a transnational focus. See, for instance, Seigel, "Beyond Compare."

1: Rotten Worlds

1   Michelmore, "Flesh-eating Bug."

2   McNeil, "Hundreds of U.S. Troops."

3   See, for instance, Jain, *Injury*.

4   Gosdsil, "Remedying Environmental Racism"; Westra, *Faces of Environmental Racism*; Park, "An Examination of International Environmental Racism."

5   Centers for Disease Control and Prevention, "Anthrax," http://www.cdc.gov/ncidod/dbmd/diseaseinfo/anthrax_g.htm.

6   See Pigg, "The Credible and the Credulous"; Cohen, *No Aging in India*; Farmer, *Pathologies of Power*; Kleinman et al., *Social Suffering*; and Rabinow, *Making PCR*.

7   For a seminal study of the impact of Western medical epistemologies on indigenous healing see Reid, *Body, Land and Spirit*.

8   See also Myers, *Pintupi Country, Pintupi Self*, and Austin-Broos, "Two Laws."

9   Watson, "Aboriginal Laws," see especially paragraphs 16 and 29–34.

10 A.P. Elkin may have been referring to Maliya when, in his field notes, he assigns "malir" to George Munggulu, whose patrilineal land was Banagiya. Maliya is located off the coast of Banagaiya. Circa 1937, Box 18, Elkin Fieldnotes, Sydney University.

11 Maggie Timber self-identified as a Marritjaben woman. She speaks here in Emiyenggal because she considers me an Emi speaker.

12 "Sorry business" is a common way of referring to various indigenous mortuary ceremonies.

13 Povinelli, *Labor's Lot*, especially chapter 3.

14 See, for instance, Fred Myers's classic study, "Burning the Truck."

15 Alwin Chong, executive officer, Aboriginal Health Research Ethics Committee of South Australia, http://www.flinders.edu.au/koko tinna/SECT02/ETH_PROC.HTM. See also Terri Janke, "Our Culture: Our Future: Report on Australian Indigenous Cultural and Intellectual Property Rights," issued by the Aboriginal and Torres Strait Islander Commission, http://www.terrijanke.com.au/fs_topics.htm.

16 National Health and Medical Research Council, *Values and Ethics*. This replaced *Guidelines on Ethical Matters in Aboriginal and Torres Strait Island Health Research, 1991*. Independent of these new guidelines, but within their general spirit, Melbourne University established a Chair of Indigenous Health in 2004 to which it appointed Ian Anderson, a Koori man and longtime health activist and researcher. For his and others' critical contribution to debates in indigenous health and ethics, see I. Anderson, "Ethical Issues"; Reid et al., *The Health of Aboriginal Australia*; and Kaplan-Myrth, "Hard Yakka."

17 National Health and Medical Research Council, *Values and Ethics*, 5.

18 Kowal and Paradies, "Ambivalent Helpers and Unhealthy Choices," 1347.

19 *Daly River Land Claim*, 79–80.

20 Povinelli, "Consuming Geist." See also Cattelino, "Casino Roots."

21 For discussions of recent legal innovations in sentencing and juridical process see Auty et al., "Koori Court Victoria."

22   Patton, *Globalizing AIDS*, 7.

23   Bond et al., *AIDS in Africa and the Caribbean*.

24   Associated Press, 15 October 1993. Available on AEGIS (AIDS Education Global Information System) Web site, http://www.aegis.com/news/ads/1993/AD931874.html.

25   See also, Willis et al., *HIV Futures II*; D. Altman, *Power and Community*; Dowsett, "Alliance Building."

26   Nicollete Casella, "Aborigines Leading in Risk of HIV," *Perth Sunday Times* 14 July 2002. Available at The Body Web site, http://www.the body.com / cdc / news_updates_archive / july18_02 / aborigines_hiv .html.

27   Pigg, "Globalizing the Facts of Life," 40.

28   For a discussion of the globalization of the hetero-homo binary, see Povinelli and Chauncey, "Thinking Sexuality Transnationally."

29   See, for instance, J. Anderson, "The Politics of Indigenous Knowledge," and Myers, *Painting Culture*, especially chapter 11.

30   Kenbi Transcripts, 5765.

31   Kenbi Transcripts, 5880.

32   See, for instance, Chapple et al., *Dangerous Liaisons*.

33   Butler, *Gender Trouble*.

34   Pearson, "Aboriginal Australia at a Crossroad." For quite different approaches to indigenous poverty, see Brock, *Outback Ghettos* and Morris, *Domesticating Resistance*.

35   For the economic and health implications of these new shared responsibility agreements, see Collard et al., "Mutual Obligation in Indigenous Health" and Calma, "Implementing New Arrangements."

36   See also the most recent Social Trends Report, published by the Australian Bureau of Statistics, on indigenous welfare in remote communities (available at http://abs.gov.au) and the Council of Australian Government's report on the social welfare of indigenous people nationwide (http://www.coag.gov.au/meetings/030605).

37   See J. Altman and Gray, "The Effects of the CDEP."

38   B. Hunter has noted, "Indigenous people are about two to three times

more likely to be impoverished than the non-indigenous population, irrespective of the equivalence scale used." Hunter, "Three Nations, Not One," 6.

39   Fifteen percent of the ATSIC budget is discretionary spending, mainly distributed to cultural programs and cultural support. Eighty-five percent of the budget was devoted to non-discretionary spending, such as CDEP. See "The Lead-Up to ATSIC's Establishment" in A. Pratt, "Make or Break?"

40   See, for instance, Apter, *The Pan-African Nation*; Kirsch, "Lost Worlds"; and Sawyer, *Crude Chronicles*.

41   Sen, *Development as Freedom*. Speaking about the African diaspora, Michael Hanchard has discussed this uneven development as "racial time." Hanchard, "Afro-Modernity," especially 252–257.

42   Feldman, "Violence and Vision," 35.

43   Lea, *Between the Pen and the Paperwork*, 26.

44   Hayden, *When Nature Goes Public*.

45   Baldwin, *Notes of a Native Son*, 106.

46   See for instance, Peterson, "Demand-sharing"; Schwab, "The Calculus of Reciprocity"; Austin-Broos, "Places, Practices and Things." In a recent policy paper, Schwab has argued that understanding these forms of sharing would critically reshape the approach to poverty alleviation, housing pricing, employment, and welfare organization and distribution in indigenous communities. Schwab, "Principles and Implications."

47   Mbembe, "Life, Sovereignty, and Terror," especially 5–12.

48   Comaroff and Comaroff, "Occult Economies"; Cohen, "The Other Kidney." For general discussion, see Das and Kleinman, introduction to *Remaking a World*; Scheper-Hughes, "Parts Unknown."

49   Maharaj, "$100,000 Compo."

50   Schmitt, *The Concept of the Political*, 48.

51   Jain, *Injury*, especially introduction.

52   Foucault, *Abnormal*, especially chapter 1.

2: Spiritual Freedom, Cultural Copyright

1   Myers, *Painting Culture*, especially chapter 3.

2   D'Andrea, "Global Nomads: Techno and New Age as Transnational Countercultures in Ibiza (Spain) and Goa (India)."

3   Weston, *Families We Chose*, especially chapters 2 and 5.

4   Hadot, *Philosophy as a Way of Life*.

5   See, for instance, D'Emilio, *Sexual Politics, Sexual Communities*; Timmons, *The Trouble With Harry Hay*; Hay, *Radically Gay*; Roscoe, *Queer Spirits*; Churchill, "Homosexual Transnationalism."

6   Churchill, "Homosexual Transnationalism."

7   See Roscoe, *Queer Spirits*; Williams, *The Spirit and the Flesh*.

8   The term *berdache* is derived from the French *bardache*, meaning catamite or male prostitute. It was used from the colonial period to the late 1960s to refer to the vast and varying array of third-gendered practices among Native American societies. It is now more typical to refer to these practices as two-spirit.

9   Hay, "The Homosexual and History," in *Radically Gay*, 139–140.

10   Hay, "A Call to Bathers," in *Radically Gay*, 24.

11   Treleaven. "Queer Rites Now."

12   Bonck, "Radical Faeries."

13   Hay, "Toward the New Frontiers of Fairy Vision," in *Radically Gay*, 255.

14   Treleaven, "Queer Rites Now."

15   For a general critical analysis of Western feminism and indigenous knowledge see J. Jacobs, "Earth Honoring"; Christ and Plaskow, *Womanspirit Rising*; Adler, "Inner Space"; Spretnak, *The Politics of Women's Spirituality*; Starhawk, *The Spiral Dance*; and LaChapelle, *Sacred Land, Sacred Sex*.

16   B. Taylor, "Earth First!" For more on the spiritual grounds of the radical green movement, see B. Taylor, "Earth and Nature-Based Spirituality (Part I)" and B. Taylor, "Earth and Nature-Based Spirituality (Part II)." For the history of the radical green movement in the words

of some of its founders, see Foreman, *Confessions of an Eco-Warrior*, and Abbey, *The Monkeywrench Gang*. For two historical studies of Earth First!, see Wall, "Earth First!" and M. Lee, "Earth First!"

17 B. Taylor, "Earth First!"

18 Morgensen, "Rooting for Queers."

19 For information about Wolf Creek, see the Nomenus Web site, http://www.nomenus.org/aboutnom.html.

20 Beltane is an ancient Gaelic holiday celebrated around 1 May by numerous New Age groups.

21 See Povinelli, "Consuming Geist."

22 According to Ade, "Aboriginal Intelligence" serves as a radical counter-public for "the political, economic and theological lifeways developed by First Nations or Aboriginal societies," a political ideology Ade calls Indigenism. Ade, "An Innovative Affair of Genocide."

23 Ibid.

24 The linguistic anthropologist Michael Silverstein has, for instance, examined semiotic techniques of ritual calibration and reflexive poetics that work in such a way that the extra-worldly realm of ritual is "removed from the quotidian." Silverstein, "Metapragmatic Discourse," 52.

25 See for instance, Turner, *The Ritual Process*; Tambiah, "A Performative Approach to Ritual"; Bloch, "Symbols, Song, Dance"; and Lee and Lipuma, "Cultures of Circulation."

26 For debates about queer public sex in the shadow of the HIV/AIDS pandemic, see Berkowitz and Callen, *How to Have Sex in an Epidemic*; Bersani, "Is The Rectum A Grave?"; Warner, "Why Gay Men Are Having Risky Sex."

27 Herbert, *Culture and Anomie*, 65. See also Pagden, *The Fall of Natural Man*.

28 Povinelli, *The Cunning of Recognition*, 111–152.

29 http://www.aboriginalartshop.com/contemporary-australian-aboriginal-art.html.

30 C. Taylor, "The Politics of Recognition," 66.

31 Ibid.

32 See D'Andrea, "The Spiritual Economy of Nightclubs and Raves."

33 Povinelli, "Might Be Something."

34 Muir, *The Marketing of Aboriginal Culture*; Michaels, *Bad Aboriginal Art*.

35 Kenbi Transcripts, 7021–7023.

36 How racial and cultural logics of genealogy complexity intertwine within different settler colonies is exemplified by *Davis v. United States* 192 F.3d 951 (10th Cir. 1999). In it, several bands of Oklahoma Seminoles sued the U.S. and various federal agencies and officials for allowing the Seminole Tribe to deny them systematically benefits provided to other members of the tribe because of their African ancestry. See Miller, "Seminoles and Africans."

37 Myers, *Pintupi Country, Pintupi Self*, 52.

38 Françoise Dussart has observed that, among the Walpiri at Yuendumu, in central Australia, the process by which any particular truth claim pertaining to the geophysical world is ratified is a matter of enormous interpretive struggle. Dussart, *The Politics of Ritual*.

39 Peirce, "Pragmatism."

40 See Povinelli, *The Cunning of Recognition*, especially chapter 5, and Beckett, *Torres Strait Islanders*.

41 For Warner, counter-publics "mark themselves off unmistakably from any general or dominant public. Their members are understood to be not merely a subset of the public but constituted through a conflictual relation to the dominant public." Warner, "Publics and Counterpublics," 117–118.

42 Gramsci, "The Modern Prince," 126.

43 In the domain of intellectual property rights, the juridical field is continually hinging the form of the denotational text to the interactional basis of its formation, foregrounding, for instance, whether a text is an original text, an innovative rift on another original text, or a plagiarized version, and whether the text is the product of an individual or community. Irrespective of these forms and social foundations, the text moves, on the basis of a temporal logic, from protected status to public

domain. See, for instance, Pottage and Mundy, *Law, Anthropology, and the Constitution of the Social*, and Coombs, *Cultural Life of Intellectual Properties*.

44 Jakobsen and Pellegrini, *Love the Sin*, 15.

45 Peyote is regulated as a Schedule 1 drug under the Controlled Substance Act, Title II of the Comprehensive Abuse Prevention and Control Act of 1970.

46 While RFRA no longer applies to the states, it is still applicable to the federal government. A second attempt to establish the strict scrutiny test for state and local legislation failed in 2000.

47 In *State of Utah v. Mooney*, the district court summarized this as: "Congress first restricted the possession and sale of peyote in the Drug Abuse Control Amendments of 1965, and classified it as a Schedule I controlled substance in 1970. 21 U.S.C. § 812(c) Schedule I(c)(12) (2004); Boyll, 774 F. Supp. at 1338; Native Am. Church, 468 F. Supp. at 1249. In 1965 and again in 1970, there were efforts in Congress to enact an explicit statutory exception for the use of peyote in bona fide religious ceremonies. Id. These efforts did not succeed, but they led the Bureau of Narcotics and Dangerous Drugs, the predecessor to the agency now known as the Drug Enforcement Administration (the 'DEA'), to promulgate a regulatory exemption for the religious use of peyote. Id. That exemption provides as follows: 'The listing of peyote as a controlled substance in Schedule I does not apply to the nondrug use of peyote in bona fide religious ceremonies of the Native American Church, and members of the Native American Church so using peyote are exempt from registration. Any person who manufactures peyote for or distributes peyote to a Native American Church is required to register annually and to comply with all other requirements of law.' "

48 Kava drinking in Arnhem Land provides an interesting potential exception. Kava was imported from the Fijian Islands, where it is used ritually, to Arnhem Land as a means of controlling alcohol abuse. See, for instance, Australian Law Reform Commission, *The Recognition of Aboriginal Customary Laws*.

49 More generally, some justices who have served as land commissioners

have also spoken out against cultural difference when it seems to violate human rights standards. For instance, Justice Michael Kirby argued, "The coming into force in 1996 of the Convention on the Elimination of All Forms of Discrimination Against Women (CEDAW) has given an impetus to legislation and judicial decision-making that is more respectful of the full equality and true dignity of women in society. It has turned the focus of the international community on such issues as violence against women, female genital mutilation, sati (widow burning), punishment according to religious law and other practices that are particular to certain cultural communities and which appear to fall short of universal human rights." Kirby, "The Challenges to Justice in a Plural Society."

50 In *Ben Ward & Ors* (2000), the High Court found that native title referred to a "bundle of rights" and not "an underlying title to land." As a result, an onus is placed on native title claimants to demonstrate (a) what bundle of rights were traditionally held for a stretch of land and whether the practices subtending and expressing these rights have continued to be practiced in an unbroken chain from the pre-settlement period to the present and (b) that these rights had not been extinguished by their inconsistency with right asserted by the Crown or the granting of pastoral, mining, freehold grants, or special purposes leases. In other words, in *Ward* the High Court insisted that the textual artifacts and the more or less shared protocols and stipulations for what is "stuff," and why it is this stuff rather than some other stuff, remain inert across historical time, rewarding those who are able to produce texts that signal the dominance of the narrative over the narrative event, the reproduced text over the person (re)producing the text—unless, of course, their rights have already been extinguished.

51 These amendments severely restricted the amount of land available for native title applications and redefined the formal application and hearing in ways that most agree gutted the substantive outcomes of even successful native title claims.

52 Muir, "Relics of Aboriginality." See also Trigger, "Indigeneity, Ferality and What 'Belongs' in the Australian Bush."

53   Strelein, "A Comfortable Existence."

54   Todorov, *The Conquest of America*, 81.

55   Sherzer, *Verbal Art in San Blas*, and Duranti, *From Grammar to Politics*.

56   Eribon, *Michel Foucault*, x.

57   Worman, *Shamans and Show Queens*.

58   Such attitudes and practices could be glimpsed, according to Foucault,
     both in Greek notions of *askesis*, the exercise of the self in the ac-
     tivity of thought, and in Kantian notions of critique as the exercise
     of knowledge in the limit of historical formations. Of course a ques-
     tion can be put to Foucault as per the correctness of his reading of the
     Greeks. Pierre Hadot's critical engagement with Foucault's reading
     of the Greek tradition of spiritual exercise makes two general critical
     interventions. The first is that the Stoics, if not the Greeks in some gen-
     eral sense, were not oriented to or interested in pleasure as the outcome
     of their exercises. "If the Stoics insist on the word *gaudium*/'joy,' it
     is precisely because they refuse to introduce the principle of pleasure
     into moral life. For them, happiness does not consist of pleasure, but
     in virtue itself, which is its own reward. Long before Kant, the Stoics
     strove jealously to preserve the purity of intention of the moral con-
     sciousness." Second, according to Hadot, the Stoics did not find joy in
     themselves but in the true good. "In fact, the goal of Stoic exercises is
     to go beyond the self, and think and act in universal reason." Hadot,
     Philosophy as a Way of Life, 207.

59   Beauvoir, *The Ethics of Ambiguity*, 43–49.

60   Bersani, *Homos*, 161. See also Vogler, "Sex and Talk."

61   See, for instance, Dawne Moon's description of debates within Meth-
     odist churches about the acceptance of openly gay and lesbian people
     in church. Moon, *God, Sex, and Politics*.

62   The idea that equal rights for gays and lesbians would assault not
     merely a kind of culture but culture itself was exemplified in debates
     in France over the *pacte civil de solidarité* (PACS), a form of civil union
     open to both heterosexual and homosexual couples. See, for instance,
     Fassin, "Same Sex, Different Politics."

63   Habermas's concept of an unregulated public sphere emerged in part

as a response to a number of class, feminist, and multiculturalist critiques of his emphasis on bourgeoise normative rationality as the end and source of Enlightenment freedom. See, for instance, Fraser, "Rethinking the Public Sphere."

64 Habermas, "Deliberative Politics," 307.

65 Ibid., 307–308.

66 Gutmann and Thompson, *Democracy and Disagreement*; Benhabib, *The Claims of Culture*; Bohman and Rehg, *Deliberative Democracy*; and Sunstein, *Democracy and the Problem of Free Speech*.

67 Habermas, "Deliberative Politics," 296, 300.

68 "According to this view, practical reason no longer resides in universal human rights, or in the ethical substance of a specific community, but in the rules of discourse and forms of argument that borrow their normative content from the validity basis of action oriented to reaching understanding." Ibid., 296–297.

69 Ibid., 304.

70 Ibid., 307.

71 McClure, "Difference, Diversity, and the Limits of Toleration," 363.

72 Duke, "The FBI's Art Attack." See also Kennedy, "The Artists in the Hazmat Suits."

73 Habermas, "Deliberative Politics," 313.

74 Ibid.

75 Ibid.

76 Gould, "Media Not Lying."

77 Foucault began to unpack some of the microtechnologies of these everyday habitudes in *Discipline and Punish*, especially 135–169.

78 See, for instance, Omi and Winant, *Racial Formation in the United States*; Goldberg, *The Racial State*; Stoler, *Race and the Education of Desire*; and Gilroy, *Against Race*.

79 Dominguez, *White By Definition*.

80 Halley, "Reasoning About Sodomy," 1722.

81 For a discussion of the force of administrative law in the reproduction of power, see Harrington, *Administrative Law and Politics*.

82 Bey, *T.A.Z.*, 99. The relation between a TAZ and radical faerie communities has been noted. The faeries have always placed "a heavy emphasis on creating a celebratory, fantasy oriented free-space." Treleaven, "Queer Rites Now."

83 Bey, *T.A.Z.*, 97.

84 Ibid., 98.

85 Ibid.

3: The Intimate Event and Genealogical Society

1 See, for instance, Kennedy, "The Marital Color Line"; Kennedy, *Interracial Intimacies*; and Kennedy, "*Loving v. Virginia* at Thirty." See also Wallenstein, *Tell the Court I Love My Wife*, and Pratt, "Crossing the Color Line."

2 Good, "Color Dynamics."

3 A position usually characterized as equality advocacy. Ida B. Wells-Barnett drew the connection between gender and race long before Sharpton. For a discussion of contributions by African American women to U.S. civil rights, see Collins, *Fighting Words* and Giddings, *Where I Enter.*

4 James, *The Black Jacobins*, 139.

5 Franke, "The Domesticated Liberty of *Lawrence v. Texas.*"

6 My emphasis. Freud, *Civilization and Its Discontents*, 57–58.

7 For a fascinating ethnography of Protestant encounters with homosexual intimacies see Moon, *God, Sex, and Politics.*

8 I am referring to the metaphorical reading of hegemony presented by Laclau and Mouffe, *Hegemony and Socialist Strategy.*

9 Kennedy, *Interracial Intimacies*, 273.

10 "One has to give up—to a greater or lesser extent—life within the (natal) family circle; further, one has to accept, as constitutive of one's own self, this more or less obligatory renunciation. Perhaps this explains, *a contrario*, why a certain number of gay men and lesbians experience such a strong desire to be recognized as legitimate couples

or families by those close to them (notably their families) and by society at large (and thus by the law). In such cases it is not simply a question of adopting heterosexual 'models,' as is sometimes asserted ('imitating the hets,' as would say those who prefer to remain outside any recognized institutional framework), but, more fundamentally, of recovering a grounding in a lost family and perhaps thereby of restoring bonds with the family one has left, or of reentering 'normal' life by joining once again the sequence of generations." Eribon, *Insult and the Making of the Gay Self*, 35–36.

11 Duggan, *The Twilight of Equality?*, especially chapter 2. See also Probyn, *Outside Belongings*, and Somerville, "Queer *Loving*."

12 Butler, "Against Proper Objects," 14.

13 Mr. Chief Justice Warren, *Loving v. Virginia*, Supreme Court of the United States, 388 us 1 (12 June 1967).

14 Balibar, "Subjection and Subjectication," 9.

15 Mafarlane, *The Origins of English Individualism*.

16 Mafarlane, *The Origins of English Individualism*, 166.

17 E.P. Thompson provides a useful example in his discussion of the struggle between woollen weavers and hand-loom factories. Thompson, *The Making of the English Working Class*, 269–313.

18 Wood, *The Radicalism of the American Revolution*, 19.

19 Thompson's *The Making of the English Working Class* is a classic archive for the historical unevenness and incompleteness of this movement. Other texts that examine radical and counter-forms of the Enlightenment in its various guises include McMahon, *Enemies of the Enlightenment* and Israel, *The Radical Enlightenment*. The feminist historian Amy Dru Stanley has forcefully described how diverse social actors before and after the American Civil War attempted to use the ideology of the free market and the marriage contract to undermine chattel slavery, only to find themselves struggling to defend against the liberal institution of "free labor." Stanley, *From Bondage to Contract*; see also Foner, *Free Soil, Free Labor, Free Men*.

20 Taylor, *Modern Social Imaginaries*.

21   Descartes, *Meditations of First Philosophy*, 59.

22   Norbert Elias modeled the intersecting relations between long-distance trade and the emergence of new forms of self-constraint and foresight. Elias, *The Civilizing Process*.

23   Habermas, *Structural Transformation of the Public Sphere*, 49. A number of scholars have examined how these experiments with subjectivity were themselves refracted across new forms of text and textual circulation. See, for instance, B. Lee, "Texuality, Mediation, and Public Discourse" and Warner, "Publics and Counterpublics."

24   Habermas, *Structural Transformation of the Public Sphere*, 28. Anthony Giddens has likewise claimed that the rise of romantic love in the bourgeois family was critical to the constitution of the modern institutional reflexivity so fundamental to deliberative democracies and cultural tolerance. Giddens, *The Transformation of Intimacy*. On a different note, scholars have examined the constitution of intimacy in relation to the rise of the welfare state. See Pedersen, *Family, Dependence, and the Origins of the Welfare State*.

25   For a fascinating ethnography of the changing languages and forms of love, intimacy, and the family in a Chinese village, see Yan, *Private Life Under Socialism*, and Friedman, *Intimate Politics*. For changes outside China, see Green, *Unrequited Conquests*; Matsuda, *Empire of Love*; and Parker et al., *Nationalities and Sexualities*.

26   Laura Kipnis, in particular, has written a series of critical essays on this phantom formation. In a recent opinion piece in the *New York Times* Kipnis noted, "marriage has long provided a metaphor for citizenship. Both are vow-making enterprises; both involve a degree of romance. Households are like small governments, and in this metaphor, divorce is a form of revolution—at least an overthrow." Kipnis, "Should This Marriage be Saved?"

27   Frederick, "Savage Instincts."

28   Donzelot, *The Policing of Families*; Stoler, *Carnal Knowledge and Imperial Power*.

29   It is hard to recapture the intensity of the threat to the community

faced by this new kind of subject, when, for the most part, we see the issue the other way around—the threat to the individual by the collectivity. Max Weber perhaps best captured the anxiety of the potential of this form of subjectivity to the social collective in his discussion of Calvinism. Weber, *The Protestant Ethic*.

30 Arendt, *The Human Condition*, 28.

31 Kennedy, quoting the decision in *Perez v. Sharp*, 32 Cal.2d 711 (1948), in Kennedy, *Interracial Intimacies*, 262.

32 Dalton, "Non-Biological Mothers"; Ragone, "Surrogate Motherhood"; Franklin, *Embodied Progress*; Ginsberg and Rapp, *Conceiving the New World Order*; and Cannell, "Concepts of Parenthood."

33 Fraser, "Rethinking the Public Sphere," 131. See also Landes, *Women and the Public Sphere in the Age of the French Revolution*.

34 Alain Badiou locates the origin of this event-form in Pauline Christianity and describes it as a singular universality in which the "non-difference between Jew and Greek establishes Christianity's potential universality" is "found the subject as division, rather than perpetuation of a tradition, renders the subjective element adequate to this universality by terminating the predicative particularity of cultural subjects." Badiou, *Saint Paul*, 57. Again, Arendt's observations about Greek antiquity are relevant here—especially her argument that post–Roman Christianity elevated a life-renouncing transcendental eternity over a life-oriented immortality. Arendt, *The Human Condition*, 28.

35 Agamben, *Means Without End*, 3.

36 A point addressed in Paul Gilroy's recent book, *Against Race*.

37 See for instance Stephen Collier et al., "Biosecurity."

38 Gordon argues that marriage, seen as threatened by polygamy, could be cured through "emotional homogeneity (the inherently anonymous 'nature' shared by all women)." Gordon, "Our National Hearthstone," 300. See also Nancy Cott's discussion of Christian monogamy in early America. Cott, *Public Vows*, especially chapter 10.

39 Hunt, *The Family Romance*, especially chapters 1 and 3; Verges, *Monsters and Revolutionaries*.

40 A classic example of this approach to the materiality of the body is Butler, *Gender Trouble*.

41 Steven Becker, Letter to the Editor, *New York Times*, April 22, 2004.

42 See, for instance, Green, *Unrequited Conquests*; Matsuda, *Empire of Love*; and Patton et al., *Queer Diasporas*.

43 It is important to remember that these reforms also occurred in the context of the long struggle among various powers within what would become Western Europe and Islamic empires. Christian forms of couplet marriage were opposed to Islamic forms of polygamy, the conjugal couple of modern marriage taking on a religious penumbra long before the emergence of European colonial empires of the sixteenth century were inflected with a civilizational penumbra.

44 For a fuller discussion, see Brundage, *Love, Sex, and Christianity*; Boswell, *Christianity, Social Tolerance, and Homosexuality*; and Dinshaw, *Getting Medieval*.

45 Duby, *The Knight, the Lady and the Priest*.

46 See, for instance, Stone, *Uncertain Unions*.

47 C. Taylor, *Modern Social Imaginaries*.

48 Howell, *The Marriage Exchange*; Stone, *Uncertain Unions*; Houlbrooke, *The English Family*; Mendelson and Crawford, *Women in Early Modern England*; Frankel and Dye, *Gender, Class, Race*.

49 Other discursive forms like the first person future (I will marry thee) were, for a long time in many places, seen as performative at the moment of sexual consummation.

50 Goody, *The Development of the Family*; see also Brown, *The Rise of Western Christendom*.

51 Le Goff, "Head or Heart?"

52 See Strathern, *After Nature*, for an excellent rethinking of intimacy as an effect of modern forms of kinship.

53 Trouillot, "Anthropology and the Savage Slot." See also, Cott, *Public Vows*, 26.

54 Strathern, *After Nature*, 16.

55 Morgan, *Systems of Consanguinity*, 10.

56   Ibid., 12.

57   Weeks, *Sex, Politics, and Society*; Stocking, *Victorian Anthropology*.

58   C. Taylor, *New Social Imaginaries*.

59   Durkheim and Mauss, *Primitive Classification*, 16–17.

60   See for example the remarkable advertising campaign mounted by the SmithKline Corporation in the *American Journal of Psychiatry* and the *Archives of General Psychiatry* during the mid-1970s for Thorazine and Stelazine, which featured masks, scepters, and statues from the Ewe of Tongo, the Ashanti in Ghana, the Tlingit, and others.

61   Stocking, *Victorian Anthropology*; Stocking, *After Tylor*.

62   Rivers, "The Genealogical Method."

63   Radcliffe Brown, *Structure and Function in Primitive Society*, 51–52.

64   Macey, *Frantz Fanon*, 70–111.

65   Lévi-Strauss, *Elementary Structures of Kinship*, 38.

66   Fassin, "Same Sex, Different Politics."

67   For instance, see the tantalizing clues in Dutton, "Mango Mao" and Grant, foreword to *The Social Organization of the Gilyak*.

68   Young, *Postcolonialism*, 238.

69   For the British School and Gluckman's contribution, see Colson, "Gluckman, Max"; Kapferer, "The Anthropology of Max Gluckman"; and Kuper, *Anthropology and Anthropologists*. For tribalism deployment in Africa, see Vail, *The Creation of Tribalism*. For an extended historical analysis of the heterogeneity of such practices within imperial Germany, see Steinmetz, *The Devil's Handwriting*.

70   Lewis, *W. E. B. Du Bois*, 42. Amy Kaplan has made a similar point. Kaplan, *The Anarchy of Empire*, 195. The international black community did not agree about how to think about the relationship between European forms of colonialism and African futures, especially under the twin shadow of communism and tribalism. See, for instance, Young, *Postcolonialism*, especially chapters 17–19. Perhaps the most well-known division was between African Francophones and African Americans. See Brent Hayes Edwards, *The Practice of Diaspora*.

71   Lewis, *W. E. B. Du Bois*, 42.

72   For the transnational nature of this struggle see Young, *Postcolonial-*

ism, especially 217–307; Brent Hayes Edwards, *The Practice of Diaspora*; Kelley, *Freedom Dreams*; Esebe, *Pan-Africanism*; Layton, *International Politics and Civil Rights Policies in the United States*; von Eschen, *Race against Empire*.

73 Kelley, *Freedom Dreams*, especially 53–54; Lewis, *W. E. B. Du Bois*, especially 554–555, 559; Young, *Postcolonialism*, especially 228–235.

74 Young, *Postcolonialism*, 223.

75 Partha Chatterjee has described this technique as the rule of colonial difference. See Chatterjee, *The Nation and Its Fragments*, especially 16–22. For an excellent study of how tradition is used as a technique of governance outside Europe and its colonies, see Kogacioglu, "The Tradition Effect."

76 Austin, "Cecil Cook"; Jacobs, "Science and Veiled Assumptions"; Wolfe, "Nation and Miscegenation"; and Cowlishaw, *Rednecks, Eggheads and Blackfellas*.

77 See Borrows, *Recovering Canada*.

78 Mbembe, "Aesthetics of Superfluity."

79 Fanon, *The Wretched of the Earth*, 47.

80 Beauvoir, *The Ethics of Ambiguity*, 16.

81 Fanon, *The Wretched of the Earth*, 47.

82 Ibid.

83 An enormous literature examines variations in national modes of racial/genealogical governance. See for example, James's classic *The Black Jacobins*. See also Todorov, *On Human Diversity*, and Mignolo, *Local Histories/Global Designs*.

84 Steinmetz, *The Devil's Handwriting*.

85 See, for instance, Chakrabarty, *Provincializing Europe*, and Segal, *Crossing Cultures*.

86 Said, *Orientalism*.

87 In an astonishing text, Jean Jacques Goux revised this argument in an attempt to provide a master synthesis of the major modernist metanarratives. See Goux, *Symbolic Economies*. See Spivak's discussion of this text in "Scattered Speculations on a Theory of Value."

88 Deleuze and Guattari, *A Thousand Plateaus*, especially 3–26.

Bibliography

Abbey, Edward. *The Monkeywrench Gang*. New York: Avon, 1975.

Ade, Sequoyah. "An Innovative Affair of Genocide." The Angry Indian Reader, http://angryindian.atspace.com/spirit.html.

Adler, Margot. "Inner Space: The Spiritual Frontier." In *Sisterhood Is Forever: The Women's Anthology for a New Millennium*, ed. Robin Morgan, 551–559. New York: Washington Square, 2003.

Agamben, Giorgio. *Means Without End: Notes on Politics*. Minneapolis: University of Minnesota Press, 2003.

Alexander, M. Jacqui. "Not Just Anyone Can be a Citizen: The Politics of Law, Sexuality, and Postcoloniality in Trinidad and Tobago." *Feminist Studies* 48 (Autumn 1994): 5–23.

Altman, Dennis. *Power and Community: Organisational and Cultural Responses to HIV/AIDS*. London: Taylor and Francis, 1992.

Altman, Jon, and M. C. Gray. "The Effects of the CDEP Scheme on the Economic Status of Indigenous Australians: Some Analyses Using the 1996 Census." Centre for Aboriginal Economic Policy Research, Discussion Paper No. 195. Canberra: Australian National University, 2000.

Anderson, Ian. "Ethical Issues in the Reform of Aboriginal Health Financing." In *Aboriginal Health: The Ethical Challenges*, ed. N. Ford, 25–34. Melbourne: Caroline Chisholm Centre for Health Ethics, 1999.

Anderson, Jane. "The Politics of Indigenous Knowledge: Australia's Proposed Communal Moral Rights Bill." *University of New South Wales Law Journal* 27, no. 3 (2004): 585–604.

Apter, Andrew. *The Pan-African Nation: Oil and the Spectacle of Culture in Nigeria*. Chicago: University of Chicago Press, 2005.

Arendt, Hannah. *The Human Condition*. Chicago: University of Chicago Press, 1958.

Arondekar, Anjali. "Border/Line Sex: Queer Postcolonialities or How Race Matters Outside the U.S." *Interventions: International Journal of Postcolonial Studies* 7, no. 2 (2005): 235–249.

Austin, Tony. "Cecil Cook, Scientific Thought and 'Half-Castes' in the Northern Territory 1927–1939." *Aboriginal History* 14, no. 1 (1990): 104–122.

Austin-Broos, Diane. "Places, Practices and Things: The Articulation of Arrernte Kinship with Welfare and Work." *American Ethnologist* 30, no. 1 (2003): 118–135.

———. "'Two Laws,' Ontologies, Histories: Ways of Being Arrernte Today." *Australian Journal of Anthropology* 7 (1996): 1–20.

Australian Law Reform Commission. *The Recognition of Aboriginal Customary Laws*. Canberra: Australian Government Publishing Service, 1986.

Auty, Kate, and Daniel Briggs. "Koori Court Victoria: Magistrates Court (Koori Court) Act 2002." *Law/Text/Culture* 8 (2004): 7–38.

Axel, Brian. "The Diasporic Imaginary." *Public Culture* 14, no. 2: 411–428.

Babb, Florence E. "Out in Nicaragua: Local and Transnational Desires after the Revolution." *Cultural Anthropology* 18, no. 3 (2003): 304–328.

Badiou, Alain. *Saint Paul: The Foundation of Universalism*. Stanford: Stanford University Press, 2003.

Baldwin, James. "Notes of a Native Son." In *Notes of a Native Son*, 85–114. Boston: Beacon, 1984.

Balibar, Etienne. "Subjection and Subjectication." In *Supposing the Subject*, ed. Joan Copjec, 1–15. London: Verso, 1994.

Beauvoir, Simone de. *The Ethics of Ambiguity*. New York: Citadel, 2000.

Beckett, Jeremy. *Torres Strait Islanders: Custom and Colonialism*. Cambridge: Cambridge University Press, 1990.

258

Benhabib, Seyla. *The Claims of Culture: Equality and Diversity in the Global Era*. Princeton: Princeton University Press, 2002.

Berkowitz, Richard, and Michael Callen. *How to Have Sex in an Epidemic*. New York: News From the Front Publications, 1993.

Berlant, Lauren. *The Queen of America Goes to Washington, D.C.: Essays on Sex and Citizenship*. Durham: Duke University Press, 1997.

Berlant, Lauren, ed. *Intimacy*. Chicago: University of Chicago Press, 2000.

Bersani, Leo. *Homos*. Cambridge, Mass.: Harvard University Press, 1996.

———. "Is The Rectum a Grave?" *October* 43 (1987): 197–222.

Bey, Hakim. *T.A.Z.: The Temporary Autonomous Zone, Ontological Anarchy, Poetic Terrorism*. New York: Autonomedia, 2003.

Bloch, Maurice. "Symbols, Song, Dance, and Features of Articulation." In *Ritual, History, and Power: Selected Papers in Anthropology*, 19–45. London School of Economics Monographs on Social Anthropology 58. London: Athlone, 1989.

Boellstorff, Tom. *The Gay Archipelago*. Princeton: Princeton University Press, 2005.

Bohman, James, and William Rehg, eds. *Deliberative Democracy: Essays on Reason and Politics*. Cambridge, Mass.: MIT Press, 1997.

Bonck, John Harry. "Radical Faeries." *glbtq: an encyclopedia of gay, lesbian, bisexual, transgender and queer culture*, http://www.glbtq.com/social-sciences/radical_faeries.html.

Bond, George C., John Kreniske, Ida Susser, and Joan Vincent, eds. *AIDS in Africa and the Caribbean*. Cambridge, Mass.: Westview, 1997.

Borrows, John. *Recovering Canada, The Resurgence of Indigenous Law*. Toronto: University of Toronto Press, 1996.

Boswell, John. *Christianity, Social Tolerance, and Homosexuality: Gay People in Western Europe from the Beginning of the Christian Era to the Fourteenth Century*. Chicago: University of Chicago Press, 2005.

Brock, P. *Outback Ghettos: Aborigines, Institutionalization, and Survival*. Cambridge: Cambridge University Press, 1993.

Brown, Peter. *The Rise of Western Christendom: Triumph and Diversity 200–1000*. London: Blackwell, 2003.

Brundage, James A. *Law, Sex, and Christianity: Society in Medieval Europe*. Chicago: University of Chicago Press, 1987.

Butler, Judith. "Against Proper Objects." *differences: A Journal of Feminist Cultural Studies* 6, no. 2/3 (1994): 1–26.

———. *Gender Trouble*. London: Routledge, 1989.

Calma, Tom. "Implementing New Arrangements for the Administration of Indigenous Affairs." *Social Justice Report 2004, Report of the Aboriginal and Torres Strait Islander Social Justice Commissioner*. Sydney: Office of the Aboriginal and Torres Strait Islander Social Justice Commissioner, 2004.

Cannell, Fenella. "Concepts of Parenthood: The Warnock Report, the Gillick Debate, and Modern Myths." *American Ethnologist* 17, no. 4 (1990): 667–686.

Carter, Lief H., and Christine Harrington. *Administrative Law and Politics*. New York: Longman. 2000.

Cattelino, Jessica. "Casino Roots: The Cultural Production of Twentieth-Century Seminole Economic Development." In *Native Pathways: Economic Development and American Indian Culture in the Twentieth Century*, ed. B. Hosmer and C. Oneill, 66–90. Boulder: University of Colorado Press, 2004.

Chakrabarty, Dipesh. *Provincializing Europe*. Princeton: Princeton University Press, 2000.

Chapple, Murray, and Sue Kippax, with assistance from Michael Bartos and Juliet Richters. *Dangerous Liaisons*. National Centre in HIV Social Research, School of Behavioural Sciences. Sydney: Macquarie University New Press, 1999.

Chatterjee, Partha. *The Nation and Its Fragments*. Princeton: Princeton University Press, 1993.

Christ, Carol, and Judith Plaskow, eds. *Womanspirit Rising: A Feminist Reader in Religion*. San Francisco: Harper and Row, 1979.

Churchill, David. "Homosexual Transnationalism: Rights and the Queer Use of Anthropology." Unpublished paper.

Cohen, Lawrence. *No Aging in India: Alzheimer's, The Bad Family, and Other Modern Things*. Berkeley: University of California Press, 2000.

———. "The Other Kidney: Biopolitics beyond Recognition." *Body and Society* 7, no. 2–3 (2001): 9–29.

Collard, Kim S., Heather A. D'Antione, Dennis G. Eggington, Barbara R. Henry, Carol A. Martin, and Gavin H. Mooney. "Mutual Obligation in Indigenous Health: Can Shared Responsibility Agreements be Truly Mutual?" *MJA* 182, no. 10 (2005): 502–504.

Collier, Stephen, Andrew Lakoff, and Paul Rabinow. "Biosecurity: Proposal for an Anthropology of the Contemporary." *Anthropology Today* 20, no. 5 (2004): 3–7.

Collins, Patricia Hill. *Fighting Words: Black Women and the Search for Justice*. Minneapolis: University of Minnesota Press, 1998.

Colson, Elizabeth. "Gluckman, Max." In *International Encyclopedia of the Social Sciences*. Biographical Supplement, 242–246. New York: Macmillan, 1979.

Comaroff, Jean, and John Comaroff. "Occult Economies and the Violence of Abstraction." *American Ethnography* 26, no. 3 (1999): 279–301.

Coombs, Rosemary. *Cultural Life of Intellectual Properties: Authorship, Appropriation and the Law*. Durham: Duke University Press, 1998.

Cott, Nancy. *Public Vows: A History of Marriage and the Nation*. Cambridge, Mass.: Harvard University Press, 2000.

Cowlishaw, Gillian. *Rednecks, Eggheads and Blackfellas: A Study of Racial Power and Intimacy in Australia*. Sydney: Allen and Unwin, 1999.

Dale, Charles V. "Affirmative Action Revisited: A Legal History and Prospectus." Report for Congress. Washington, D.C.: Congressional Research Service, 2002.

Dalton, Susan. "Non-Biological Mothers and the Legal Boundaries of Motherhood." In *Ideologies and Technologies of Motherhood*, ed. Heléna Ragoné and France Winddance Twine, 191–232. London: Routledge, 2000.

Daly River Land Claim. Indooroopilly: Transcripts Australia, 2001.

D'Andrea, Anthony. "Global Nomads: Techno and New Age as Transnational Countercultures in Ibiza (Spain) and Goa (India)." PhD diss., University of Chicago, 2006.

———. "Global Nomads: Techno and New Age in Ibiza and Goa." In *Rave*

Culture and Religion, ed. Graham Saint-John, 236–255. London: Routledge, 2004.

———. "The Spiritual Economy of Nightclubs and Raves: Osho Sannyasins as Party Promoters in Ibiza and Pune–Goa." *Culture and Religion*. Forthcoming.

Das, Veena, and Arthur Kleinman. Introduction to *Remaking a World, Violence, Social Suffering and Recovery*, ed. Veena Das and Arthur Kleinman, 1–30. Berkeley: University of California Press, 2001.

Deleuze, Gilles, and Felix Guattari. *A Thousand Plateaus: Capitalism and Schizophrenia*. Trans. Brian Massumi. Minneapolis: University of Minnesota Press, 1987.

D'Emilio, John. *Sexual Politics, Sexual Communities*. Chicago: University of Chicago Press, 1998.

Descartes, Jean-Jacques. *Meditations on First Philosophy*. Trans. Ronald Cress. Indianapolis: Hackett, 1993.

Dinshaw, Carolyn. *Getting Medieval: Sexual Communities, Pre- and Postmodern*. Durham: Duke University Press, 1999.

Dominguez, Virginia. *White By Definition: Social Classification in Creole in Louisiana*. New Brunswick: Rutgers University Press, 1986.

Donzelot, Jacques. *The Policing of Families*. Baltimore: Johns Hopkins University Press, 1997.

Dowsett, G. "Alliance Building. HIV/AIDS Case Study: Community Perspectives." Sir Gustav Nossal International Fellowship Leadership Reform Seminar. Melbourne: University of Melbourne, 2001.

Duby, Georges. *The Knight, the Lady and the Priest: The Making of Modern Marriage in Medieval France*. Trans. Barbara Bray. Chicago: University of Chicago Press, 1994.

Duggan, Lisa. *The Twilight of Equality? Neoliberalism, Cultural Politics, and the Attack on Democracy*. Boston: Beacon, 2003.

Duke, Lynne. "The FBI's Art Attack: Offbeat Materials at Professor's Home Set Off Bioterror Alarm." *Washington Post*, 2 June 2004, C1.

Duranti, Alessandro. *From Grammar to Politics: Linguistic Anthropology in a Western Samoan Village*. Berkeley: University of California Press, 1994.

Durkheim, Emile, and Marcel Mauss. *Primitive Classification*. Chicago: University of Chicago Press, 1963.

Dussart, Françoise. *The Politics of Ritual in an Aboriginal Settlement: Kinship, Gender, and the Currency of Knowledge*. Washington, D.C.: Smithsonian Books, 2000.

Dutton, Michael. "Mango Mao: Inflections of the Sacred." *Public Culture* 16, no. 2 (2004): 161–187.

Edwards, Brent Hayes. *The Practice of Diaspora: Literature, Translation, and the Rise of Black Internationalism*. Cambridge, Mass.: Harvard University Press, 2003.

Edwards, Brian T. *Morocco Bound: Disorienting America's Maghreb, from Casablanca to the Marrakech Express*. Durham: Duke University Press, 2005.

Elias, Norbert. *The Civilizing Process*. London: Blackwell, 2000.

Eribon, Didier. *Insult and the Making of the Gay Self*. Durham: Duke University Press, 2004.

———. *Michel Foucault*. Trans. Betsy Wing. Cambridge, Mass.: Harvard University Press, 1991.

Esedebe, P. Olisanwuche. *Pan-Africanism: The Idea and the Movement, 1776–1963*. Washington, D.C.: Howard University Press, 1977.

Fanon, Frantz. *The Wretched of the Earth*. New York: Grove Press, 1963.

Farmer, Paul. *Pathologies of Power: Health, Human Rights, and the New War on the Poor*. Berkeley: University of California Press, 2003.

Fassin, Eric. "Same Sex, Different Politics: 'Gay Marriage' Debates in France and the United States." *Public Culture* 13, no. 2 (2001): 215–232.

Faubion, James. *Shadow and Lights of Waco*. Princeton: Princeton University Press, 2001.

Feldman, Allen. "Violence and Vision: The Prosthetics and Aesthetics of Terror." *Public Culture* 10, no. 1 (1997): 24–60.

Foner, Eric. *Free Soil, Free Labor, Free Men*. Oxford: Oxford University Press, 1995.

Foreman, Dave. *Confessions of an Eco-Warrior*. Bourbon, Ind.: Harmony Books, 1991.

Foreman, Dave, and Bill Haywood, eds. *Ecodefense: A Field Guide to Monkey-wrenching*. Chico, Calif.: Abbzug Press, 1993.

Foucault, Michel. *Abnormal: Lectures at the Collège de France, 1974–1975*. London: Picador, 2003.

———. *Discipline and Punish: The Birth of the Prison*. Trans. Alan Sheridan. New York: Vintage, 1977.

Franke, Katherine. "The Domesticated Liberty of *Lawrence v. Texas*." *Columbia Law Review* 104 (2004): 1399.

Frankel, Noralee, and Nancy S. Dye, eds. *Gender, Class, Race, and Reform in the Progressive Era*. Lexington: University Press of Kentucky, 1991.

Franklin, Sarah. *Embodied Progress: A Cultural Account of Assisted Conception*. London: Routledge, 1997.

Fraser, Nancy. "Rethinking the Public Sphere: A Contribution to the Critique of Actually Existing Democracies." In *Habermas and the Public Sphere*, ed. Craig Calhoun, 109–142. Cambridge, Mass.: MIT Press, 1993.

Frederick, Kathleen. "Savage Instincts: Sex, Social Science, and Some Imperatives of Categories." PhD diss., University of Chicago, 2006.

Freud, Sigmund. *Civilization and Its Discontents*. New York: W.W. Norton, [1961] 1989.

Friedman, Sara. *Intimate Politics: Marriage, the Market, and State Power in Southeastern China*. Harvard University East Asian Monograph Series. Cambridge, Mass.: Harvard University, 1996.

Gal, Susan. "A Semiotics of the Public/Private Distinction." *differences: A Journal of Feminist Cultural Studies* 13, no. 1 (2002): 77–95.

Giddens, Anthony. *The Transformation of Intimacy: Love, Sexuality and Eroticism in Modern Societies*. Cambridge: Polity Press, 1993.

Giddings, Paula. *Where I Enter: The Impact of Black Women on Race and Sex in America*. New York: William Morrow, 1984.

Gilroy, Paul. *Against Race: Imagining Political Culture Beyond the Color Line*. Cambridge, Mass.: Harvard University Press, 2000.

Ginsberg, Faye D., and Rayna Rapp, eds. *Conceiving the New World Order: The Global Politics of Reproduction*. Berkeley: University of California Press, 1995.

Goldberg, David Theo. *The Racial State*. Oxford: Blackwell, 2002.

Good, Regan. "Color Dynamics: Questions for Randall Kennedy." *New York Times Magazine*, 9 February 2003, 19.

Goode, Erica. "Certain Words Can Trip Up AIDS Grants, Scientists Say." *New York Times*, 18 April 2003, 10.

Goody, Jack. *The Development of the Family and Marriage in Europe*. Cambridge: Cambridge University Press, 1983.

Gordon, Sarah Barringer. " 'Our National Hearthstone': Anti-Polygamy Fiction and the Sentimental Campaign against Moral Diversity in Ante-Bellum America." *Yale Journal of Law and the Humanities* 8, no. 2 (Summer 1996): 295–349.

Gosdsil, Rachel D. "Remedying Environmental Racism." *Michigan Law Review* 90 (November 1991): 394–401.

Gould, Annette M. "Media Not Lying On Rhea County Gay Ban Issue." *Watts Bar Lake Observer*, 18 April 2004.

Goux, Jean Jacques. *Symbolic Economies after Marx and Freud*. Trans. Jennifer Curtis Gage. Ithaca: Cornell University Press, 1990.

Gramsci, Antonio. "The Modern Prince." In *Selections from the Prison Notebooks*, 123–209. New York: International Publishers, 1971.

Grant, Bruce. Foreword to *The Social Organization of the Gilyak*, by Lev Shternberg, ed. Bruce Grant, xxiii–lvi. New York and Seattle: American Museum of Natural History and the University of Washington Press, 1999.

Green, Roland. *Unrequited Conquests: Love and Empire in the Colonial Americas*. Chicago: University of Chicago Press, 2000.

Gutmann, Amy, and Dennis Thompson. *Democracy and Disagreement*. Cambridge, Mass.: Belknap Press, 1996.

Habermas, Jürgen. "Deliberative Politics: A Procedural Concept of Democracy." In *Between Facts and Norms*, 287–328. Cambridge: Cambridge University Press, 1998.

———. *Structural Transformation of the Public Sphere*. Cambridge, Mass.: MIT Press, 1989.

Hadot, Pierre. *Philosophy as a Way of Life: Spiritual Exercises from Socrates to Foucault*. Ed. Arnold I. Davidson. London: Blackwell, 1995.

Halley, Janet E. "Reasoning About Sodomy: Act and Identity In and After *Bowers v. Hardwick.*" *Virginia Law Review* 79 (1993): 1721–1780.

Halperin, David. *How to Do the History of Homosexuality.* Chicago: University of Chicago Press, 2002.

Hanchard, Michael. "Afro-Modernity: Temporality, Politics, and the African Diaspora." *Public Culture* 11, no. 1 (1999): 245–268.

Hay, Harry. *Radically Gay: Gay Liberation in the Words of its Founder.* Ed. Will Roscoe. Boston: Beacon, 1996.

Hayden, Cori. *When Nature Goes Public: The Making and Unmaking of Bioprospecting in Mexico.* Princeton: Princeton University Press, 2003.

Herbert, Christopher. *Culture and Anomie: Ethnographic Imagination in the Nineteenth Century.* Chicago: University of Chicago Press, 1991.

Hobsbawm, Eric. *The Age of Revolution: 1789–1848.* New York: Vintage, 1962.

Houlbrooke, R. A. *The English Family, 1450–1700.* London: Books Britain, 1984.

Howell, Martha. *The Marriage Exchange: Property, Social Place, and Gender in Cities of the Low Countries, 1300–1550.* Chicago: University of Chicago Press, 1998.

Hunt, Lynn Avery. *The Family Romance of the French Revolution.* Berkeley: University of California Press, 1992.

Hunter, B. "Three Nations, Not One: Indigenous and Other Australian Poverty." Centre for Aboriginal Economic Policy Research Working Paper No. 1. Canberra: Australian National University, 1999.

Israel, Jonathon I. *The Radical Enlightenment: Philosophy and the Making of Modernity, 1650–1750.* Oxford: Oxford University Press, 2002.

Jacobs, Jane M. "Earth Honoring: Western Desires and Indigenous Knowledges." In *Writing Women and Space: Colonial and Postcolonial Geographies*, ed. A. Blunt and G. Rose, 169–196. London: Routledge, 1994.

Jacobs, Patricia. "Science and Veiled Assumptions: Miscegenation in W.A. 1930–1937." *Australian Aboriginal Studies* 2 (1986): 15–23.

Jain, Sarah. *Injury: The Politics of Product Design and Safety Law in the United States.* Princeton: Princeton University Press, 2006.

Jakobsen, Janet, and Ann Pellegrini. *Love the Sin: Sexual Recognition and the Limits of Religious Tolerance*. Boston: Beacon, 2004.

James, C. L. R. *The Black Jacobins, Toussaint L'Ouverture and the San Domingo Revolution*. New York: Vintage, 1963.

Kapferer, Bruce. "The Anthropology of Max Gluckman." *Social Analysis* 22 (1987): 2–19.

Kaplan, Amy. *The Anarchy of Empire in the Making of U.S Culture*. Cambridge, Mass.: Harvard University Press, 2002.

Kaplan-Myrth, Nili. "Hard Yakka: A Study of the Community-Government Relations that Shape Australian Aboriginal Health Policy and Politics." PhD diss., Yale University, 2003.

Kelley, Robin D. G. *Freedom Dreams, The Black Radical Imagination*. Boston: Beacon, 2002.

Kenbi Transcripts. Indooroopilly: Transcripts Australia, 1995–1998.

Kennedy, Randall. *Interracial Intimacies: Sex, Marriage, Identity, and Adoption*. New York: Vintage, 2003.

———. *"Loving v. Virginia* at Thirty." SpeakOut, http://speakout.com/ activism/opinions/3208-1.html.

———. "The Marital Color Line." *The Nation*, 25 December 2000.

Kennedy, Randy. "The Artists in the Hazmat Suits." *New York Times*, 3 July 2005, sec. 2, 1.

Kipnis, Laura. "Should This Marriage be Saved?" *New York Times*, 25 January 2004, sec. 4, 14.

Kirby, Michael. "The Challenges to Justice in a Plural Society." Speech given at the Commonwealth Lawyers' Association Judicial Conference, Kuala Lumpur, Malaysia, 4 April 2002. High Court of Australia, http:// www.hcourt.gov.au/speeches/kirbyj/kirbyj_plural.htm.

Kirsch, Stuart. "Lost Worlds: Environment Disaster, 'Culture Loss' and the Law." *Current Anthropology* 42, no. 2 (2001): 167–198.

Kleinman, Arthur, Veena Das, and Margaret Locke, eds. *Social Suffering*. Berkeley: University of California Press, 1997.

Kogacioglu, Dicle. "The Tradition Effect: Framing Honor Crimes in Turkey." *differences: A Journal of Feminist Cultural Studies* 15, no. 2 (2004): 118–151.

Kowal, Emma, and Yin Paradies. "Ambivalent Helpers and Unhealthy Choices. Public Health Practitioners' Narrative of Indigenous Ill-health." *Social Science Medicine* 60, no. 6 (March 2005): 1347–1357.

Kuper, Adam. *Anthropology and Anthropologists: The Modern British School*. London: Routledge, 1983.

LaChapelle, Dolores. *Sacred Land, Sacred Sex: Rapture of the Deep*. Silverton, Colo.: Finn Hill Arts, 1988.

Laclau, Ernesto, and Chantal Mouffe. *Hegemony and Socialist Strategy: Towards a Radical Democratic Politics*. London: Verso, 1985.

Landes, Joan. *Women and the Public Sphere in the Age of the French Revolution*. Ithaca: Cornell University Press, 1988.

Layton, Azza Salama. *International Politics and Civil Rights Policies in the United States, 1941–1960*. Cambridge: Cambridge University Press, 2000.

Lea, Tess. "Between the Pen and the Paperwork: A Native Ethnography of Learning to Govern Indigenous Health in the Northern Territory." PhD diss., University of Sydney, 2002.

Lee, Benjamin. "Texuality, Mediation, and Public Discourse." In *Habermas and the Public Sphere*, ed. Craig Calhoun, 402–418. Cambridge, Mass.: MIT Press, 1993.

Lee, Benjamin, and Edward Lipuma. "Cultures of Circulation: The Imaginations of Modernity." *Public Culture* 14, no. 1 (2002): 191–213.

Lee, Martha F. *Earth First!: Environmental Apocalypse*. Syracuse: Syracuse University Press, 1995.

Le Goff, Jacques. "Head or Heart? The Political Use of Body Metaphors in the Middle Ages." In *Fragments for a History of the Human Body*, vol. 3, ed. Michael Feher with Ramona Naddaff and Nadia Tazi, 12–27. New York: Zone, 1989.

Lévi-Strauss, Claude. *Elementary Structures of Kinship*. Boston: Beacon, 1971.

Lewis, David Levering. *W. E. B. Du Bois, the Fight for Equality and the American Century, 1919–1963*. New York: Henry Holt, 2000.

Macey, David. *Frantz Fanon, A Biography*. New York: Picador, 2002.

Macfarlane, Alan. *The Origins of English Individualism: The Family, Property, and Social Transition*. London: Blackwell, 1978.

Madigan, Nick. "After Fleeing Polygamist Community, An Opportunity for Influence." *New York Times*, 29 June 2005, sec. A, 16.

Maharaj, Rajiv. "$100,000 Compo for Disfigured Right Hand." *Northern Territory News*, 30 August 2003, 3.

Mahmood, Saba. *Politics of Piety, the Islamic Revival and the Feminist Subject*. Princeton: Princeton University Press, 2004.

Manalansan, Martin F. *Global Divas: Filipino Gay Men in the Diaspora*. Durham: Duke University Press, 2003.

Martin, Biddy. "Feminism, Criticism, and Foucault." In *Feminism Played Straight: The Significance of Being Lesbian*, 185–214. London: Routledge, 1997.

Massumi, Brian. *A User's Guide to Capitalism and Schizophrenia: Deviations from Deleuze and Guattari*. Cambridge, Mass.: MIT Press, 1992.

Matsuda, Matt. *Empire of Love: Histories of France and the Pacific*. Oxford: Oxford University Press, 2004.

Mbembe, Achille. "Aesthetics of Superfluity." *Public Culture* 16, no. 3 (2004): 373–405.

———. "Life, Sovereignty, and Terror in the Fiction of Amos Tutuola." *Research in African Literatures* 34, no. 4 (2003): 1–26.

McClure, Kirstie. "Difference, Diversity, and the Limits of Toleration." *Political Theory* 18, no. 3 (1990): 361–391.

McMahon, Darrin M. *Enemies of the Enlightenment: The French Counter-Enlightenment and the Making of Modernity*. Oxford: Oxford University Press, 2001.

McNeil, Donald G. "Hundreds of U.S. Troops Infected by Parasite Borne by Sand Flies, Army Says." *New York Times*, 6 December 2003, sec. A, 8.

Mendelson, S. H., and P. Crawford, eds. *Women in Early Modern England, 1550–1720*. Oxford: Clarendon Press, 1998.

Michaels, Eric. *Bad Aboriginal Art, and Other Essays*. Minneapolis: University of Minnesota Press, 1993.

Michelmore, Karen. "Flesh-Eating Bug Found in Northern Territory." *Northern Territory News*, 11 September 2003, 3.

Mignolo, Walter. *Local Histories/Global Designs*. Princeton: Princeton University Press, 2000.

Miller, Susan A. "Seminoles and Africans under Seminole Law: Sources and Discourses of Tribal Sovereignty and 'Black Indian' Entitlement." *Wicazo Sa Review* 20, no. 1 (2005): 23–47.

Moon, Dawne. *God, Sex, and Politics: Homosexuality and Everyday Theologies*. Chicago: University of Chicago Press, 2004.

Morgan, Lewis Henry. *Systems of Consanguinity and Affinity of the Human Family*. Washington, D.C.: Smithsonian Institution Press, 1870.

Morgensen, Scott. "Metropolitan Desires, Utopian Practices: Contesting Race, Sex and Other Colonial Legacies in U.S. Queer Communities." PhD diss., University of California, Santa Cruz, 2001.

Morris, Barry. *Domesticating Resistance: The Dhan-Gadi and the Australian State*. Oxford: Oxford University Press, 1989.

Muir, Stewart. "The Marketing of Aboriginal Culture: The New Age and Aboriginality." PhD diss., La Trobe University, 2006.

———. "Relics of Aboriginality in Victorian and Australian Commonwealth Cultural Heritage Legislation." Paper presented to Anthropology of Law Workshop, Birkbeck College, University of London, April 2005.

Myers, Fred. "Burning the Truck and Holding the Country: Forms of Property, Time, and the Negotiation of Identity among Pintupi Aborigines." In *We Are Here: Politics of Aboriginal Land Tenure*, ed. E. Wilmsen, 15–42. Berkeley: University of California Press, 1988.

———. *Painting Culture: The Making of an Aboriginal High Art*. Durham: Duke University Press, 2002.

———. *Pintupi Country, Pintupi Self: Sentiment, Place and Politics among Western Desert Aborigines*. Washington, D.C.: Smithsonian Institution Press, 1986.

National Health and Medical Research Council. *Values and Ethics: Guidelines for Ethical Conduct in Aboriginal and Torres Strait Island Health Research*. Canberra: Commonwealth of Australia, 2003.

Navarro, Mireya. "Experts in Sex Field Say Conservatives Interfere with Health and Research." *New York Times*, 11 July 2004, sec. A, 16.

Omi, Michael, and Howard Winant. *Racial Formation in the United States: From the 1960s to the 1990s*. New York: Routledge, 1993.

Pagden, Anthony. *The Fall of Natural Man: The American Indian and the Origins of Comparative Ethnology*. Cambridge: Cambridge University Press, 1987.

Park, Rozelia S. "An Examination of International Environmental Racism Through the Lens of Transboundary Movement of Hazardous Wastes." *Indiana Journal of Global Legal Studies* 5 (Spring 1998): 659–701.

Parker, Andrew, Mary Russo, Doris Sommer, Patricia Yaeger, eds. *Nationalisms and Sexualities*. London: Routledge, 1991.

Pateman, Carol. *The Sexual Contract*. Stanford: Stanford University Press, 1988.

Patton, Cindy. *Globalizing AIDS*. Minneapolis: University of Minnesota Press, 2002.

Patton, Cindy, and Benigno Sánchez-Eppler, eds. *Queer Diasporas*. Durham: Duke University Press, 2000.

Pearson, Noel. "Aboriginal Australia at a Crossroads: Reciprocity, Initiative and Community." Edited text of an address to the Brisbane Institute, 26 July 1999. http://www.mrcltd.org.au/uploaded_documents/ACF1277.htm.

Pedersen, Susan. *Family, Dependence, and the Origins of the Welfare State: Britain and France, 1914–1945*. Cambridge: Cambridge University Press, 1993.

Peirce, Charles S. "Pragmatism." In *The Essential Peirce: Selected Philosophical Writings, 1893–1913*, ed. Nathan Houser and Christian Kloesel, 398–433. Bloomington: Indiana University Press, 1989.

Peterson, Nicholas. "Demand-sharing: Reciprocity and the Pressure for Generosity among Foragers." *American Anthropologist* 95, no. 4 (1993): 860–874.

Pigg, Stacy Leigh. "The Credible and the Credulous: The Question of Villagers' Belief in Nepal." *Cultural Anthropology* 11, no. 2 (1996): 160–201.

———. "Globalizing the Facts of Life." In *Sex in Development, Sciences, Sexuality, and Morality in Global Perspective*, ed. Vincanne Adams and Stacy Leigh Pigg, 39–65. Durham: Duke University Press, 2005.

Pottage, Alain, and Martha Mundy, eds. *Law, Anthropology, and the Constitution of the Social: Making Persons and Things*. Cambridge: Cambridge University Press, 2004.

Povinelli, Elizabeth A. "Consuming Geist: Popontology and the Spirit of Capital in Indigenous Australia." *Public Culture* 12, no. 2 (2000): 501–528.

——. *The Cunning of Recognition: Indigenous Alterities and the Making of Australian Multiculturalism*. Durham: Duke University Press, 2002.

——. *Labor's Lot: The Power, History and Culture of Aboriginal Action*. Chicago: University of Chicago Press, 1994.

——. " 'Might Be Something': The Language of Indeterminacy in Australian Aboriginal Land Use." *Man* 28, no. 4 (December 1993): 679–704.

——. "Radical Worlds: The Anthropology of Incommensurability and Inconceivability." *The Annual Review of Anthropology* 30 (2001): 319–334.

Povinelli, Elizabeth A., and George Chauncey. "Thinking Sexuality Transnationally: An Introduction." *glq: A Journal of Lesbian and Gay Studies* 5, no. 4 (1999): 1–11.

Pratt, Angela. "Make or Break? A Background to the ATSIC Changes and the ATSIC Review." Australian Parliamentary Library, Current Issues Brief no. 29 2002–03. http://www.aph.gov.au/library/pubs/CIB/2002-03/03cib29.htm.

Pratt, Richard A. "Crossing the Color Line: A Historical and Personal Narrative of *Loving v. Virginia*." *Howard Law Journal* 41 (1998): 229.

Probyn, Elspeth. *Outside Belongings*. London: Routledge, 1996.

Quiroga, José. *Tropics of Desire: Interventions from Queer Latino America*. New York: New York University Press, 2000.

Rabinow, Paul. *Making PCR: A Story of Biotechnology*. Chicago: University of Chicago Press, 1997.

Radcliffe-Brown, A. R. *Structure and Function in Primitive Society*. New York: Free Press, 1965.

Rafael, Vicente. *White Love and Other Events in Filipino History*. Durham: Duke University Press, 2000.

Ragone, Helena. "Surrogate Motherhood: Rethinking Biological Models, Kinship, and Family." In *Gender in Cross-Cultural Perspective*, ed. Caroline Brettell and Carolyn Sargent, 470–480. New York: Prentice Hall, 2001.

Reid, Janice, ed. *Body, Land and Spirit: Health and Healing in Aboriginal Society*. Brisbane: Queensland University Press, 1982.

Reid, Janice, and P. Trompf, eds. *The Health of Aboriginal Australia*. Sydney: Harcourt Brace, 1991.

Rivers, W. H. R. "The Genealogical Method of Anthropological Inquiry." *Sociological Review* 3 (1910): 1–12.

Roscoe, Will. *Queer Spirits: A Gay Men's Myth Book*. Boston: Beacon, 1998.

Roy, Parama. "Discovering India, Imagining Thuggee." *Yale Journal of Criticism* 9, no. 1 (Spring 1996): 121–145.

Rubin, Gayle. "Thinking Sex: Notes for a Radical Theory of the Politics of Sexuality." In *The Lesbian and Gay Studies Reader*, ed. Henry Abelove, Michele Aina Barale, and David Halperin, 3–44. London: Routledge, 1992.

Said, Edward. *Orientalism*. New York: Vintage, 1979.

Sawicki, Jana. *Disciplining Foucault: Feminism, Power, and the Body*. London: Routledge, 1991.

Sawyer, Suzana. *Crude Chronicles: Indigenous Politics, Multinational Oil, and Neoliberalism in Ecuador*. Durham: Duke University Press, 2004.

Scheper-Hughes, Nancy. "Parts Unknown: Undercover Ethnography of the Organs-Trafficking Underworld." *Ethnography* 5, no. 1 (2004): 29–73.

Schmitt, Carl. *The Concept of the Political*. Chicago: University of Chicago Press, 1996.

Schwab, R. G. "The Calculus of Reciprocity: Principles and Implications of Aboriginal Sharing." Discussion Paper no. 100, Centre for Aboriginal Economic Policy Research, 1995.

———. "Principles and Implications of Aboriginal Sharing." Issue Brief 17, Centre for Aboriginal Economic Policy Research, March 1997.

Segal, Daniel A. *Crossing Cultures: Essays in the Displacement of Western Civilization*. Tuscon: University of Arizona Press, 1992.

Seigel, Micol. "Beyond Compare: Comparative Method after the Transnational Turn." *Radical History Review* 91 (Winter 2005): 62–90.

Sen, Amartya. *Development as Freedom*. New York: Knopf, 1999.

Sharpe, Jenny. "Is the United States Postcolonial? Transnationalism, Immigration, and Race." *Diaspora* 4, no. 2 (1995): 181–199.

Sherzer, Joel. *Verbal Art in San Blas: Kuna Culture through its Discourse*. Cambridge: Cambridge University Press, 1990.

Silverstein, Michael. "Metapragmatic Discourse and Metapragmatic Function." In *Reflexive Language*, ed. John Lucy, 33–58. Cambridge: Cambridge University Press, 1993.

Somerville, Siobhan. "Queer *Loving*." *glq: A Journal of Lesbian and Gay Studies* 11, no. 3 (2005): 335–370.

Spivak, Gayatri. "Scattered Speculations on a Theory of Value." In *In Other Worlds: Essays in Cultural Politics*, 154–175. London: Methuen, 1987.

Spretnak, Charlene. *The Politics of Women's Spirituality*. New York: Anchor Press, 1982.

Stanley, Amy Dru. *From Bondage to Contract: Wage Labor, Marriage, and the Market in the Era of Slave Emancipation*. Cambridge: Cambridge University Press, 1998.

Starhawk. *The Spiral Dance: A Rebirth of the Ancient Religion of the Great Goddess*. San Francisco: Harper and Row, 1979.

Steinmetz, George. *The Devil's Handwriting: Precoloniality and the German Colonial State in Qingdao, Samoa, and Southwest Africa*. Chicago: University of Chicago Press, 2006.

Stocking, George W. *After Tylor: British Social Anthropology 1888–1951*. Madison: University of Wisconsin Press, 1995.

———. *Victorian Anthropology*. New York: Free Press, 1991.

Stoler, Ann L. *Carnal Knowledge and Imperial Power: Race and the Intimate in Colonial Rule*. Berkeley: University of California Press, 2002.

———. *Race and the Education of Desire*. Durham: Duke University Press, 1995.

Stone, Lawrence. *Uncertain Unions: Marriage in England, 1660–1753*. Oxford: Oxford University Press, 1992.

Strathern, Marilyn. *After Nature: English Kinship in the Late Twentieth Century*. Cambridge: Cambridge University Press, 1992.

Strelein, Lisa. "A Comfortable Existence: Commercial Fishing and the Concept of the Traditional in Native Title." *Balayi: Law, Culture, and Colonialism* 5 (2003): 94–123.

Sunstein, Cass. *Democracy and the Problem of Free Speech*. New York: Free Press, 1993.

Tambiah, Stanley. "A Performative Approach to Ritual." In *Culture, Thought, and Social Action: An Anthropological Perspective*, 122–166. Cambridge, Mass.: Harvard University Press, 1985.

Taylor, Bron. "Earth and Nature-Based Spirituality (Part I): From Deep Ecology to Radical Environmentalism." *Religion* 30, no. 2 (2001): 175–193.

———. "Earth and Nature-Based Spirituality (Part II): From Deep Ecology to Scientific Paganism." *Religion* 30, no. 3 (2001): 225–245.

———. "Earth First! And the Earth Liberation Front." In *The Encyclopedia of Religion and Nature*, ed. Bron Taylor, 518–524. London: Thoemmes Continuum, 2005.

Taylor, Charles. *Modern Social Imaginaries*. Durham: Duke University Press, 2004.

———. "The Politics of Recognition." In *Multiculturalism*, ed. Amy Gutmann, 25–73. Princeton: Princeton University Press, 1994.

Thompson, E. P. *The Making of the English Working Class*. New York: Vintage, 1966.

Timmons, Stuart. *The Trouble With Harry Hay: Founder of the Modern Gay Movement*. Los Angeles: Alyson Publications, 1990.

Todorov, Tzvetan. *The Conquest of America: The Question of the Other*. Trans. Richard Howard. Norman: University of Oklahoma Press, 1999.

———. *On Human Diversity: Nationalism, Racism, and Exoticism in French Thought*. Cambridge, Mass.: Harvard University Press, 1993.

Treleaven, Scott. "Queer Rites Now: A Brief History of the Radical Faeries." Disinformation, http://www.disinfo.com/archive/pages/dossier/id767/pg1/index.html.

Trigger, David S. "Indigeneity, Ferality and What 'Belongs' in the Australian Bush: Nature, Culture and Identity in a Settler Society." Paper prepared for CHAGS 9 (Conference on Hunting and Gathering Societies), Edinburgh, September 2002.

Trouillot, Michel-Rolph. "Anthropology and the Savage Slot: The Poetics and Politics of Otherness." In *Global Transformations: Anthropology and the Modern World*, 7–28. New York: Palgrave Macmillan, 2003.

Turner, Victor. *The Ritual Process: Structure and Anti-Structure*. New York: Aldine, 1969.

Vail, Leroy. *The Creation of Tribalism in Southern Africa*. Berkeley: University of California Press, 1989.

Verges, Françoise. *Monsters and Revolutionaries: Colonial Family Romance and Métissage*. Durham: Duke University Press, 1999.

Vogler, Candace. "Sex and Talk." *Critical Inquiry* 24, no. 2 (1998): 328–365.

Von Eschen, Penny M. *Race against Empire: Black Americans and Anticolonialism, 1937–1957*. Ithaca: Cornell University Press, 1996.

Wall, Derek. *Earth First! And the Anti-Roads Movement: Radical Environmentalism and Comparative Social Movements*. London: Routledge, 1999.

Wallenstein, Peter. *Tell the Court I Love My Wife: Race, Marriage, and Law — An American History*. New York: Palgrave Macmillan, 2002.

Warner, Michael. "The Mass Public and the Mass Subject." In *Habermas and the Public Sphere*, ed. Craig Calhoun, 377–401. Cambridge, Mass.: MIT Press, 1993.

———. "Publics and Counterpublics." In *Publics and Counterpublics*, 65–124. New York: Zone, 2002.

———. *The Trouble with Normal: Sex, Politics and the Ethics of Queer Life*. Cambridge, Mass.: Harvard University Press, 2000.

———. "Why Gay Men Are Having Risky Sex." *Village Voice*, 21 January 1995, 33–36.

Watson, Irene. "Aboriginal Laws and the Sovereignty of *Terra Nullius*." *borderlands e-journal* 1, no. 2 (2002).

Weber, Max. *The Protestant Ethic and the Spirit of Capitalism*. London: Routledge, 2001.

Weeks, Jeffrey. *Sex, Politics, and Society: The Regulation of Sexuality Since 1800*. London: Longman, 1989.

Weston, Kath. *Families We Choose: Lesbians, Gays, Kinship*. New York: Columbia University Press, 1997.

Westra, Laura, and Bill Lawson, eds. *Faces of Environmental Racism: Confronting Issues of Global Justice*. Lanham, Md.: Rowman and Littlefield, 2001.

Wiegman, Robyn. "Intimate Publics: Race, Property, and Personhood." *American Literature* 74, no. 4 (December 2002): 859–885.

Williams, Walter L. *The Spirit and the Flesh: Sexual Diversity in American Indian Culture*. Boston: Beacon, 1992.

Willis, J., K. McDonald, M. Saunders, and J. Grierson. *HIV Futures II: Aboriginal and Torres Strait Islander People Living with HIV*. Monograph Series no. 30, Australian Research Centre in Sex, Health & Society. Melbourne: La Trobe University, 2002.

Wilson, Ara. *The Intimate Economies of Bangkok: Tomboys, Tycoons, and Avon Ladies in the Global City*. Berkeley: University of California Press, 2004.

Wilson, Elizabeth A. *Psychosomatic: Feminism and the Neurological Body*. Durham: Duke University Press, 2004.

Wittgenstein, Ludwig. *On Certainty*. Trans. Denis Paul and G. E. M. Anscombe. New York: Harper Perennial, 1972.

Wolfe, Patrick. "Nation and Miscegenation: Discursive Continuity in the Post-Mabo Era." *Social Analysis* 36 (1994): 93–152.

Wood, Gordon S. *The Radicalism of the American Revolution*. New York: Vintage, 1991.

Yan, Yunxiang. *Private Life Under Socialism: Love, Intimacy, and Family Change in a Chinese Village, 1949–1999*. Stanford: Stanford University Press, 2003.

Young, Robert J. C. *Postcolonialism: An Historical Introduction*. London: Blackwell, 2001.

Index

282

Elizabeth A. Povinelli is a professor of anthropology at Columbia University. She is the author of *The Cunning of Recognition: Indigenous Alterities and the Making of Australian Multiculturalism* and *Labor's Lot: The Power, History, and Culture of Aboriginal Action.*

Library of Congress Cataloging-in-Publication Data
Povinelli, Elizabeth A.
The empire of love : toward a theory of intimacy, genealogy, and carnality /
Elizabeth A. Povinelli.
p. cm. — (Public planet books)
Includes bibliographical references and index.
ISBN-13: 978-0-8223-3836-9 (cloth : alk. paper)
ISBN-10: 0-8223-3836-x (cloth : alk. paper)
ISBN-13: 978-0-8223-3889-5 (pbk. : alk. paper)
ISBN-10: 0-8223-3889-0 (pbk. : alk. paper)
1. Social structure. 2. Intimacy (Psychology) 3. Love. 4. Power (Social sciences) I. Title. II. Series.
HM706.P68 2006
306.701—dc22   2006008054